A Catholic Book of Hymns

✟

A Catholic Book of Hymns

✝

Four-Part Sacred Songs
For a Singing Congregation

Sacred Music Library
Augusta, Kentucky

Nihil obstat: Very Reverend Ryan L. Stenger, J.V.
Censor librorum

Imprimatur: † Most Reverend Roger J. Foys, D.D.
Bishop of Covington

January 20, 2021

Editors:
George Baclay, Ellen Doll Jones, Noel Jones, Mary C. Weaver

This edition © 2020 Sacred Music Library, Augusta, Kentucky

www.sacredmusiclibrary.com

All the hymns are in the public domain, aside from hymns 20, 32, 75, 154, and 168. These few are protected under Creative Commons 3.0, which freely permits printing, copying, and sharing for non-commercial purposes. Use this music freely, there are no restrictions nor permissions required for sharing, podcast, streaming or other such use by churches.

Table of Contents

HYMNS BY ALPHABET   PAGE

A	1
B	20
C	38
D	62
E	70
F	71
G	88
H	98
I	122
J	134
K	148
L	149
M	172
N	181
O	184
P	237
R	242
S	247
T	264
V	292
W	292
Y	312

INDICES

I.	First Lines with Tunes	320
II.	Tunes with First Lines	326
III.	Liturgical	331
	Proper of the Seasons	331
	Proper of the Saints	333
	Commons	333
	Rites	334
	Masses for Various Needs and Occasions	335
IV.	Topical	336
V.	Metrical	342
VI.	Scriptural Passages Related to Hymns	ONLINE

WWW.CATHOLICBOOKOFHYMNS.COM/INDEX/

Introduction

"Music and silence—how I detest them both!"

Screwtape, under-secretary to the devil,
The Screwtape Letters by C. S. Lewis

It's easy to see why the enemies of mankind would hate and fear both sacred silence and sacred music. Both bring joy, spur contemplation, and draw the soul nearer to the Lord. Both have been part of our private prayer as well as our communal liturgy for thousands of years.

The Psalms—biblical songs of praise, supplication, and wonder—have been sung for three thousand years. Naturally, Jesus, his disciples, and later the early Christian community also sang hymns (from the Greek word meaning "songs of praise"), as The New Testament makes clear.

We sing because we love, and sung praise elevates our words, takes them out of the realm of the commonplace, and increases our joy. The holy pleasure of singing to God involves the entire person—spirit, heart, mind, and body—and unites us not only with the Divine but also with one another as a worshiping community.

This collection of hymns for the singing Catholic congregation exemplifies the best of the genre. These songs are religiously orthodox, beautiful, sacred, and—for the most part—familiar. But here you will also find worthy hymn tunes and texts that are new to you.

Sung hymns have been an important part of the Liturgy of the Hours for century upon century, so they are nothing new, although singing them at Mass is relatively recent.

We present this book to propose not that hymns replace the proper chants for a particular day's Mass but live happily alongside them. In most instances the chants for processions are the prerogative of cantors and choirs and, as the texts change with every Sunday and solemnity, it's not practical for the congregation to learn and sing them.

Hymns, on the other hand, belong to all the faithful and serve as a key means of the "active participation" spoken of in Vatican II's Constitution on the Sacred Liturgy.

May this book bring joy to all who sing from it!

1 Abide With Me
10 10 10 10

EVENTIDE   WILLIAM H. MONK, 1823–1889

1. A - bide with me: fast falls the e - ven-tide; The dark-ness deep - ens; Lord, with me a - bide. When oth - er help - ers fail and com - forts flee, Help of the help - less, O a - bide with me.

2. Swift to its close ebbs out life's lit - tle day; Earth's joys grow dim, its glo - ries pass a - way. Change and de - cay in all a - round I see. O thou who chang - est not, a - bide with me.

3. I need thy pres - ence ev - ery pass-ing hour. What but thy grace can foil the tempt - er's power? Who like thy - self my guide and stay can be? Through cloud and sun - shine, Lord, a - bide with me.

4. I fear no foe, with thee at hand to bless;
Ills have no weight, and tears no bitterness.
Where is death's sting? where, grave, thy victory?
I triumph still, if thou abide with me.

5. Hold thou thy cross before my closing eyes;
Shine through the gloom, and point me to the skies;
Heav'n's morning breaks, and earth's vain shadows flee:
In life, in death, O Lord, abide with me. Amen.

BASED ON LUKE 24:29
HENRY F. LYTE, 1793–1847

2 Accept, Almighty Father
76 76 D

L. Herold's *Gesangbuch*, 1908

1. Accept, Almighty Father, These gifts of bread and wine;
Which now the Priest doth offer For us before thy shrine;
But soon the word will make them His body and his blood,

2. That blest and consecrated, The Sacrifice may plead
For mercy unabated, As we poor sinners need;
Alas, we are frail mortals, But through his flesh and blood,

3. With these although unworthy, Some off'ring we would make
But all we have thou gavest Then what thou gavest take
Our hearts, our souls, our senses We give through Mary's hands

4. O God, by that comingling Of water and of wine,
May he who took our nature Give us his life divine.
Come, thou who makest holy And bless this Sacrifice.

2 • A CATHOLIC BOOK OF HYMNS

The Sac - ri - fice re - new - ing, Once of - fered on the Rood.
Who o - pen'd heav - en's por - tals, We hope to rise to God.
Who by the Cross once stand - ing Now by the al - tar stands.
Then shall our gift be pleas - ing To thee a - bove the skies.

Nimm an, o Herr, die Gaben; Franz Seraph von Kohlbrenner, 1728–1783
TR. BY ANON.

3. All Glory, Laud, and Honor

76 76 D

ST. THEODULPH

MELCHIOR TESCHNER, 1584–1635
HARM. BY WILLIAM H. MONK, 1823–1889

All glory, laud, and honor To thee, Redeemer, King!
To whom the lips of children Made sweet hosannas ring.

1 Thou art the King of Is - ra - el, Thou David's royal Son,
2 The company of angels Are praising thee on high;
3 The people of the Hebrews With palms before thee went:

Who in the Lord's Name comest, The King and Blessed One.
And mortal men, and all things Created, make reply.
Our praise and prayers and anthems Before thee we present.

4 To thee before thy passion They sang their hymns of praise:
To thee, now high exalted, Our melody we raise.

5 Thou didst accept their praises; Accept the prayers we bring,
Who in all good delightest, Thou good and gracious King.

GLORIA, LAUS ET HONOR; THEODULPH OF ORLEANS, C. 760–821
TR. BY JOHN M. NEALE, 1818–1866, ALT.

4 All Hail the Power of Jesus' Name
86 86 86

CORONATION OLIVER HOLDEN, 1765–1836

1. All hail the pow'r of Jesus' name! Let angels prostrate fall; Bring forth the royal diadem And crown him Lord of all; Bring forth the royal diadem And crown him Lord of all.

2. Ye chosen seed of Israel's race, Ye ransomed from the fall, Hail him who saves you by his grace, And crown him Lord of all; Hail him who saves you by his grace, And crown him Lord of all.

3. Let ev'ry kindred, ev'ry tribe, On this terrestrial ball, To him all majesty ascribe, And crown him Lord of all; To him all majesty ascribe, And crown him Lord of all.

4. O that with yonder sacred throng, We at his feet may fall, We'll join the everlasting song, And crown him Lord of all; We'll join the everlasting song, And crown him Lord of all.

EDWARD PERRONET, 1726–1792
ALT. BY JOHN RIPPON, 1751–1836

5. All People That on Earth Do Dwell
88 88

OLD HUNDREDTH

MELODY FROM *GENEVAN PSALTER*, 1551
ATTR. TO LOUIS BOURGEOIS, C. 1510–1561, ALT.

1. All people that on earth do dwell, Sing to the Lord with cheerful voice; Him serve with fear, his praise forth tell, Come ye before him and rejoice.

2. Know that the Lord is God indeed; Without our aid he did us make; We are his folk, he doth us feed, And for his sheep he doth us take.

3. O enter then his gates with praise; Approach with joy his courts unto; Praise, laud, and bless his name always, For it is seemly so to do.

4. For why? The Lord our God is good: His mercy is forever sure; His truth at all times firmly stood, And shall from age to age endure.

5. To Father, Son, and Holy Ghost, The God whom heav'n and earth adore, From men and from the angel host Be praise and glory evermore.

6. Praise God, from whom all blessings flow; Praise him, all creatures here below; Praise him above, ye heav'nly host: Praise Father, Son, and Holy Ghost.

BASED ON PSALM 100
VSS. 1–5, WILLIAM KETHE, D. C. 1594, ALT.
VS. 6, THOMAS KEN, 1637–1711

6 All You Who Seek a Comfort Sure
86 86 D

KINGSFOLD

TRADITIONAL ENGLISH FOLK SONG
HARM. BY RALPH VAUGHAN WILLIAMS, 1872–1958

1. All you who seek a comfort sure In trouble and distress,
Whatever sorrow vex the mind, Or guilt the soul oppress,
Jesus, who gave himself for you Upon the cross to die,
Opens to you his Sacred Heart; Oh, to that heart draw nigh.

2. You hear how kindly he invites; You hear his words so blest:
"All you that labor come to me, And I will give you rest."
Christ Jesus, joy of saints on high, The hope of sinners here,
Attracted by those loving words To you we lift our prayer.

QUINCUMQUE CERTUM QUAERITIS, 18TH CENT.
TR. BY EDWARD CASWALL, 1814–1878, ALT.

7 Alleluia! Alleluia! Hearts to Heaven
87 87 D

HYMN TO JOY

LUDWIG VAN BEETHOVEN, 1770–1827
ADAPT. AND HARM. BY EDWARD HODGES, 1796–1867

1 Alleluia! Alleluia! Hearts to heav'n and voices raise;
Sing to God a hymn of gladness, Sing to God a hymn of praise.
He, who on the cross as Savior For the world's salvation bled,
Jesus Christ, the King of glory, Now is risen from the dead.

2 Now the iron bars are broken, Christ from death to life is born,
Glorious life and life immortal, On this resurrection morn.
Christ has triumphed, and we conquer By his mighty enterprise,
We with him to life eternal By his resurrection rise.

3 Alleluia! Alleluia! Glory be to God on high;
Alleluia to the Savior Who has won the victory;
Alleluia to the Spirit, Fount of love and sanctity;
Alleluia! Alleluia! To the Triune Majesty.

CHRISTOPHER WORDSWORTH, 1807–1885, ALT.

8 Alleluia! Alleluia! Let the Holy Anthem Rise
87 87 D

ALLELUIA! ALLELUIA!   TRADITIONAL AMERICAN MELODY

1. Alleluia! Alleluia! Let the holy anthem rise,
And the choirs of heaven chant it In the temple of the skies;
Let the mountain skip with gladness, And the joyful valleys ring
With Hosannas in the highest To our Savior and our King.

2. Alleluia! Alleluia! Like the sun from out the wave,
He has risen up in triumph From the darkness of the grave,
He's the splendor of the nations, He's the lamp of endless day;
He's the very Lord of glory Who is risen up today.

3. Alleluia! Alleluia! Blessed Jesus, make us rise
From the life of this corruption To the life that never dies.
May your glory be our portion When the days of time are past,
And the dead shall be awakened By the trumpet's mighty blast.

EDWARD CASWALL, 1814–1878

9 Alleluia! Sing to Jesus
87 87 D

HYFRYDOL

ROWLAND H. PRITCHARD, 1811–1887

1. Alleluia! Sing to Jesus! His the scepter, his the throne. Alleluia! His the triumph, His the victory alone. Hark! The songs of peaceful Zion Thunder
2. Alleluia! Not as orphans Are we left in sorrow now; Alleluia! He is near us, Faith believes, nor questions how; Though the cloud from sight received him When the
3. Alleluia! Bread of angels, Thou on earth our food, our stay; Alleluia! Here the sinful Flee to thee from day to day: Intercessor, Friend of sinners, Earth's Re-

lyrics under music (three verses aligned):

like a migh-ty flood, Je - sus out of
for - ty days were o'er, Shall our hearts for -
deem - er, plead for me, Where the songs of

ev - ery na - tion Hath re-deemed us by his blood.
get his prom - ise, "I am with you ev - er - more"?
all the sin - less Sweep a - cross the crys-tal sea.

4 Alleluia! King eternal, Thee the Lord of lords we own;
Alleluia! Born of Mary, Earth thy footstool, Heav'n thy throne:
Thou within the veil hast entered, Robed in flesh our great high priest:
Thou on earth both priest and victim In the Eucharistic feast.

5 Alleluia! Sing to Jesus! His the scepter, his the throne.
Alleluia! His the triumph, His the victory alone.
Hark! The songs of holy Zion Thunder like a mighty flood,
Jesus out of every nation Hath redeemed us by his blood.

BASED ON REVELATION 5:9–14
WILLIAM C. DIX, 1837–1898

10 Almighty God, Your Word Is Cast
86 86

DUNDEE
MELODY FROM *SCOTTISH PSALTER*, 1615
ADAPT. AND HARM. BY THOMAS RAVENSCROFT, 1592–1635

1. Almighty God, Your Word is cast Like seed into the ground;
Now let the dew of Heav'n descend And righteous fruits abound.

2. Nor let Your Word so kindly sent To raise us to Your throne
Return to You, and sadly tell That we reject Your Son.

3. Great God, come down and on Your Word Your mighty power bestow,
That all who hear the joyful sound Your saving grace may know.

JOHN CAWOOD, 1775–1852, ALT.

11 Angels, From the Realms of Glory
87 87 87

REGENT SQUARE HENRY T. SMART, 1813–1879

1. An-gels, from the realms of glo-ry, Wing your flight o'er all the earth;
   Ye who sang cre-a-tion's sto-ry Now pro-claim Mes-si-ah's birth.
   Come and wor-ship, come and wor-ship, Wor-ship Christ, the new-born King.

2. Shep-herds, in the field a-bid-ing, Watch-ing o'er your flocks by night,
   God with man is now re-sid-ing; Yon-der shines the in-fant light:
   Come and wor-ship, come and wor-ship, Wor-ship Christ, the new-born King.

3. Sag-es, leave your con-tem-pla-tions, Bright-er vi-sions beam a-far;
   Seek the great De-sire of na-tions; Ye have seen his na-tal star.
   Come and wor-ship, come and wor-ship, Wor-ship Christ, the new-born King.

4. Saints before the altar bending, Watching long in hope and fear;
   Suddenly the Lord, descending, In his temple shall appear.

5. All creation, join in praising God, the Father, Spirit, Son,
   Evermore your voices raising, to the eternal Three-in-One:

VSS. 1–4, JAMES MONTGOMERY, 1771–1854
VS. 5, *SALISBURY HYMN BOOK*, 1857

12 Angels We Have Heard on High

77 77 WITH REFRAIN

GLORIA

TRADITIONAL FRENCH CAROL

1. Angels we have heard on high Sweetly singing o'er the plains,
And the mountains in reply Echo back their joyous strains.

2. Shepherds, why this jubilee? Why your joyous strains prolong?
Say, what may the tidings be Which inspire your heav'nly song?

3. Come to Bethlehem, and see Him whose birth the angels sing;
Come, adore on bended knee Christ the Lord, the newborn King.

Gloria in excelsis Deo!

Gloria in excelsis Deo!

LES ANGES DANS NOS CAMPAGNES; TRADITIONAL FRENCH CAROL, C. 18TH CENT.
TR. BY JAMES CHADWICK, 1813–1882, AND OTHERS, ALT.

13 As With Gladness Men of Old
77 77 77

DIX

CONRAD KOCHER, 1786–1872
ADAPT. AND HARM. BY WILLIAM H. MONK, 1823–1889

1. As with gladness men of old Did the guiding star behold;
As with joy they hailed its light, Leading onward, beaming bright;
So, most gracious Lord, may we Evermore be led to thee.

2. As with joyful steps they sped To that lowly manger-bed,
There to bend the knee before Him whom heav'n and earth adore;
So may we with willing feet Ever seek thy mercy seat.

3. As they offered gifts most rare At that manger rude and bare;
So may we with holy joy, Pure and free from sin's alloy,
All our costliest treasures bring, Christ, to thee, our heav'nly King.

4. Holy Jesus, ev'ry day Keep us in the narrow way;
And, when earthly things are past, Bring our ransomed souls at last
Where they need no star to guide, Where no clouds thy glory hide.

5. In the heav'nly country bright Need they no created light;
Thou its light, its joy, its crown, Thou its sun which goes not down;
There for ever may we sing Alleluias to our King.

WILLIAM C. DIX, 1837–1898

14 At the Cross Her Station Keeping
8 8 7

STABAT MATER *Maintzisch Gesangbuch*, 1661

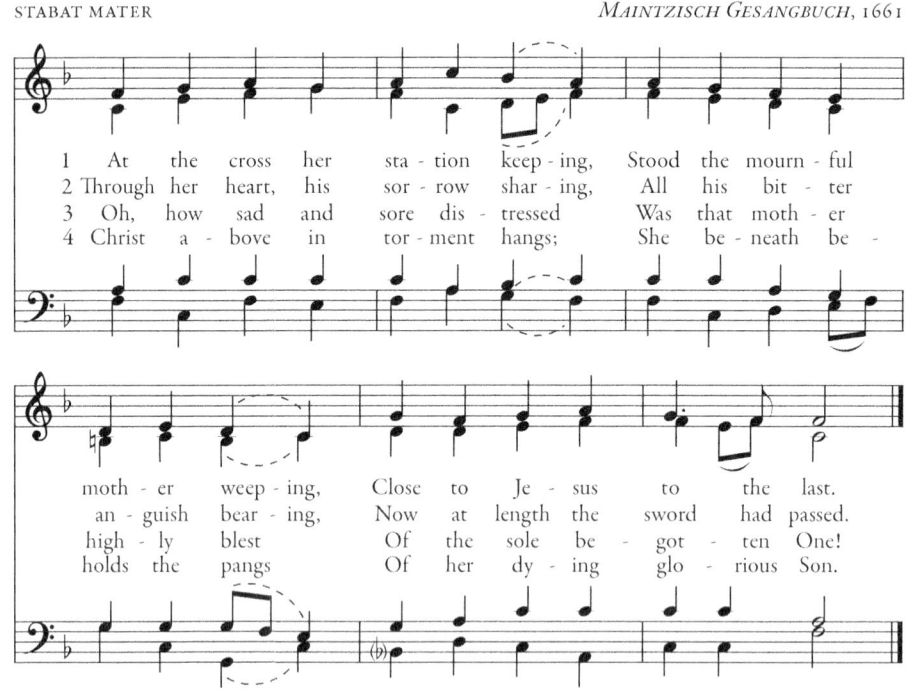

1. At the cross her station keeping,
   Stood the mournful mother weeping,
   Close to Jesus to the last.

2. Through her heart, his sorrow sharing,
   All his bitter anguish bearing,
   Now at length the sword had passed.

3. Oh, how sad and sore distressed
   Was that mother highly blest
   Of the sole begotten One!

4. Christ above in torment hangs;
   She beneath beholds the pangs
   Of her dying glorious Son.

5. Is there one who would not weep,
   Whelmed in miseries so deep
   Christ's dear Mother to behold?

6. Can the human heart refrain
   From partaking in her pain,
   In that Mother's pain untold?

7. Bruised, derided, cursed, defiled,
   She beheld her tender Child
   All with bloody scourges rent;

8. For the sins of his own nation,
   Saw him hang in desolation,
   Till his Spirit forth he sent.

9. O thou Mother! Fount of love!
   Touch my spirit from above,
   Make my heart with thine accord:

10. Make me feel as thou hast felt;
    Make my soul to glow and melt
    With the love of Christ my Lord.

11. Holy Mother! pierce me through;
    In my heart each wound renew
    Of my Savior crucified:

12. Let me share with thee his pain,
    Who for all my sins was slain,
    Who for me in torment died.

13. Let me mingle tears with thee,
    Mourning him who mourned for me,
    All the days that I may live:

14. By the Cross with thee to stay;
    There with thee to weep and pray;
    Is all I ask thee to give.

15. Virgin of all virgins blest!
    Listen to my fond request:
    Let me share thy grief divine;

16. Let me, to my lastest breath,
    In my body bear the death
    Of that dying Son of thine.

17. Wounded with his ev'ry wound,
    Steep my soul till it hath swooned
    In his very blood away.

18. Be to me, O Virgin, nigh,
    Lest in flames I burn and die,
    In that awful Judgment day.

19. Christ, when thou shalt call me hence,
    Be thy Mother my defence,
    Be thy Cross my victory;

20. While my body here decays,
    May my soul thy goodness praise,
    Safe in Paradise with thee.   Amen.

Stabat mater dolorosa; Jacapone da Todi, 1230–1306
tr. by Edward Caswall, 1814–1878, alt.

15 At the Lamb's High Feast We Sing
77 77 D

SALZBURG

JAKOB HINTZE, 1622–1702
HARM. BY JOHANN SEBASTIAN BACH, 1685–1750

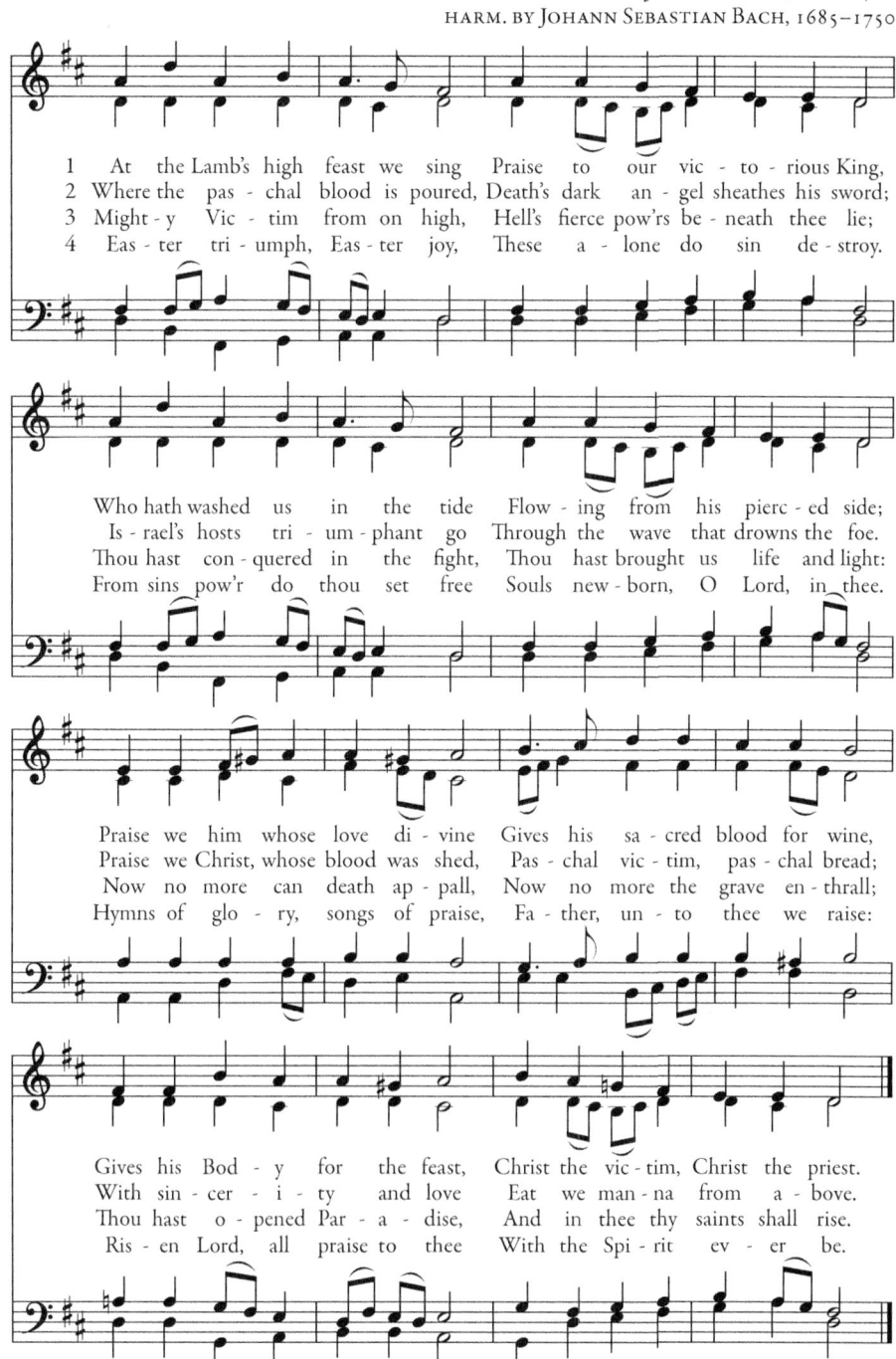

1. At the Lamb's high feast we sing Praise to our victorious King, Who hath washed us in the tide Flowing from his pierced side; Praise we him whose love divine Gives his sacred blood for wine, Gives his Body for the feast, Christ the victim, Christ the priest.

2. Where the paschal blood is poured, Death's dark angel sheathes his sword; Israel's hosts triumphant go Through the wave that drowns the foe. Praise we Christ, whose blood was shed, Paschal victim, paschal bread; With sincerity and love Eat we manna from above.

3. Mighty Victim from on high, Hell's fierce pow'rs beneath thee lie; Thou hast conquered in the fight, Thou hast brought us life and light: Now no more can death appall, Now no more the grave enthrall; Thou hast opened Paradise, And in thee thy saints shall rise.

4. Easter triumph, Easter joy, These alone do sin destroy. From sin's pow'r do thou set free Souls new-born, O Lord, in thee. Hymns of glory, songs of praise, Father, unto thee we raise: Risen Lord, all praise to thee With the Spirit ever be.

AD REGIAS AGNI DAPES, 17TH CENT.
TR. BY ROBERT CAMPBELL, 1814–1868, ALT.

16 Ave Maria! Thou Virgin and Mother
11 10 11 10

AUGUSTUS EDMONDS TOZER, 1857–1919

1. A-ve Ma-ri-a! thou Virgin and Mother, Fond-ly thy chil-dren are call-ing to thee; Thine are the grac-es, un-claimed by an-oth-er, Sin-less and beau-ti-ful Star of the Sea.

2. A-ve Ma-ri-a! the night shades are fall-ing, Soft-ly our voic-es a-rise un-to thee! Earth's lone-ly ex-iles for suc-cor are call-ing, Sin-less and beau-ti-ful Star of the Sea.

3. A-ve Ma-ri-a! thy chil-dren are kneel-ing, Words of en-dear-ment are whis-pered to thee; Soft-ly thy spi-rit up-on us is steal-ing, Sin-less and beau-ti-ful Star of the Sea.

4. A-ve Ma-ri-a! thy arms are ex-tend-ing, Glad-ly with-in them for shel-ter we flee; Are thy sweet eyes on thy lone-ly ones bend-ing, Sin-less and beau-ti-ful Star of the Sea.

AUGUSTUS EDMONDS TOZER, 1857–1919

17 Away in a Manger
11 11 11 11

CRADLE SONG · WILLIAM JAMES KIRKPATRICK, 1838–1921

1. A-way in a man-ger, no crib for a bed,
The lit-tle Lord Je-sus laid down his sweet head.
The stars in the bright sky looked down where he lay,
The lit-tle Lord Je-sus a-sleep on the hay.

2. The cat-tle are low-ing, the Ba-by a-wakes,
But lit-tle Lord Je-sus, no cry-ing he makes;
I love thee, Lord Je-sus, look down from the sky
And stay by my cra-dle till morn-ing is nigh.

3. Be near me, Lord Je-sus, I ask thee to stay
Close by me for-ev-er, and love me, I pray;
Bless all the dear chil-dren in thy ten-der care,
And fit us for Heav-en to live with thee there.

VSS. 1–2, *LITTLE CHILDREN'S BOOK FOR SCHOOLS AND FAMILIES*, C. 1885
VS. 3, JOHN T. MCFARLAND, 1851–1913

18 Be Joyful, Mary
85 84 7

REGINA CAELI   *Catholicum Hymnologium Germanicum*, 1584

1. Be joyful, Mary, heav'nly Queen, *Gaude, María:*
Your Son who died was living seen,
Alleluia; *laetare, O María.*

2. The Son you bore by heaven's grace, *Gaude, María:*
Did all our guilt and sin efface,
Alleluia; *laetare, O María.*

3. The Lord has risen from the dead, *Gaude, María:*
He rose with might as he had said,
Alleluia; *laetare, O María.*

Regina caeli, jubila, 17th cent.
tr. anon. in *Psallite*, 1901, alt.

19 Be Thou My Vision

10 10 10 10

SLANE
TRADITIONAL IRISH MELODY

1. Be thou my vision, O Lord of my heart;
All else be nought to me, save that thou art.
Thou my best thought, by day or by night,
Waking or sleeping, thy presence my light.

2. Be thou my wisdom, and thou my true word;
I ever with thee and thou with me, Lord;
Thou my great Father, thine own may I be:
Thou in me dwelling, and I one with thee.

3. High King of heaven, when vict'ry is won,
May I reach heaven's joys, bright heaven's Sun!
Heart of my heart, whatever befall,
Still be my vision, O Ruler of all.

ANCIENT IRISH
TR. BY MARY E. BYRNE, 1905

20 Beautiful Savior, Mightiest in Mercy
56 56 56 5

ST. RICHARD GWYN NOEL JONES, 1947–

1 Beau-ti-ful Sa-vior, Migh-ti-est in Mer-cy, Light pier-cing darkness, Joy be-yond all sorrow, Woun-ded for heal-ing, Dy-ing for our sav-ing, Vic-tim and High Priest.

2 Son of the Fa-ther, Child of Ma-ry Mo-ther, Just Jo-seph's dear boy, Cause of Great John's leap-ing, Ma-ry's De-liv'-rer, Tru-est friend to Laz'-rus True God, our High King.

3 All laud we bring now Prais-ing our Be-lov-ed, Christ Je-sus, Sa-vior, Vic-tor, and Re-deem-er Judge of the Liv-ing, Judge of the de-par-ted, Come quick-ly, Je-sus.

VINCENT UHER, 1963–

21 Before the Day's Last Moments Fly

88 88

TE LUCIS ANTE TERMINUM

ANDERNACH GESANGBUCH, 1608
ADAPT. BY A. GREGORY MURRAY, 1905–1992

1. Be-fore the day's last mo-ments fly,
Mak-er of all, to thee we cry;
Be-neath thy kind pro-tec-tion take,
And shield us for thy mer-cy's sake.

2. Let no ill dreams our souls a-larm,
No pow'rs of night ap-proach to harm;
De-fend us from the tempt-er's art,
And keep us ev-er pure in heart.

3. Fa-ther of mer-cies, hear our cry;
O hear, co-e-qual Son most high;
Whom with the Spir-it we a-dore,
One on-ly God for ev-er-more.

TE LUCIS ANTE TERMINUM, 7TH CENT.
TR. BY ROBERT CAMPBELL, 1814–1868

22. Bethlehem, of Noblest Cities
87 87

MERTON
WILLIAM H. MONK, 1823–1889

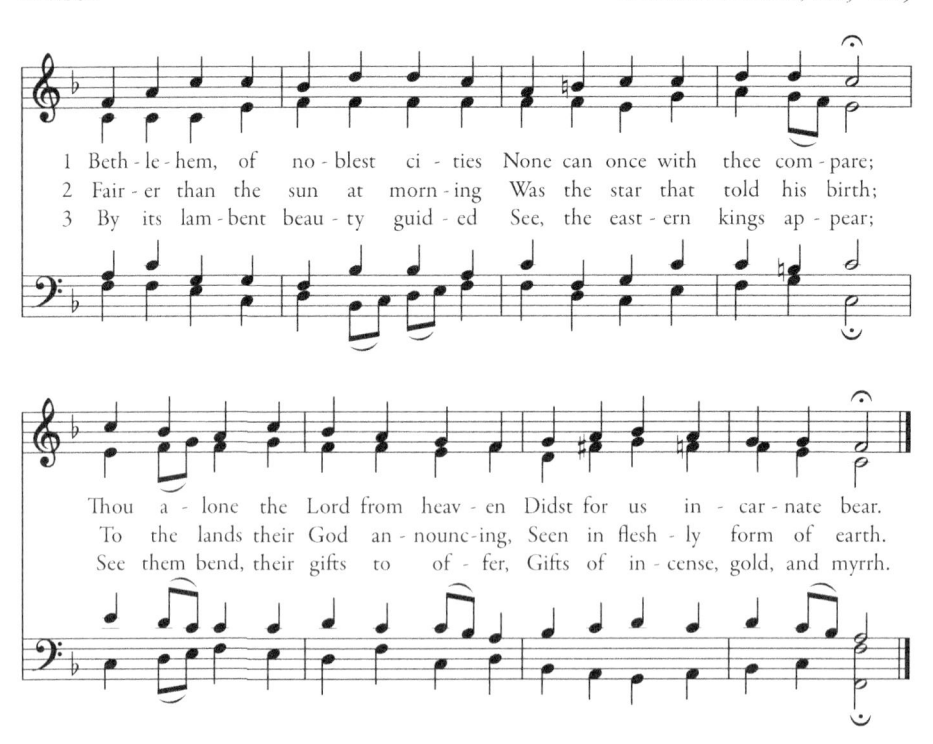

1. Beth-le-hem, of no-blest ci-ties None can once with thee com-pare; Thou a-lone the Lord from heav-en Didst for us in-car-nate bear.
2. Fair-er than the sun at morn-ing Was the star that told his birth; To the lands their God an-nounc-ing, Seen in flesh-ly form of earth.
3. By its lam-bent beau-ty guid-ed See, the east-ern kings ap-pear; See them bend, their gifts to of-fer, Gifts of in-cense, gold, and myrrh.

4. Solemn things of mystic meaning:
   Incense doth the God disclose,
   Gold a royal Child proclaimeth,
   Myrrh a future tomb foreshows.

5. Holy Jesus, in thy brightness
   To the Gentile world displayed,
   With the Father and the Spirit
   Endless praise to thee be paid.

O SOLA MAGNARUM URBIUM; AURELIUS CLEMENS PRUDENTIUS, 348-410
TR. BY EDWARD CASWALL, 1814–1878

23 Bethlehem, of Noblest Cities
87 87

STUTTGART

WITT's *PSALMODIA SACRA*, GOTHA, 1715
ADAPT. BY HENRY J. GAUNTLETT, 1805–1876

1. Bethlehem, of noblest cities
None can once with thee compare;
Thou alone the Lord from heaven
Didst for us incarnate bear.

2. Fairer than the sun at morning
Was the star that told his birth;
To the lands their God announcing,
Seen in fleshly form of earth.

3. By its lambent beauty guided
See, the eastern kings appear;
See them bend, their gifts to offer,
Gifts of incense, gold, and myrrh.

4. Solemn things of mystic meaning:
Incense doth the God disclose,
Gold a royal Child proclaimeth,
Myrrh a future tomb foreshows.

5. Holy Jesus, in thy brightness
To the Gentile world displayed,
With the Father and the Spirit
Endless praise to thee be paid.

O SOLA MAGNARUM URBIUM; AURELIUS CLEMENS PRUDENTIUS, 348-410
TR. BY EDWARD CASWALL, 1814–1878

24   Bless Me, Befriend Me
10 10 10 10

ST. BASIL'S HYMNAL, 1918

1. Bless me, befriend me, sweet angel, I pray;
Watch me, defend me by night and by day.
Shelter, enfold me, with in thy bright wings:
Guide me, uphold me in life's wanderings.

2. Beam on my gladness, thy joy shall I share;
Shine on my sadness, and sorrow I'll bear.
Go thou before me, my path shall be clear,
Hover thou o'er me, no foe shall I fear.

3. Angel so holy! whom God sends to me,
Sinful and lowly, my guardian to be.
Wilt thou not cherish the child of thy care?
Let me not perish, my trust is thy prayer.

4. O, may I never forget thou art near;
Keep, keep me ever in love and in fear.
Waking and sleeping, in labor and rest,
In thy sweet keeping my life shall be blest.

5. Till my last sorrow I'll walk in thy light;
Till the tomorrow eternal and bright.
Till thy soft pinions shall waft me on high,
To those dominions more fair than the sky.

E. F. MACGONIGLE'S *THE SODALIST'S HYMNAL*, PHILADELPHIA, 1887

25 Blessed Jesus, at Thy Word
78 78 88

LIEBSTER JESU

JOHANN R. AHLE, 1625–1673
ADAPT. BY JOHANN SEBASTIAN BACH, 1685–1750

1. Blessed Jesus, at thy word we are gathered all to hear thee; Let our hearts and souls be stirred now to seek and love and fear thee, By thy teachings, sweet and holy, Drawn from earth to love thee solely.

2. Glorious Lord, thyself impart, Light of Light, from God proceeding; Open thou our ears and heart, help us by thy Spirit's pleading; Hear the cry thy people raises, Hear and bless our prayers and praises.

3. Father, Son, and Holy Ghost, Praise to thee and adoration! Grant that we thy Word may trust and obtain true consolation While we here below must wander, Till we sing thy praises yonder.

LIEBSTER JESU, WIR SIND HIER; TOBIAS CLAUSNITZER, 1619–1684
TR. BY CATHERINE WINKWORTH, 1828–1878

26   Blest Guardian of All Virgin Souls
88 88

H. Farmer, sj

1. Blest guardian of all virgin souls! Portal of bliss to man forgiven! Pure Mother of Almighty God! Thou hope of earth, and joy of heaven!

2. Fair Lily found amid the thorns! Most beauteous Dove with wings of gold! Rod from whose tender root upspring That healing Flower long since foretold.

3. Thou Tower, against the dragon proof! Thou Star, to storm-tossed voy'gers dear! Our course lies o'er a treach'rous deep, Thine be the light by which we steer.

4. Scatter the mists that round us hang;
   Keep far the fatal shoals away;
   And while through darkling waves we sweep,
   Open a path to light and day.

5. O Jesu, born of Virgin bright,
   Immortal glory be to Thee;
   Praise to the Father infinite
   And Holy Ghost eternally.

Præclara custos virginum, 17th cent.
tr. by Edward Caswall, 1814–1878

27. Bread of the World
98 98

EUCHARISTIC HYMN
JOHN S. B. HODGES, 1830–1915

1. Bread of the world, in mercy broken,
Wine of the soul, in mercy shed,
By whom the words of life were spoken,
And in whose death our sins are dead:

2. Oh, see the heart by sorrow broken,
Here too the tears by Mary shed;
Blest is this Feast more than mere token,
The body broken, thy blood red.

3. Eternal Word, our Lord, our Savior,
Taking away our sin and shame,
Incarnate Love, our hope, our Treasure,
We worship and adore thy name.

4. O Lamb of God, our Friend and Brother,
We cry for joy to meet thee here;
Now send us out to do thee honor;
Stay with us till that day appear.

REGINALD HEBER, 1783–1826

28 Bread of the World
98 98 D

RENDEZ Á DIEU   LOUIS BOURGEOIS, 1510–1561

1 Bread of the world, in mercy broken, Wine of the soul, in mercy shed, by whom the words of life were spoken, and in whose death our sins are dead: O, see thy Heart by sorrow broken, here too the tears by Mary shed; Blest is this Feast more than mere token, Thy Body broken, thy blood red.

2 Eternal Word, our Lord, our Savior, Taking away our sin and shame, Incarnate Love, our Hope, our Treasure, we worship and adore thy name. O Lamb of God, our Friend and Brother, we cry for joy to meet thee here; Now send us out to do thee honor; Stay with us till that day appear.

REGINALD HEBER, 1783–1826

29 Bright the Vision That Delighted
87 87

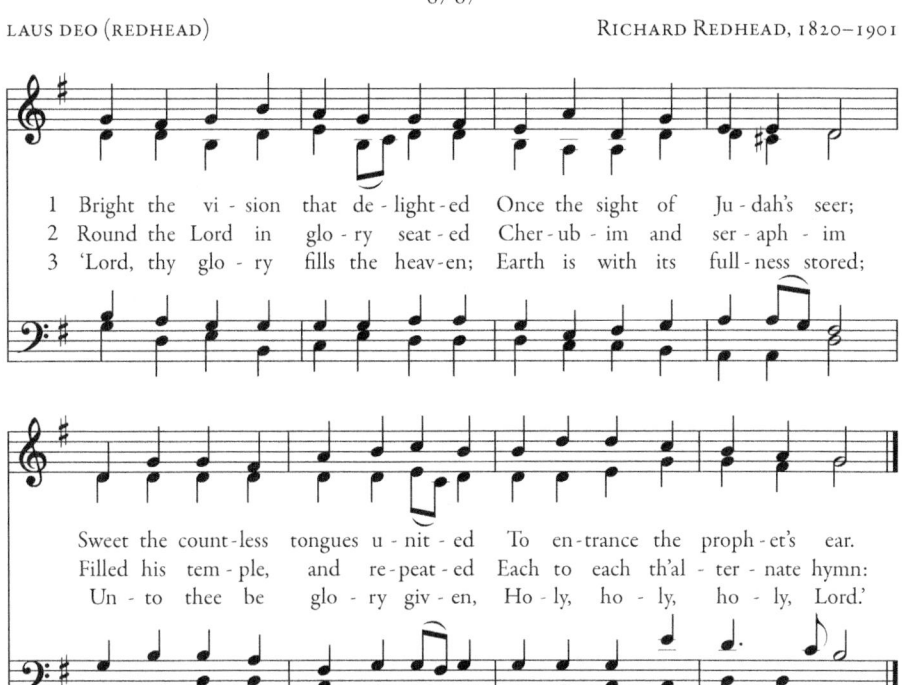

LAUS DEO (REDHEAD) — RICHARD REDHEAD, 1820–1901

1. Bright the vision that delighted
Once the sight of Judah's seer;
Sweet the countless tongues united
To entrance the prophet's ear.

2. Round the Lord in glory seated
Cherubim and seraphim
Filled his temple, and repeated
Each to each th'alternate hymn:

3. 'Lord, thy glory fills the heaven;
Earth is with its fullness stored;
Unto thee be glory given,
Holy, holy, holy, Lord.'

4. Heaven is still with glory ringing,
Earth takes up the angels' cry,
'Holy, holy, holy,' singing,
'Lord of hosts, the Lord most high.'

5. With his seraph train before him,
With his holy Church below,
Thus unite we to adore him,
Bid we thus our anthem flow:

6. 'Lord, thy glory fills the heaven;
Earth is with its fullness stored;
Unto thee be glory given,
Holy, holy, holy, Lord.'

BASED ON ISAIAH 6
Hymn commemorative of the "Thrice Holy"; RICHARD MANT, 1776–1848

30 Brightest and Best
11 10 11 10

LIEBSTER IMMANUEL

HIMMELSLUST, JENA, 1679
HARM. BY JOHANN SEBASTIAN BACH, 1685–1750

1. Brightest and best of the stars of the morning,
Dawn on our darkness, and lend us thine aid;
Star of the east, the horizon adorning,
Guide where our infant Redeemer is laid.

2. Cold on his cradle the dew-drops are shining,
Low lies his head with the beasts of the stall;
Angels adore him in slumber reclining,
Maker and Monarch and Savior of all.

3. Say, shall we yield him, in costly devotion,
Odors of Edom, and of f'rings divine,
Gems of the mountain, and pearls of the ocean,
Myrrh from the forest, and gold from the mine?

4. Vainly we offer each ample oblation,
Vainly with gifts would his favor secure,
Richer by far is the heart's adoration,
Dearer to God are the prayers of the poor.

REGINALD HEBER, 1783–1826

31 Brightest and Best
11 10 11 10

MORNING STAR
JAMES P. HARDING, 1850–1911

1. Brightest and best of the stars of the morning,
Dawn on our darkness, and lend us thine aid;
Star of the east, the horizon adorning,
Guide where our infant Redeemer is laid.

2. Cold on his cradle the dewdrops are shining,
Low lies his head with the beasts of the stall;
Angels adore him in slumber reclining,
Maker and Monarch and Savior of all.

3. Say, shall we yield him, in costly devotion,
Odors of Edom, and off'rings divine,
Gems of the mountain, and pearls of the ocean,
Myrrh from the forest, and gold from the mine?

4. Vainly we offer each ample oblation,
Vainly with gifts would his favor secure,
Richer by far is the heart's adoration,
Dearer to God are the prayers of the poor.

REGINALD HEBER, 1783–1826

32 Bring Flowers of the Rarest

12 11 WITH REFRAIN

QUEEN OF THE ANGELS

WREATH OF MARY, 1883
HARM. ALT. BY NOEL JONES, 1947–

1. Bring flow'rs of the rarest, bring blossoms the fairest,
From garden and woodland and hillside and vale;
Our full hearts are swelling, our glad voices telling

2. Our voices ascending, in harmony blending,
O thus may our hearts turn, dear Mother, to thee;
O thus shall we prove thee how truly we love thee,

3. O Virgin most tender, our homage we render,
Thy love and protection, sweet Mother, to win;
In danger defend us, in sorrow befriend us,

4. Of Mothers the dearest, oh, wilt thou be nearest
When life with temptation is darkly replete?
Forsake us, O never! our hearts be they ever

34 • A CATHOLIC BOOK OF HYMNS

The praise of the love - li - est Rose of the vale.
How dark with - out Ma - ry life's jour - ney would be.
And shield our hearts from con - ta - gion and sin.
As pure as the lil - ies we lay at thy feet.

O Ma - ry, we crown thee with blos - soms to-day, Queen of the An - gels, Queen of the May. O Ma - ry, we crown thee with blos - soms to - day, Queen of the An - gels, Queen of the May.

MARY E. WALSH

33 By the Blood That Flowed From Thee
77 77 D

AUGUSTUS EDMONDS TOZER, 1857–1919

1. By the blood that flowed from thee, In thy bitter agony;
   By the scourge so meekly borne; By thy purple robe of scorn,
   Jesus, Savior, hear our cry; Thou wert suff'ring once as we;
   Hear the loving Litany We thy children sing to thee.

2. By the thorns that crowned thy head; By thy scepter of a reed;
   By thy footstep faint and slow, Weighed beneath thy Cross of woe,
   Jesus, Savior, hear our cry; Thou wert suff'ring once as we;
   Hear the loving Litany We thy children sing to thee.

3. By the nails and pointed spear; By thy people's cruel jeer;
   By thy dying prayer which rose Begging mercy for thy foes.
   Jesus, Savior, hear our cry; Thou wert suff'ring once as we;
   Hear the loving Litany We thy children sing to thee.

4. By the darkness thick as night
   Blotting out the sun from sight;
   By the cry with which in death
   Thou didst yield thy parting breath.

5. By thy weeping Mother's woe;
   By the sword that pierced her through,
   When, in anguish standing by,
   On the Cross she saw thee die.

ATTR. TO FREDERICK W. FABER, 1814–1863

34. By the First Bright Easter Day

77 77 D

MENDELSSOHN
FELIX MENDELSSOHN, 1809–1847

1. By the first bright Easter day, / When the stone was rolled away; / By the glory round thee shed / At the rising from the dead. / King of glory, hear our cry; / Make us soon thy joy to see, / Where enthroned in majesty / Countless angels sing to thee.

2. By thy parting blessing giv'n / As thou didst ascend to heav'n; / By the cloud of living light / That received thee out of sight. / King of glory, hear our cry; / Make us soon thy joy to see, / Where enthroned in majesty / Countless angels sing to thee.

3. By that rushing sound of might / Coming down from heaven's height; / By the cloven tongues of fire, / Holy Ghost, our hearts inspire. / King of glory, hear our cry; / Make us soon thy joy to see, / Where enthroned in majesty / Countless angels sing to thee.

4. See the Virgin Mother rise, / Angels bear her to the skies; / Mount aloft, imperial Queen, / Plead on high the cause of men!

5. Mary reigns upon the throne / Pre-ordained for her alone; / Saints and angels round her sing, / Mother of our God and King.

ATTR. TO FREDERICK W. FABER, 1814–1863

35. Christ Is Made the Sure Foundation
87 87 87

WESTMINSTER ABBEY
HENRY PURCELL, 1659–1695

1. Christ is made the sure foundation, Christ the head and cornerstone; Chosen of the Lord, and precious, Binding all the Church in one, Holy Zion's help forever, And her confidence alone.

2. To this temple, where we call thee, Come, O Lord of hosts, today; With thy wonted loving-kindness Hear thy servants as they pray. And thy fullest benediction Shed within its walls alway.

3. Here vouchsafe to all thy servants What they ask of thee to gain; What they gain from thee forever With the blessed to retain, And hereafter in thy glory Evermore with thee to reign.

4. Laud and honor to the Father, Laud and honor to the Son, Laud and honor to the Spirit, Ever three and ever one; Consubstantial, coeternal, While unending ages run.

ANGULARIS FUNDAMENTUM, 7TH CENT.
TR. BY JOHN M. NEALE, 1818–1866, ALT.

36 Christ, the Fair Glory of the Holy Angels
11 11 11 5

CAELITES PLAUDANT

ANTIPHONER, ROUEN, 1728
HARM. BY RALPH VAUGHAN WILLIAMS, 1872–1958

1. Christ, the fair glory of the holy angels, Ruler of all, and author of creation, Grant us in thy mercy grace to win by patience Realms everlasting.

2. Send forth thine angel Michael from thy presence: Peacemaker blessed, may he hover o'er us Hallow our dwellings, that for us thy children All things may prosper.

3. Send forth thine angel Gabriel the mighty; On strong wings flying, may he come from heaven, Drive from thy temple Satan the old foeman, Succor our weakness.

4. Send forth thine angel Raphael the healer,
   Through him with wholesome medicines of salvation,
   Heal our backsliding, and in paths of goodness
   Guide our steps daily.

5. May the blest mother of God and Savior,
   May the celestial company of angels,
   May the assembly of the saints in heaven,
   Help us to praise thee.

6. Father almighty, Son, and Holy Spirit,
   God ever blessèd, hear our thankful praises;
   Thine is the glory which from all creation
   Ever ascendeth.

CHRISTE SANCTORUM DECUS ANGELORUM; ATTR. TO RABANUS MAURUS, C. 776–856
TR. BY J. ATHELSTAN L. RILEY, 1858–1945, ALT.

37   Christ, the Glory of the Sky
77 77

CULBACH   SHEFFLER'S *HEILIGE SEELELUST*, 1657

1. Christ, the glory of the sky, Christ, of earth the hope secure, Only Son of God most high, Offspring of a Maiden pure.
2. Help us now thy praise to sing, Praise for this returning day; Light and life let morning bring, Clouds and darkness flee away.
3. Purest Light, within us dwell, Never from our souls depart; Come, the shades of earth dispel, Fill and purify the heart.

    4   Faith in him whose name we bear
           In our heart of hearts abound;
           Hope, thy brightest torch prepare;
           All with holy love be crowned.

    5   Praise the Father; praise the Son;
           Spirit blest, to thee be praise;
           To the eternal Three in One
           Glory be through endless days.

AETERNA CAELI GLORIA, 5TH CENT.
TR. BY ROBERT CAMPBELL, 1814–1866

38 Christ, the Lord, Is Risen Today
77 77 WITH ALLELUIAS

EASTER HYMN *Lyra Davidica*, 1708

1. Christ, the Lord, is ris'n to-day, Alleluia!
2. Lives a-gain our glo-rious King; Alleluia!
3. Love's re-deem-ing work is done, Alleluia!
4. Soar we now where Christ has led, Alleluia!

Sons of man and an-gels say! Alleluia!
Where, O death, is now thy sting? Alleluia!
Fought the fight, the bat-tle won, Alleluia!
Fol-l'wing our ex-alt-ed head; Alleluia!

Raise your joys and tri-umphs high, Alleluia!
Once he died our souls to save, Alleluia!
Death in vain for-bids him rise; Alleluia!
Made like him, like him we rise, Alleluia!

Sing, ye heav'ns and earth re-ply, Alleluia!
Where thy vic-to-ry, O grave? Alleluia!
Christ has o-pened par-a-dise. Alleluia!
Ours the cross, the grave, the skies. Alleluia!

Charles Wesley, 1707–1788, ALT.

39 Christ, the Lord, Is Risen Today
77 77 WITH ALLELUIAS

LLANFAIR · ROBERT WILLIAMS, 1781–1821

1. Christ, the Lord, is ris'n to-day,
2. Lives a-gain our glo-rious King;
3. Love's re-deem-ing work is done,
4. Soar we now where Christ has led,

Al - le - lu - ia!

Sons of men and an-gels say!
Where, O death, is now thy sting?
Fought the fight, the bat-tle won.
Fol-l'wing our ex-alt-ed head;

Al - le - lu - ia!

Raise your joys and tri-umphs high,
Once he died our souls to save,
Death in vain for-bids him rise;
Made like him, like him we rise,

Al - le - lu - ia!

Sing, ye heav'ns, and earth re-ply,
Where thy vic-to-ry, O grave?
Christ has o-pened par-a-dise.
Ours the cross, the grave, the skies.

Al - le - lu - ia!

CHARLES WESLEY, 1707–1788, ALT.

40   Christ, the Lord, Is Risen Today
77 77 D

VICTIMAE PASCHALI   WÜRTH'S *KATHOLISCHES GESANGBUCH*, 1859

1. Christ, the Lord, is ris'n to-day; Christians, haste your vows to pay;
   Offer ye your praises meet At the Paschal Victim's feet,
   For the sheep the Lamb hath bled, Sinless in the sinner's stead;
   Christ the Lord is ris'n on high; Now he lives, no more to die.

2. Christ, the Victim undefiled, Man to God hath reconciled;
   When in strange and awful strife Met together death and life;
   Christians, on this happy day, Haste with joy your vows to pay.
   Christ the Lord is ris'n on high; Now he lives, no more to die.

3. Say, O wond'ring Mary, say, What thou sawest on thy way;
   I beheld where Christ had lain, Empty tomb and angels twain.
   I beheld the glory bright Of the risen Lord of Light;
   Christ, my hope, is ris'n again; Now he lives, and lives to reign.

4. Christ, who once for sinners bled, Now the first-born from the dead,
   Throned in endless might and pow'r, Lives and reigns forevermore.
   Hail, eternal Hope on high! Hail, thou King of Victory!
   Hail, thou Prince of Life adored! Help and save us, gracious Lord.

VICTIMAE PASCHALI LAUDES; ATTR. TO WIPO OF BURGUNDY, C. 1000–1050
TR. BY JANE E. LEESON, 1807–1882, ALT.

41 Christ, the True Light of Us
88 88

O AMOR QUAM EXSTATICUS

OLD FRENCH MELODY
ADAPT. BY A. GREGORY MURRAY, 1905–1992

1. Christ, the true light of us, true morn, Dispersing far the shades of night, Light whereof ev'ry light is born, Pledge of the beatific light.

2. Thou all the night our guardian be, Whose watch no sleep or slumber knows; Thou be our peace, that stayed on thee Through darkness we may find repose.

3. But let no sloth our will be dim Nor Satan steal the burdened sense, Lest the frail flesh, in league with him, Lose before thee its innocence.

4. Sleep then our eyes, but never sleep
The watchful heaven-directed heart,
And may thy hand in safety keep
The servants whose desire thou art.

5. Look on us thou, and at our side
Our foes and thine repulse afar;
Through every ill the faithful guide
Who in thy blood redeemèd are.

6. While soul within the body clings,
Body and soul defend us, Lord,
Sure in the shadow of thy wings,
Kept in thy lasting watch and ward.

CHRISTE QUI LUX ES ET DIES, 8TH CENT.
TR. BY WALTER H. SHEWRING, 1906–1990

42. Come Down, O Love Divine
66 11 D

DOWN AMPNEY
RALPH VAUGHAN WILLIAMS, 1872–1958

1. Come down, O Love divine; Seek thou this soul of mine, And visit it with thine own ardor glowing. O Comforter, draw near, Within my heart appear, And kindle it, thy holy flame bestowing.

2. O let it freely burn, Till earthly passions turn To dust and ashes in its heat consuming; And let thy glorious light Shine ever on my sight, And clothe me round, the while my path illuming.

3. Let holy charity Mine outward vesture be, And lowliness become mine inner clothing; True lowliness of heart, Which takes the humbler part, And o'er its own shortcomings weeps with loathing.

4. And so the yearning strong, With which the soul will long, Shall far outpass the pow'r of human telling. For none can guess its grace, Till he become the place Wherein the Holy Spirit makes his dwelling.

DISCENDI, AMOR SANTO; BIANCO DA SIENA, D. 1434
TR. BY RICHARD F. LITTLEDALE, 1833–1890

43 Come, Holy Ghost, Creator Blest

88 88 WITH REPEAT

LAMBILLOTTE   LOUIS LAMBILLOTTE SJ, 1796–1855

1. Come, Holy Ghost, Creator blest, And in our hearts take up thy rest; Come with thy grace and heav'nly aid To fill the hearts which thou hast made. To fill the hearts which thou hast made.

2. O Comforter, to thee we cry, Thou heav'nly gift of God most high, Thou font of life and fire of love, And sweet anointing from above. And sweet anointing from above.

3. Praise be to thee, Father and Son, And Holy Spirit, Three in one; And may the Son on us bestow The gifts that from the Spirit flow. The gifts that from the Spirit flow.

VENI, CREATOR SPIRITUS; ATTR. TO RABANUS MAURUS, 776–856
TR. BY EDWARD CASWALL, 1814–1878, ALT.

44 Come, Holy Ghost, Creator Blest
88 88

KOMM, GOTT SCHÖPFER   J. KLUG'S *GEISTLICHE LIEDER*, 1543

1. Come, Holy Ghost, Creator blest, And in our hearts take up thy rest, Come with thy grace and heav'nly aid To fill the hearts which thou hast made.

2. O Comforter, to thee we cry; Thou heav'nly gift of God most high. Thou font of life and fire of love, And sweet anointing from above.

3. Praise be to thee, Father and Son, And Holy Spirit, Three in one; And may the Son on us bestow The gifts that from the Spirit flow.

VENI, CREATOR SPIRITUS; ATTR. TO RABANUS MAURUS, 776–856
TR. BY EDWARD CASWALL, 1814–1878, ALT.

45 Come, Holy Ghost, Creator, Come
86 86

SOUTHWOLD CHRISTOPHER DEARNLEY, 1930–2000

1 Come, Holy Ghost, Creator, come, From thy bright heav'nly throne; Come, take possession of our souls, And make them all thine own.

2 Thou who art called the Paraclete, Best gift of God above, The living spring, the living fire, Sweet unction and true love.

3 Thou who art sev'nfold in thy grace, Finger of God's right hand; His promise, teaching little ones To speak and understand.

4 O guide our minds with thy blest light,
With love our hearts inflame;
And with thy strength, which ne'er decays,
Confirm our mortal flame.

5 Far from us drive our deadly foe;
True peace unto us brings;
And through all perils lead us safe
Beneath thy sacred wing.

6 Through thee may we the Father know,
Through thee th'eternal Son,
And thee the Spirit of them both,
Thrice-blessèd Three in One.

7 All glory to the Father be,
With his co-equal Son:
The same to thee, great Paraclete,
While endless ages run.

VENI, CREATOR SPIRITUS; ATTR. TO RABANUS MAURUS, 776–856
TR. BY ANON.

46 Come, Holy Ghost, Who Ever One
88 88

LUDBOROUGH TIMOTHY R. MATTHEWS, 1826–1910

1. Come, Holy Ghost, who ever one Are with our Father and the Son; Come, Holy Ghost, our souls possess With your full flood of holiness.
2. In will and deed, by heart and tongue, With all our pow'rs, your praise be sung; And love light up our mortal frame, Till others catch the living flame.
3. Almighty Father, hear our cry Through Jesus Christ our Lord most high, Whom with the Spirit we adore And sing your praise for evermore.

NUNC SANCTE NOBIS SPIRITUS; AMBROSE OF MILAN, 340–397
TR. BY JOHN HENRY NEWMAN, 1801–1890, ALT.

47 Come, Holy Ghost, Who Ever One
88 88

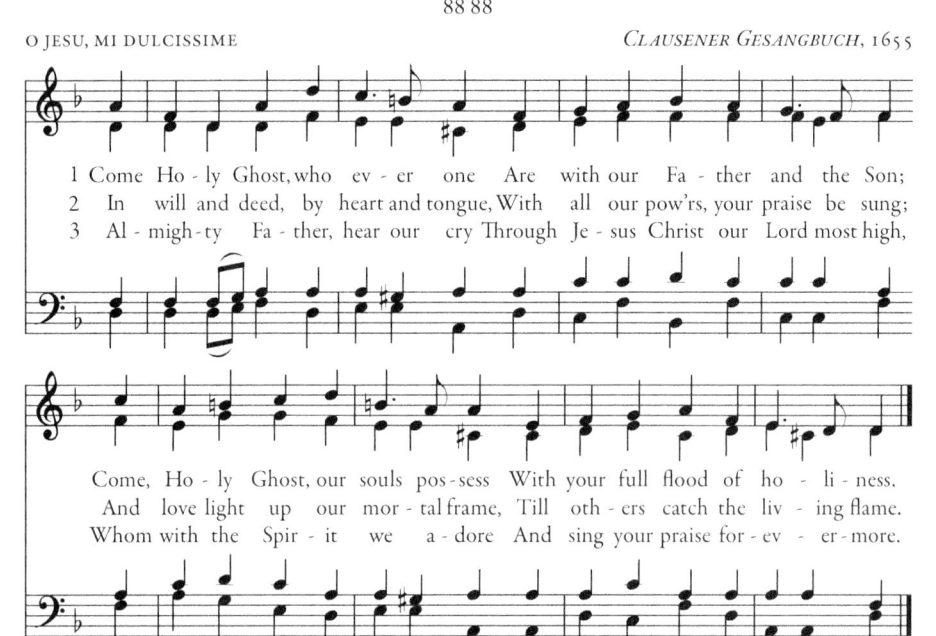

O JESU, MI DULCISSIME
CLAUSENER GESANGBUCH, 1655

1. Come Holy Ghost, who ever one Are with our Father and the Son;
   Come, Holy Ghost, our souls possess With your full flood of holiness.
2. In will and deed, by heart and tongue, With all our pow'rs, your praise be sung;
   And love light up our mortal frame, Till others catch the living flame.
3. Almighty Father, hear our cry Through Jesus Christ our Lord most high,
   Whom with the Spirit we adore And sing your praise forevermore.

Nunc Sancte nobis Spiritus; AMBROSE OF MILAN, 340–397
TR. BY JOHN HENRY NEWMAN, 1801–1890, ALT.

48 Come, My Way, My Truth, My Life
77 77

THE CALL
RALPH VAUGHAN WILLIAMS, 1872–1958

1. Come, my Way, my Truth, my Life: Such a way as gives us breath; Such a truth as ends all
2. Come, my Light, my Feast, my Strength: Such a light as shows a feast; Such a feast as mends in
3. Come, my Joy, my Love, my Heart: Such a joy as none can move; Such a love as none can

strife; Such a life as kill - eth death.
length; Such a strength as makes his guest.
part; Such a heart as joys in love.

GEORGE HERBERT, 1593–1633

49 Come, My Way, My Truth, My Life
77 77

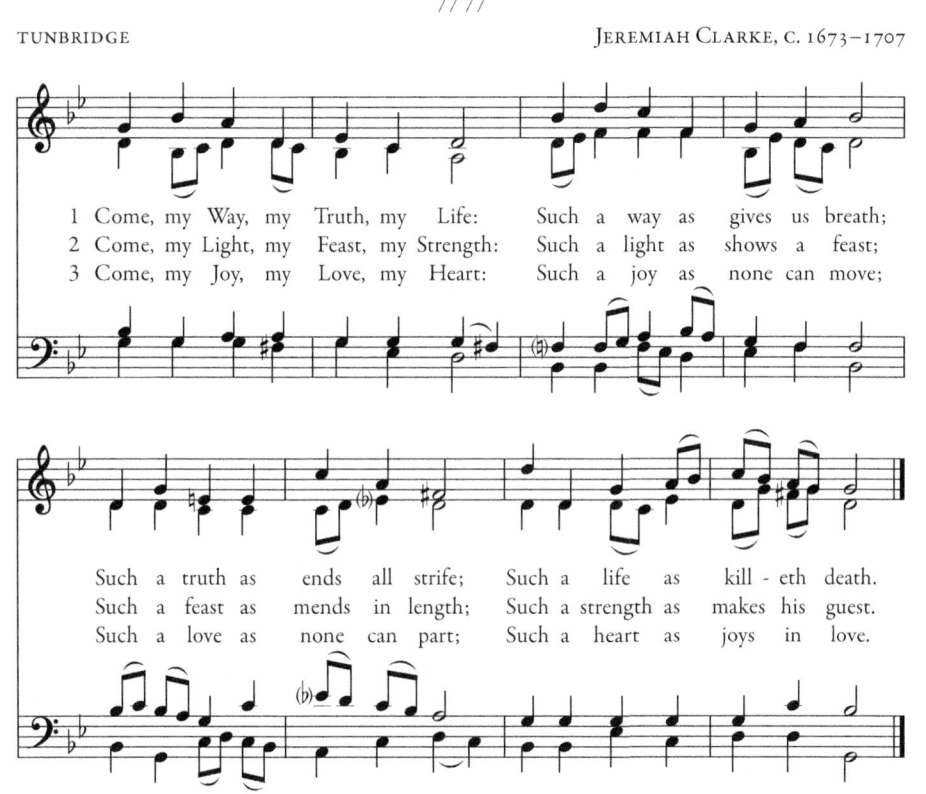

TUNBRIDGE

JEREMIAH CLARKE, C. 1673–1707

1 Come, my Way, my Truth, my Life: Such a way as gives us breath;
2 Come, my Light, my Feast, my Strength: Such a light as shows a feast;
3 Come, my Joy, my Love, my Heart: Such a joy as none can move;

Such a truth as ends all strife; Such a life as kill-eth death.
Such a feast as mends in length; Such a strength as makes his guest.
Such a love as none can part; Such a heart as joys in love.

GEORGE HERBERT, 1593–1633

50. Come, Thou Almighty King

66 4 666 4

ITALIAN HYMN — FELICE DE GIARDINI, 1716–1796

1. Come, thou Almighty King, Help us thy name to sing, Help us to praise. Father all glorious, O'er all victorious, Come, and reign over us, Ancient of Days.

2. Come, thou Incarnate Word, Who for us death endured, Our prayer attend; Come and thy people bless, And give thy word success; Fill us with righteousness, Savior and friend.

3. Come, Holy Comforter, Thy sacred witness bear In this glad hour: To us thy grace impart; And rule in ev'ry heart! Never from us depart, Spirit of pow'r!

4. To thee, O Trinity, Eternal praises be Forevermore! Thy sov'reign majesty May we in glory see, And to eternity Love and adore!

ANON., C. 1757, ALT.

51 Come, Thou Holy Spirit, Come
777 777

VENI SANCTE SPIRITUS   SAMUEL WEBBE, SR., 1740–1816

1. Come, thou Holy Spirit, come! And from thy celestial home
Shed a ray of light divine! Come, thou Father of the poor!
Come, thou Source of all our store! Come, within our bosoms shine!

2. Thou of comforters the best; Thou, the soul's most welcome Guest;
Sweet refreshment here below; In our labor rest most sweet;
Grateful coolness in the heat; Solace in the midst of woe.

3. O most blessed Light divine, Shine within these hearts of thine,
And our inmost being fill! Where thou art not, man hath naught,
Nothing good in deed or thought, Nothing free from taint of ill.

4. Heal our wounds; our strength renew;
On our dryness pour thy dew;
Wash the stains of guilt away;
Bend the stubborn heart and will;
Melt the frozen, warm the chill;
Guide the steps that go astray.

5. On the faithful, who adore
And confess thee, evermore
In thy sev'nfold gift descend:
Give them virtue's sure reward,
Give them thy salvation, Lord,
Give them joys that never end.

FROM THE SEQUENCE FOR PENTECOST SUNDAY
VENI, SANCTE SPIRITUS; ATTR. TO STEPHEN LANGTON, 1160–1228
TR. BY EDWARD CASWALL, 1814–1878

52. Come, Thou Long-Expected Jesus
87 87

STUTTGART

WITT'S *PSALMODIA SACRA*, GOTHA, 1715
ADAPT. BY HENRY J. GAUNTLETT, 1805–1876

1. Come, thou long-expected Jesus, Born to set thy people free; From our fears and sins release us; Let us find our rest in thee.
2. Israel's strength and consolation, Hope of all the earth thou art: Dear desire of ev'ry nation, Joy of ev'ry longing heart.
3. Born thy people to deliver, Born a child, and yet a king, Born to reign in us forever, Now thy gracious kingdom bring.
4. By thine own eternal Spirit Rule in all our hearts alone; By thine all-sufficient merit Raise us to thy glorious throne.

CHARLES WESLEY, 1707–1788

53. Come, Ye Faithful, Raise the Strain
76 76 D

GAUDEAMUS PARITER
JOHANN HORN, C. 1495–1547

1. Come, ye faithful, raise the strain Of triumphant gladness;
God hath brought his Israel Into joy from sadness;
Loosed from Pharaoh's bitter yoke Jacob's sons and daughters;
Led them with unmoistened foot Through the Red Sea waters.

2. 'Tis the spring of souls today; Christ hath burst his prison,
And from three days' sleep in death As a sun hath risen;
All the winter of our sins, Long and dark, is flying
From his light, to whom we give Laud and praise undying.

3. Now the queen of seasons, bright With the day of splendor,
With the royal feast of feasts, Comes its joy to render;
Comes to glad Jerusalem, Who with true affection
Welcomes in unwearied strains Jesus' resurrection.

4. Neither might the gates of death, Nor the tomb's dark portal,
Nor the watchers, nor the seal Hold thee as a mortal;
But today amidst the twelve Thou didst stand, bestowing
That thy peace which evermore Passeth human knowing.

BASED ON EXODUS 15
Ἀίσωμεν, πάντες λαοί; JOHN OF DAMASCUS, C. 675–749
TR. BY JOHN M. NEALE, 1818–1866

54. Come, Ye Thankful People, Come
77 77 D

ST. GEORGE'S WINDSOR — GEORGE J. ELVEY, 1816–1893

1. Come, ye thankful people, come, Raise the song of harvest home; All is safely gathered in Ere the winter storms begin; God, our Maker, doth provide For our wants to be supplied; Come, to God's own temple come; Raise the song of harvest home.

2. We ourselves are God's own field, Fruit unto his praise to yield; Wheat and tares together sown Unto joy or sorrow grown; First the blade and then the ear, Then the full corn shall appear; Grant, O harvest Lord, that we Wholesome grain and pure may be.

3. Ev-en so, Lord, quickly come Bring thy final harvest home; Gather all thy people in, Free from sorrow, free from sin; There, forever purified, In thy presence to abide: Come, with all thine angels, come; Raise the glorious harvest home.

BASED ON PSALM 100:4
AFTER HARVEST; HENRY ALFORD, 1810–1871, ALT.

55 Comfort, Comfort Ye My People
87 87 77 88

GENEVAN 42

LOUIS BOURGEOIS, C. 1510–1561
HARM. BY CLAUDE GOUDIMEL, C. 1505–1572

1. Comfort, comfort ye my people, Speak ye peace, thus saith our God;
Comfort those who sit in darkness, Mourning 'neath their sorrow's load.
Speak ye to Jerusalem Of the peace that waits for them;
Tell her that her sins I cover, And her warfare now is over.

2. Hark, the voice of one that crieth In the desert far and near,
Bidding all men to repentance Since the kingdom now is here.
O that warning cry obey! Now prepare for God a way;
Let the valleys rise to meet him And the hills bow down to greet him.

3. Make ye straight what long was crooked, Make the rougher places plain;
Let your hearts be true and humble, As befits his holy reign.
For the glory of the Lord Now o'er earth is shed abroad;
And all flesh shall see the token That his word is never broken.

BASED ON ISAIAH 40:1–8
TRÖSTET, TRÖSTET MEINE LIEBEN; JOHANN G. OLEARIUS, 1611–1684
TR. BY CATHERINE WINKWORTH, 1827–1878, ALT.

56 Creator of the Stars of Night
88 88

CONDITOR ALME SIDERUM

SARUM PLAINSONG, MODE IV
HARM. BY J. ALFRED SCHEHL, 1882–1959

1 Cre - a - tor of the stars of night, Thy peo-ple's ev - er - last-ing Light;
  Je - su, Re-deem - er, save us all, And hear thy ser - vants when they call.

2 Thou, griev-ing that the an - cient curse Should doom to death a u - ni - verse,
  Hast found the med'-cine, full of grace, To save and heal a ru - ined race.

3 Thou cam'st, the Bridegroom of the Bride, As drew the world to e - ven - tide;
  Pro - ceed-ing from a Vir - gin shrine, The spot-less Vic - tim all di - vine.

4 At whose dread Name, majestic now,
   All knees must bend, all hearts must bow:
   And things celestial thee shall own,
   And things terrestrial, Lord alone.

5 O thou, whose coming is with dread
   To judge and doom the quick and dead,
   Preserve us, while we dwell below,
   From ev'ry insult of the foe.

6 To God the Father, God the Son,
   And God the Spirit, Three in One,
   Laud, honor, might, and glory be
   From age to age eternally.

CONDITOR (CREATOR) ALME SIDERUM; 7TH CENT.
TR. BY JOHN M. NEALE, 1818–1866, ALT.

57 Cross of Jesus
87 87

CROSS OF JESUS
JOHN STAINER, 1840–1901

1 Cross of Jesus, cross of sorrow, Where the blood of Christ was shed, Perfect Man on thee did suffer, Perfect God on thee has bled!
2 Here the King of all the ages, Throned in light ere worlds could be, Robed in mortal flesh is dying, Crucified by sin for me.
3 O mysterious condescending! O abandonment sublime! Very God himself is bearing All the sufferings of time.
4 Cross of Jesus, cross of sorrow, Where the blood of Christ was shed, Perfect Man on thee did suffer, Perfect God on thee has bled!

WILLIAM J. SPARROW-SIMPSON, 1860–1952

58. Crown Him With Many Crowns
66 86 D

DIADEMATA
GEORGE J. ELVEY, 1816–1893

1. Crown him with many crowns, The Lamb upon his throne; Hark! how the heav'nly anthem drowns All music but its own. Awake, my soul, and sing Of him who died for thee, And hail him as thy matchless King Through all eternity.

2. Crown him the Lord of life, Who triumphed o'er the grave, And rose victorious in the strife For those he came to save. His glories now we sing, Who died and rose on high, Who died, eternal life to bring, And lives that death may die.

3. Crown him the Lord of love, Behold his hands and side, Rich wounds yet visible above In beauty glorified. No angel in the sky Can fully bear that sight, But downward bends his burning eye At mysteries so bright.

4 Crown him the Lord of peace,
　　Whose pow'r a scepter sways
　　From pole to pole, that wars may cease,
　　Absorbed in prayer and praise.
　　His reign shall know no end,
　　And round his piercèd feet
　　Fair flow'rs of Paradise extend
　　Their fragrance ever sweet.

5 Crown him the Lord of years,
　　The Potentate of time,
　　Creator of the rolling spheres,
　　Ineffably sublime,
　　All hail, Redeemer, hail!
　　For thou hast died for me;
　　Thy praise and glory shall not fail
　　Throughout eternity.

vss. 1, 3–5, Matthew Bridges, 1800–1894, alt.
vs. 2, Godfrey Thring, 1823–1903

59   Daily, Daily, Sing to Mary
87 87 D

DAILY, DAILY   19TH CENT. FORM OF MARIA ZU LIEBEN

1. Daily, daily, sing to Mary; Sing, my soul, her praises due:
All her feasts, her actions worship With the heart's devotion true.
Lost in wond'ring contemplation, Be her Majesty confess'd;
Call her Mother, call her Virgin, Happy Mother, Virgin blest.

2. She is mighty to deliver; Call her, trust her lovingly,
When the tempest rages round thee; She will calm the troubled sea.
Gifts of heaven she has given, Noble Lady, to our race:
She, the Queen, who decks her subjects With the light of God's own grace.

3. Sing, my tongue, the Virgin's trophies Who for us her Maker bore,
For the curse of old inflicted, Peace and blessing to restore.
Sing in songs of peace unending, Sing the world's majestic Queen:
Weary not nor faint in telling, All the gifts she gives to men.

4. All our joys do flow from Mary; All then join her praise to sing:
Trembling sing the Virgin Mother, Mother of our Lord and King.
While we sing her awful glory, Far above our fancy's reach,
Let our hearts be quick to offer Love alone the heart can teach.

OMNI DIE DIC MARIAE; ATTR. TO BERNARD OF CLUNY, 12TH CENT.
TR. BY HENRY BITTLESTON, 1818–1886

62 • A CATHOLIC BOOK OF HYMNS

60 Daughter of a Mighty Father
87 87 with refrain

St. Basil's Hymnal, 1918

1. Daughter of a mighty Father, Stainless Maiden Queen of May;
Angel forms around thee gather: Mácula non est in te.
2. Mother of the Son and Savior, Of the Truth, the Life, the Way;
Guide our footsteps, calm our passions: Mácula non est in te.
3. Spouse of the Eternal Spirit, Listen to our earnest lay;
Grant we may thy love inherit: Mácula non est in te.
4. Brightest Star in heaven's glory, Let thy splendor light our way;
Guide and help us, love and bless us: Mácula non est in te.

Refrain: Mácula non est in te, Mácula non est in te, Mácula non est in te, Mácula non est in te.

Mácula non est in te, Anonymous
The Catholic Youth's Hymn Book, 1871

61 Dear Angel! Ever at My Side
86 86

NICOLA A. MONTANI, 1880–1948

1. Dear Angel! ever at my side, How loving must thou be,
To leave thy home in Heav'n to guide A sinful child like me.

2. Thy beautiful and shining face, I see not, tho' so near;
The sweetness of thy soft low voice Too deaf am I to hear.

3. But when, dear Spirit, I kneel down, Both morn and night to prayer,
Something there is within my heart, Which tells me thou art there.

4. Oh! when I pray thou prayest too,
Thy prayer is all for me;
But when I sleep, thou sleepest not,
But watchest patiently.

5. Then, for thy sake, dear Angel! now
More humble will I be:
But I am weak, and when I fall,
O weary not of me.

6. Then love me, love me, Angel dear!
And I will love thee more;
And help me when my soul is cast
Upon th'eternal shore.

FREDERICK W. FABER, 1814–1863

62. Dear Guardian of Mary
11 11 11 11

Bro. Bonitus

1. Dear Guardian of Mary! dear nurse of her Child! Life's ways are full weary, the desert is wild, Bleak sands are all round us, no home can we see; Sweet Spouse of our Lady, we lean safe on thee.

2. For thou to the pilgrim art father and guide, And Jesus and Mary felt safe at thy side. O Glorious Patron, secure shall I be, Sweet Spouse of our Lady, if thou stay with me!

3. God chose thee for Jesus and Mary; wilt thou Forgive a poor exile for choosing thee now? There's no saint in heaven, Saint Joseph like thee, Sweet Spouse of our Lady, do thou plead for me.

4. When the treasures of God were unsheltered on earth, Safekeeping was found for them both in thy worth, O Father of Jesus! be father to me, Sweet Spouse of our Lady, and I will love thee.

Frederick W. Faber, 1814–1863, alt.

63 Deck Thyself, My Soul, With Gladness
88 88 D

SCHMÜCKE DICH

JOHANN CRÜGER, 1598–1662
HARM. BY J. ALFRED SCHEHL, 1882–1959

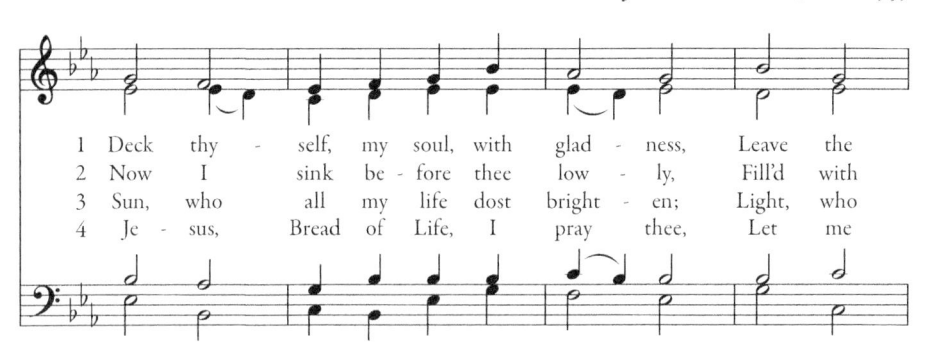

1 Deck thy-self, my soul, with glad - ness, Leave the gloom-y haunts of sad - ness; Come in - to the day - light's splen - dor, There with joy thy prais - es ren - der,

2 Now I sink be - fore thee low - ly, Fill'd with joy most deep and ho - ly, As with trem - bling awe and won - der On thy might - y works I pon - der;

3 Sun, who all my life dost bright - en; Light, who dost my soul en - light - en; Joy, the sweet - est man e'er know - eth; Fount, whence all my be - ing flow - eth:

4 Je - sus, Bread of Life, I pray thee, Let me glad - ly here o - bey thee; Nev - er to my hurt in - vit - ed, Be thy love with love re - quit - ed:

Un - to him, whose grace un - bound - ed Hath this won-drous ban-quet found - ed; High o'er all the heav'ns he reign - eth, Yet to dwell with thee he deign - eth.
How, by mys - ter - y sur - round - ed, Depths no man hath ev - er sound - ed, None may dare to pierce un - bid - den Se - crets that with thee are hid - den.
At thy feet I cry, my Mak - er, Let me be a fit par - tak - er Of this bless - ed food from heav - en, For our good, thy glo - ry giv - en.
From this ban - quet let me meas - ure, Lord, how vast and deep its treas - ure; Through the gifts thou here dost give me, As thy guest in heav'n re - ceive me.

Schmücke dich, o liebe Seele; Johann Franck, 1618–1677
tr. by Catherine Winkworth, 1827–1878

64 Down in Adoration Falling
87 87 87

ST. THOMAS (WADE)   JOHN F. WADE, 1711–1786

1. Down in adoration falling, This great sacrament we hail; Over ancient forms of worship, Newer rites of grace prevail; Faith will tell us Christ is present When our human senses fail.

2. To the everlasting Father And the Son who made us free And the Spirit God proceeding From them each eternally, Be salvation, honor, blessing, Might, and endless majesty. A - men.

Tantum ergo; ATTR. TO THOMAS AQUINAS, 1227–1274
TR. BY EDWARD CASWALL, 1814–1878, ALT.

65 Draw Near and Take the Body of the Lord
10 10

COENA DOMINI ARTHUR S. SULLIVAN, 1842–1900

1. Draw near and take the body of the Lord,
   And drink with faith the blood for you outpoured;
2. Saved by his body, hallowed by his blood,
   With souls refreshed we give our thanks to God.
3. Salvation's giver, Christ, the only Son,
   By his dear cross and blood the vict'ry won.

4. With heav'nly bread he makes the hungry whole,
   Gives living waters to the thirsting soul.

5. Before thy presence, Lord, all people bow.
   In this thy feast of love be with us now.

SANCTI, VENITE, CHRISTE CORPUS SUMITE, 7TH CENT.
TR. BY JOHN M. NEALE, 1818–1866, ALT.

66 Eternal Father, Strong to Save
88 88 88

MELITA

JOHN B. DYKES, 1823–1876

1. E-ternal Father, strong to save, Whose arm doth bind the restless wave, Who bidst the mighty ocean deep Its own appointed limits keep: O hear us when we cry to thee For those in peril on the sea.

2. O Christ, the Lord of hill and plain O'er which our traffic runs amain By mountain pass or valley low; Wherever, Lord, thy brethren go, Protect them by thy guarding hand From ev'ry peril on the land.

3. O Spirit, whom the Father sent To spread abroad the firmament; O Wind of heaven, by thy might Save all who dare the eagle's flight, And keep them by thy watchful care From ev'ry peril in the air.

4. O Trinity of love and pow'r, Our brethren shield in danger's hour; From rock and tempest, fire and foe, Protect them where-so-e'er they go; Thus evermore shall rise to thee Glad praise from air and land and sea.

VSS. 1, 4, WILLIAM WHITING, 1825–1878, ALT.
VSS. 2–3, ROBERT N. SPENCER, 1877–1961, ALT.

67 Fairest Lord Jesus
5 6 8 5 5 8

SCHÖNSTER HERR JESU

MÜNSTER GESANGBUCH, 1677

1. Fair-est Lord Je-sus, Rul-er of all na-ture,
O thou of God and man the Son,
Thee will I cher-ish, Thee will I hon-or,
Thou, my soul's glo-ry, joy, and crown.

2. Fair are the mead-ows, Fair-er still the wood-lands,
Robed in the bloom-ing garb of spring:
Je-sus is fair-er, Je-sus is pur-er,
Who makes the woe-ful heart to sing.

3. Fair is the sun-shine, Fair-er still the moon-light,
And all the twin-kling, star-ry host:
Je-sus shines bright-er, Je-sus shines pur-er,
Than all the an-gels heav'n can boast.

4. Beau-ti-ful Sav-ior! Lord of all the na-tions!
Son of God and Son of Man!
Glo-ry and hon-or, Praise, a-do-ra-tion,
Now and for-ev-er-more be thine.

SCHÖNSTER HERR JESU; ANON. GERMAN HYMN, *MÜNSTER GESANGBUCH*, 1677
VSS. 1–3, TR. SOURCE UNKNOWN
VS. 4, TR. BY JOSEPH AUGUSTUS SEISS, 1823–1904

68 Fairest Lord Jesus
5 6 8 55 8

ST. ELIZABETH *SCHLESISCHE VOLKSLIEDER*, LEIPZIG, 1842

1. Fair-est Lord Je-sus, Rul-er of all na-ture, O thou of God and man the Son, Thee will I cher-ish, Thee will I hon-or, Thou, my soul's glo-ry, joy, and crown.
2. Fair are the mead-ows, Fair-er still the wood-lands, Robed in the bloom-ing garb of spring: Je-sus is fair-er, Je-sus is pur-er, Who makes the woe-ful heart to sing.
3. Fair is the sun-shine, Fair-er still the moon-light, And all the twin-kling star-ry host: Je-sus shines bright-er, Je-sus shines pur-er, Than all the an-gels heav'n can boast.
4. Beau-ti-ful Sav-ior! Lord of all the na-tions! Son of God and Son of Man! Glo-ry and hon-or, Praise, a-do-ra-tion, Now and for-ev-er-more be thine.

SCHÖNSTER HERR JESU; ANON. GERMAN HYMN, *MÜNSTER GESANGBUCH*, 1677
VSS. 1–3, TR. SOURCE UNKNOWN
VS. 4, TR. BY JOSEPH AUGUSTUS SEISS, 1823–1904

69 Faith of Our Fathers
88 88 88

ST. CATHERINE

HENRI F. HEMY, 1818–1888
ADAPT. BY JAMES G. WALTON, 1821–1905

1. Faith of our fathers, living still, In spite of dungeon, fire and sword; O how our hearts beat high with joy, When-e'er we hear that glorious word: Faith of our fathers, holy faith! We will be true to thee till death.

2. Our fathers, chained in prisons dark, Were still in heart and conscience free; And blest would be their children's fate If we, like them, should die for thee. Faith of our fathers, holy faith! We will be true to thee till death.

3. Faith of our fathers, Mary's prayers Shall win all nations unto thee; And through the truth that comes from God, Mankind shall then indeed be free. Faith of our fathers, holy faith! We will be true to thee till death.

4. Faith of our fathers, we will love Both friend and foe in all our strife; And preach thee, too, as love knows how By kindly deeds and virtuous life. Faith of our fathers, holy faith! We will be true to thee till death.

FREDERICK W. FABER, 1814–1863, ALT.

70 Faith of Our Fathers

88 88 88 WITH REPEAT

SAWSTON

TRADITIONAL IRISH MELODY
ADAPT. BY A. GREGORY MURRAY, 1905–1992

1. Faith of our fathers! living still In spite of dungeon, fire and sword. O how our hearts beat high with joy When-e'er we hear that glorious word!

2. Our fathers, chained in prisons dark, Were still in heart and con-science free; And blest would be their chil-dren's fate If we, like them, should die for thee.

3. Faith of our fathers! Ma-ry's prayers Shall win all na-tions un-to thee; And through the truth that comes from God, Man-kind shall then in-deed be free.

4. Faith of our fathers! we will love Both friends and foe in all our strife, And preach thee, too, as love knows how By kind-ly words and vir-tuous life.

Faith of our fathers, holy faith! We will be true to thee till death. We will be true to thee till death.

FREDERICK W. FABER, 1814–1863, ALT.

71 Faith of Our Fathers

88 88 87 WITH REPEAT

ST. BASIL'S HYMNAL, 1918

1. Faith of our fathers! living still In spite of dungeon, fire, and sword. O how our hearts beat high with joy When-e'er we hear that glorious word!
2. Our fathers, chained in prisons dark, Were still in heart and conscience free; And blest would be their children's fate If we, like them, should die for thee.
3. Faith of our fathers! Mary's prayers Shall win all nations unto thee; And through the truth that comes from God, Mankind shall then indeed be free:
4. Faith of our fathers! we will love Both friend and foe in all our strife, And preach thee, too, as love knows how By kindly words and virtuous life:

76 • A CATHOLIC BOOK OF HYMNS

Faith of our fa-thers, ho-ly faith! We'll be true to thee till death.

Faith of our fa-thers, ho-ly faith! We'll be true to thee till death.

FREDERICK W. FABER, 1814–1863, ALT.

72. Father, See Thy Children

11 11 11 11

GHENT

MELODY OF *ADORO TE*, CANON VAN DAMME OF GHENT
HARM. BY J. ALFRED SCHEHL, 1882–1959

1. Father, see thy children bending at thy throne,
Pleading here the Passion of thine only Son;
Pleading here before thee all his dying love,
As he pleads it ever in the courts above.

2. Not for our wants only we this Off'ring plead,
But for all thy children, who thy mercy need:
Bless thy faithful people, win thy wand'ring sheep,
Keep the souls departed, who in Jesus sleep.

WILLIAM HENRY HAMMOND JERVOIS, 1852–1905
AND W. B. TREVELYAN, 1853–1929

73. Firmly I Believe and Truly
87 87

DRAKE'S BROUGHTON — EDWARD ELGAR, 1857–1934

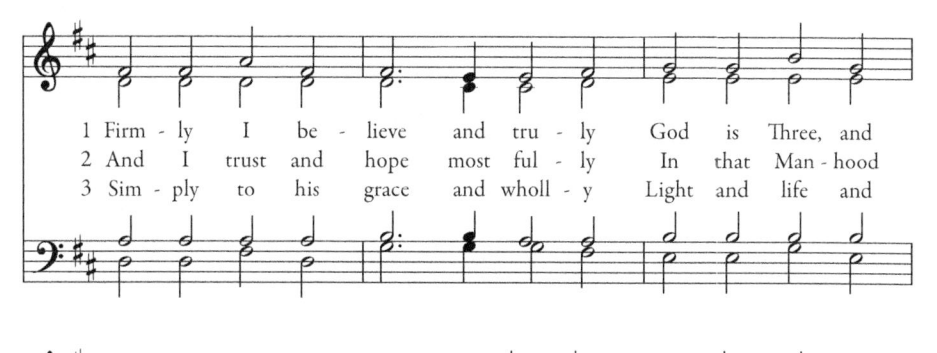

1. Firmly I believe and truly
   God is Three, and God is One;
   And I next acknowledge duly
   Manhood taken by the Son.

2. And I trust and hope most fully
   In that Manhood crucified;
   And each thought and deed unruly
   Do to death, as he has died.

3. Simply to his grace and wholly
   Light and life and strength belong,
   And I love supremely, solely,
   Him the holy, him the strong.

4. And I hold in veneration,
   For the love of him alone,
   Holy Church as his creation,
   And her teachings as his own.

5. Adoration aye be given,
   With and through th'angelic host,
   To the God of earth and heaven,
   Father, Son, and Holy Ghost.

6. And I take with joy whatever
   Now besets me, pain or fear,
   And with a strong will I sever
   All the ties which bind me here.

7. Sanctus fortis, Sanctus Deus,
   De profundis oro te,
   Miserere, Judex meus,
   Parce mihi, Domine.

Sanctus fortis; JOHN HENRY NEWMAN, 1801–1890

74. Firmly I Believe and Truly
87 87

MERTON   WILLIAM H. MONK, 1823–1889

1. Firmly I believe and truly
God is Three, and God is One;
And I next acknowledge duly
Manhood taken by the Son.

2. And I trust and hope most fully
In that Manhood crucified;
And each thought and deed unruly
Do to death, as he has died.

3. Simply to his grace and wholly
Light and life and strength belong,
And I love supremely, solely,
Him the holy, him the strong.

4. And I hold in veneration,
For the love of him alone,
Holy Church as his creation,
And her teachings as his own.

5. Adoration aye be given,
With and through th'angelic host,
To the God of earth and heaven,
Father, Son, and Holy Ghost.

6. And I take with joy whatever
Now besets me, pain or fear,
And with a strong will I sever
All the ties which bind me here.

7. Sanctus fortis, Sanctus Deus,
De profundis oro te,
Miserere, Judex meus,
Parce mihi, Domine.

SANCTUS FORTIS; JOHN HENRY NEWMAN, 1801–1890

75 For All the Saints

10 10 10 WITH ALLELUIAS

SINE NOMINE

RALPH VAUGHAN WILLIAMS, 1872–1958
HARM. ALT. BY NOEL JONES, 1947–

1. For all the saints who from their labors rest, Who thee by faith before the world confessed; Thy name, O Jesus, be forever blest. Alleluia, Alleluia!

2. Thou wast their Rock, their Fortress and their Might; Thou, Lord, their Captain in the well-fought fight; Thou, in the darkness drear, their one true light. Alleluia, Alleluia!

3. O blest communion, fellowship divine! We feebly struggle, they in glory shine; Yet all are one in thee, for all are thine. Alleluia, Alleluia!

4. And when the strife is fierce, the warfare long, Steals on the ear the distant triumph song, And hearts are brave again, and arms are strong. Alleluia, Alleluia!

5. But then there breaks a still more glorious day: The saints triumphant rise in bright array; The King of glory passes on his way. Alleluia, Alleluia!

6. From earth's wide bounds, from ocean's farthest coast, Through gates of pearl streams in the countless host, Singing to Father, Son, and Holy Ghost. Alleluia, Alleluia!

WILLIAM WALSHAM HOW, 1823–1897

A CATHOLIC BOOK OF HYMNS • 81

76   For the Beauty of the Earth
77 77 77

DIX

CONRAD KOCHER, 1786–1872
HARM. BY WILLIAM H. MONK, 1823–1889

1. For the beauty of the earth, For the glory of the skies,
For the love which from our birth Over and around us lies:
Lord of all, to thee we raise This our hymn of grateful praise.

2. For the beauty of each hour Of the day and of the night,
Hill and vale, and tree and flower, Sun and moon, and stars of light:
Lord of all, to thee we raise This our hymn of grateful praise.

3. For the joy of human love, Brother, sister, parent, child,
Friends on earth, and friends above; For all gentle thoughts and mild:
Lord of all, to thee we raise This our hymn of grateful praise.

4. For thy Church, that evermore
Lifteth holy hands above,
Off'ring up on ev'ry shore
Her pure sacrifice of love:

5. For thyself, best Gift Divine!
To our race so freely giv'n;
For that great, great love of thine,
Peace on earth and joy in heav'n:

THE SACRIFICE OF PRAISE; FOLLIOT S. PIERPOINT, 1835–1917, ALT.

77   Forty Days and Forty Nights
77 77

HEINLEIN

Nürnbergisches Gesang-Buch, Nuremberg, 1676
attr. to Martin Herbst, 1654–1681
harm. by William H. Monk, 1823–1889

1. Forty days and forty nights Thou wast fasting in the wild;
Forty days and forty nights, Tempted, and yet undefiled.

2. Shall not we thy sorrow share And from worldly joys abstain,
Fasting with unceasing prayer, Glad with thee to suffer pain?

3. Then, if Satan on us press, Flesh or spirit to assail,
Victor in the wilderness, Grant we may not faint nor fail!

4. Keep, O keep us, Savior dear, Ever constant at thy side;
That with thee we may appear At the eternal Eastertide.

George H. Smyttan, 1822–1870, alt.

78 From All Thy Saints in Warfare
76 76 D

KING'S LYNN

ENGLISH MELODY
HARM. BY RALPH VAUGHAN WILLIAMS, 1872–1958

1. From all thy saints in warfare, For all thy saints at rest,
To thee, O blessèd Jesus, All praises be addressed.
Thou, Lord, didst win the battle That they might conquerors be;
Their crowns of living glory Are lit with rays from thee.

2. Apostles, prophets, martyrs, And all the sacred throng
Who wear the spotless raiment, Who raise the ceaseless song—
For these, passed on before us, Savior, we thee adore,
And walking in their footsteps, Would serve thee more and more.

3. Then praise we God the Father, And praise we God the Son
And God the Holy Spirit, Eternal Three in One,
Till all the ransomed number Fall down before the throne,
And honor, power, and glory Ascribe to God alone.

HORATIO NELSON, 1823–1913

79 From All Thy Saints in Warfare
76 76 D

ST. THEODULPH
MELCHIOR TESCHNER, 1584–1635
HARM. BY WILLIAM H. MONK, 1823–1889

1. From all thy saints in warfare, For all thy saints at rest,
To thee, O blessed Jesus, All praises be addressed.
Thou, Lord, didst win the battle That they might conquerors be;
Their crowns of living glory Are lit with rays from thee.

2. Apostles, prophets, martyrs, And all the sacred throng
Who wear the spotless raiment, Who raise the ceaseless song—
For these, passed on before us, Savior, we thee adore,
And walking in their footsteps, Would serve thee more and more.

3. Then praise we God the Father, And praise we God the Son
And God the Holy Spirit, Eternal Three in One,
Till all the ransomed number Fall down before the throne,
And honor, power, and glory Ascribe to God alone.

HORATIO NELSON, 1823–1913

80 From the Depths We Cry to Thee
77 77

HEINLEIN

Nürnbergisches Gesang-Buch, Nuremberg, 1676
attr. to Martin Herbst, 1654–1681
harm. by William H. Monk, 1823–1889

1. From the depths we cry to thee, God of sov-'reign maj-es-ty!
   Hear our prayers and hymns of praise; Bless our Lent of for-ty days.
2. Lord, ac-cept our Lent-en fast And for-give our sin-ful past,
   That we may par-take with thee In the Eas-ter mys-ter-y.

Alan Gordon McDougal, 1895–1965, alt.

81 Full in the Panting Heart of Rome
88 88 with refrain

WISEMAN

C.A. Cox, 1853–1916
harm. by A. Gregory Murray, 1905–1992

1. Full in the pant-ing heart of Rome, Be-neath the A-
2. The gol-den roof, the mar-ble walls, The Va-ti-
3. Then surg-ing through each hal-lowed gate, Where mar-tyrs'

86 • A CATHOLIC BOOK OF HYMNS

post - le's crown - ing dome, From pil - grims' lips that
can's ma - jes - tic halls, The note re - dou - ble,
glo - ry, in peace, a - wait, It sweeps be - yond the

kiss the ground, Breathes in all tongues one on - ly sound:
till it fills With e - choes sweet the se - ven hills:
so - lemn plain, Peals o - ver Alps, a - cross the main:

"God bless our Pope, God bless our Pope,

God bless our Pope, the great, the good."

NICHOLAS PATRICK WISEMAN, 1802–1865

82 Glorious Things of Thee Are Spoken

87 87 D

BEACH SPRING

TRADITIONAL AMERICAN MELODY, *THE SACRED HARP*, 1844
ATTR. TO BENJAMIN F. WHITE, 1800–1879

1. Glorious things of thee are spoken, Zion, city of our God; He whose word cannot be broken Formed thee for his own abode; On the Rock of Ages founded, What can shake thy sure repose? With salvation's walls surrounded, Thou may'st smile at all thy foes.

2. See! The streams of living waters, Springing from eternal love, Well supply thy sons and daughters And all fear of want remove. Who can faint, when such a river Ever will their trust assuage? Grace which, like the Lord, the giver, Never fails from age to age.

3. Round each habitation hov'ring, See the cloud and fire appear For a glory and a cov'ring Showing that the Lord is near. Thus deriving from their banner, Light by night, and shade by day, Safe they feed upon the manna Which he gives them when they pray.

4. Blest inhabitants of Zion, Washed in the Redeemer's blood! Jesus, whom their souls rely on, Makes them kings and priests to God. 'Tis his love his people raises Over self to reign as kings: And as priests, his solemn praises Each for a thank off'ring brings.

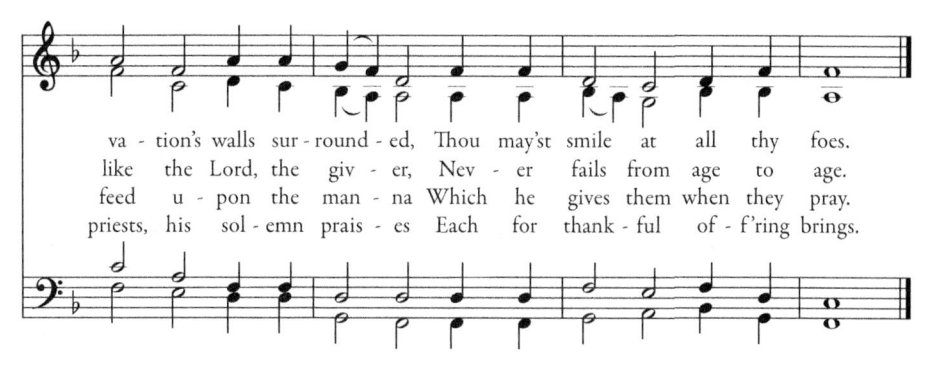

va - tion's walls sur - round - ed, Thou may'st smile at all thy foes.
like the Lord, the giv - er, Nev - er fails from age to age.
feed u - pon the man - na Which he gives them when they pray.
priests, his sol - emn prais - es Each for thank - ful of - f'ring brings.

Zion, or the City of God; John Newton, 1725–1807, alt.

83 Glory Be to Jesus
65 65

WEM IN LEIDENSTAGEN   FRIEDRICH FILITZ, 1804–1876

1 Glo - ry be to Je - sus, Who, in bit - ter pains,
2 Grace and life e - ter - nal In that blood I find;
3 Blest through end - less a - ges Be the pre - cious stream,

Poured for me the life - blood From his sa - cred veins.
Blest be his com - pas - sion, In - fi - nite - ly kind.
Which from end - less tor - ment Doth the world re - deem.

4 Abel's blood for vengeance
   Pleaded to the skies;
   But the blood of Jesus
   For our pardon cries.

5 Oft as it is sprinkled
   On our guilty hearts,
   Satan in confusion
   Terror-struck departs.

6 Oft as earth exulting
   Wafts its praise on high,
   Hell with terror trembles,
   Heav'n is filled with joy.

7 Lift ye then your voices;
   Swell the mighty flood;
   Louder still and louder
   Praise the precious blood.

Viva! viva! Gesù; anon., 18th cent.
tr. by Edward Caswall, 1814–1878

84 God of Mercy and Compassion
87 87 D

AU SANG QU'UN DIEU
TRADITIONAL FRENCH MELODY

1. God of mercy and compassion, Look with pity upon me.
Father, let me call thee Father, 'Tis thy child returns to thee.
Jesus, Lord, I ask for mercy; Let me not implore in vain.
All my sins, I now detest them, Never will I sin again.

2. By my sins I have deservèd Death and endless misery,
Hell with all its pains and torments, And for all eternity.

3. By my sins I have abandoned Right and claim to heav'n above
Where the saints rejoice for ever In a boundless sea of love.

4. See our Savior, bleeding, dying, On the cross of Calvary;
To that cross my sins have nailed him, Yet he bleeds and dies for me.

EDMUND VAUGHAN, C.SS.R., 1827–1908

85 God of Our Fathers
10 10 10 10

NATIONAL HYMN GEORGE W. WARREN, 1828–1902

1 God of our fathers, whose almighty hand
2 Thy love divine hath led us in the past,
3 From war's alarms, from deadly pestilence,
4 Refresh thy people on their toilsome way;

Leads forth in beauty all the starry band
In all our days by thee our lot is cast;
Be thy strong arm our ever sure defense;
Lead us from night to never-ending day;

Of shining worlds in splendor through the skies,
Be thou our ruler, guardian, guide, and stay;
Thy true religion in our hearts increase,
Fill all our lives with love and grace divine,

Our grateful songs before thy throne arise.
Thy word our law, thy paths our chosen way.
Thy bounteous goodness nourish us in peace.
And glory, laud, and praise be ever thine.

DANIEL C. ROBERTS, 1841–1907, ALT.

86   God Rest You Merry, Gentlemen
86 86 86 with refrain

GOD REST YOU MERRY   ENGLISH CAROL, 18TH CENT.
HARM. BY JOHN STAINER, 1840–1901

1. God rest you merry, gentlemen, Let nothing you dismay;
Remember Christ our Savior Was born on Christmas day,
To save us all from Satan's pow'r When we were gone astray:

2. In Bethlehem in Jewry This blessed Babe was born,
And laid within a manger Upon this blessed morn:
The which his Mother Mary Did nothing take in scorn:

3. From God our heav'nly Father A blessed angel came,
And unto certain shepherds Brought tidings of the same;
How that in Bethlehem was born The Son of God by name:

O tidings of comfort and joy, comfort and joy;

92 • A CATHOLIC BOOK OF HYMNS

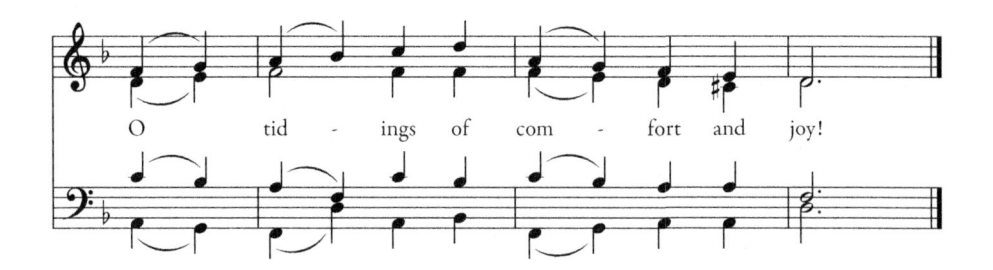

O tidings of comfort and joy!

4. The shepherds at those tidings
   Rejoicèd much in mind,
   And left their flocks afeeding
   In tempest, storm, and wind,
   And went to Bethlehem straightway,
   The Son of God to find:

5. Now to the Lord sing praises,
   All you within this place,
   And with true love and brotherhood
   Each other now embrace.
   This holy tide of Christmas
   Doth bring redeeming grace.

ENGLISH CAROL, 18TH CENT.

87 Good Christian Men, Rejoice
66 77 78 55

IN DULCI JUBILO

GERMAN CAROL, 14TH CENT.
HARM. BY ROBERT L. PEARSALL, 1795–1856

1 Good Christian men, rejoice With heart and soul and voice;
Give ye heed to what we say: Jesus Christ is born today!
Ox and ass before him bow, And he is in the manger now.
Christ is born today! Christ is born today!

2 Good Christian men, rejoice With heart and soul and voice;
Now ye hear of endless bliss: Jesus Christ was born for this!
He hath op'd the heav'nly door, And man is blessed evermore.
Christ was born for this! Christ was born for this!

3 Good Christian men, rejoice With heart and soul and voice;
Now ye need not fear the grave: Jesus Christ was born to save!
Calls you one and calls you all To gain his everlasting hall.
Christ was born to save! Christ was born to save!

In dulci jubilo; GERMAN CAROL, 14TH CENT.
TR. BY JOHN M. NEALE, 1818–1866, ALT.

88. Great Saint in Heaven

11 10 11 10 WITH REFRAIN

CAJETAN ELSHOFF, O.F.M., 1888–1956

1. Great Saint in heav-en, our Pa-tron we greet thee! Be thou our well-spring of cour-age and light! Guide thou our steps so that once we may meet thee; Bright be thy bea-con, tho' dark be the night.

2. Lead thou us on-ward through earth's pain and an-guish, Cross-es and tri-als dis-heart-en us here; Temp-er our sor-rows, whilst here we still an-guish, Make us wax strong in Christ's love and his fear.

Refrain: To God be glo-ry, who gave thee thy crown; To us be cour-age and to thee re-nown; So may we ev-er find strength in thy name, Thee as our pa-tron-al Saint, we ac-claim!

REV. HENRY MEYER

89 Great Saint Joseph
87 87 D
HURLBURT'S *A TREASURY OF CATHOLIC SONG*, NEW YORK, 1915

1. Great Saint Joseph, son of David, Foster father of our Lord,
Spouse of Mary ever-Virgin, Keeping o'er them watch and ward:
In the stable thou didst guard them With a father's loving care;
Thou by God's command didst save them From the cruel Herod's snare.

2. Three long days, in grief, in anguish, With his Mother sweet and mild,
Mary Virgin, didst thou wander, Seeking the beloved Child.
In the temple thou didst find him: O what joy then filled thy heart!
In thy sorrows, in thy gladness, Grant us, Joseph, to have part.

3. Clasped in Jesus' arms and Mary's, When death gently came at last,
Thy pure spirit, sweetly sighing, From its earthly dwelling passed.
Dear Saint Joseph, by that passing, May our death be like to thine,
And with Jesus, Mary, Joseph, May our souls for ever shine. A-men.

ANONYMOUS

90 Guardian Angel! From Heaven So Bright
10 10 10 10 WITH REFRAIN

ANONYMOUS
HARM. BY J. ALFRED SCHEHL, 1882–1959

1. Guardian Angel! from heaven so bright, Watching beside me to lead me aright, Fold thy wings round me, oh, guard me with love. Softly sing songs to me of heav'n above.
2. Angel so holy! whom God sends to me, Sinful and lowly, my guardian to be, Wilt thou not cherish the child of thy care? Let me not perish; my trust is thy prayer.
3. O may I never forget thou art near: But keep me ever in love and in fear. Waking and sleeping, in labor and rest, In thy sweet keeping my life shall be blest.
4. Angel, dear Angel! Oh, close by me stay; Safe from harm shield me, all ill keep away. Then thou wilt lead me when this life is o'er To Jesus and Mary to praise evermore.

Refrain: Beautiful Angel, my guardian so mild, Tenderly guide me, for I am thy child.

ANONYMOUS

91 Hail, Glorious Saint Patrick

11 11 11 11 WITH REFRAIN

HENRI F. HEMY, 1818–1888

1. Hail, glorious Saint Patrick, dear saint of our isle!
   On us, thy poor children, bestow a sweet smile;
   And now thou art high in thy mansions above,
   On Erin's green valleys look down in thy love.

2. Hail, glorious Saint Patrick, thy words were once strong,
   Against Satan's wiles and a heretic throng;
   Not less in thy might where in heaven thou art;
   Oh, come to our aid, in our battle take part.

3. In the war against sin, in the fight for the faith,
   Dear saint, may thy children resist to the death;
   May their strength be in meekness, in penance, and prayer,
   Their banner the cross which they glory to bear.

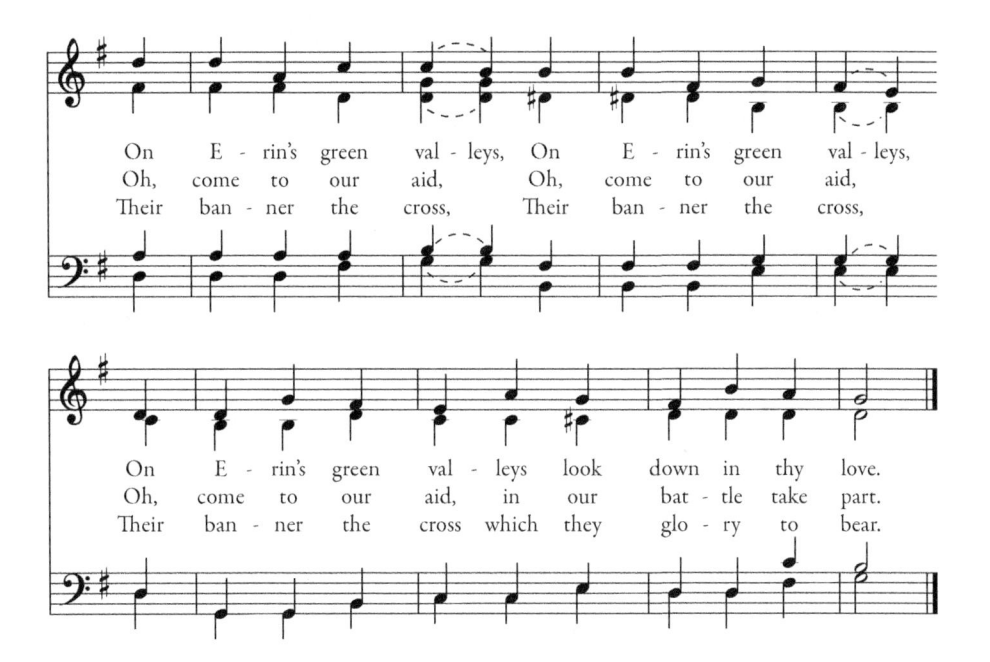

On Erin's green valleys, On Erin's green valleys,
Oh, come to our aid, Oh, come to our aid,
Their banner the cross, Their banner the cross,

On Erin's green valleys look down in thy love.
Oh, come to our aid, in our battle take part.
Their banner the cross which they glory to bear.

4 Thy people, now exiles on many a shore,
Shall love and revere thee till time be no more;
And the fire thou hast kindled shall ever burn bright,
Its warmth undiminished, undying its light.
Its warmth undiminished, its warmth undiminished,
Its warmth undiminished, undying its light.

5 Ever bless and defend the sweet land of our birth,
Where the shamrock still blooms as when thou wert on earth;
And our hearts shall yet burn wheresoever we roam,
For God and Saint Patrick, and our native home.
For God and Saint Patrick, For God and Saint Patrick,
For God and Saint Patrick, and our native home.

SISTER AGNES

92. Hail, Holy Queen Enthroned Above

84 84 WITH REFRAIN

SALVE REGINA COELITUM

MELCHIOR LUDWIG HEROLD, 1753–1810

1. Hail, holy Queen enthroned above, O Maria,
Hail, Mother of mercy and of love, O Maria.
2. The cause of joy to all below, O Maria,
The spring through which all graces flow, O Maria.
3. O gentle, loving, holy one, O Maria,
The God of light became your Son, O Maria.

Refrain:
Triumph, all ye Cherubim, Sing with us, ye Seraphim, Heav'n and earth resound the hymn: Salve, Salve, Salve, Regina.

Gegrüßet seist du, Königin (Salve, regina coelitum);
Johann Georg Seidenbusch, 1641–1729
tr. Anonymous in Roman Hymnal, 1884

93 Hail, O Star That Pointest
66 66

AVE MARIS STELLA
18TH CENT. MELODY

1. Hail, O star that point - est T'wards the port of Hea - ven,
   Thou to whom as maid - en God for Son was giv - en.

2. When the sa - lu - ta - tion Ga - bri - el had spo - ken,
   Peace was shed up - on us, E - va's bonds were bro - ken.

3. Bound by Sa - tan's fet - ters, Health and vi - sion need - ing,
   God will aid and light us At thy gen - tle plead - ing.

4. Jesus' tender mother,
   Make thy supplication
   Unto him who chose thee
   At his incarnation;

5. That, O matchless maiden,
   Passing meek and lowly,
   Thy dear Son may make us
   Blameless, chaste, and holy.

6. So, as now we journey,
   Aid our weak endeavor,
   Till we gaze on Jesus,
   And rejoice forever.

7. Father, Son, and Spirit,
   Three in One confessing,
   Give we equal glory,
   Equal praise and blessing.

AVE MARIS STELLA; ANONYMOUS, C. 9TH CENT.
TR. BY J. ATHELSTAN L. RILEY, C. 1858–1945

94 Hail, Queen of Heaven
88 88 88

STELLA (ENGLISH) — HENRI FRIEDRICH HEMY, 1818–1888

1. Hail, Queen of heav'n, the ocean star, Guide of the wand'rer here below! Thrown on life's surge we claim thy care, Save us from peril and from woe. Mother of Christ, Star of the sea, Pray for the wanderer, pray for me!

2. O gentle, chaste, and spotless maid, We sinners make our prayers through thee, Remind thy Son that he has paid The price of our iniquity. Virgin most pure, Star of the sea, Pray for the sinner, O pray for me!

3. Sojourners in this vale of tears, To thee, blest Advocate, we cry, Pity our sorrows, calm our fears, And soothe with hope our misery. Refuge in grief, Star of the sea, Pray for the mourner, O pray for me!

4. And while to him who reigns above, In Godhead one, in persons three, The source of life, of grace, of love, Homage we pay on bended knee. Do thou bright Queen, Star of the sea, Pray for thy children, O pray for me!

JOHN LINGARD, 1771–1851

95. Hail the Day That Sees Him Rise

77 77 WITH ALLELUIAS

LLANFAIR

ATTR. TO ROBERT WILLIAMS, 1781–1821

1. Hail the day that sees him rise, Alleluia!
   To the throne above the skies; Alleluia!
   Paschal Lamb for sinners giv'n, Alleluia!
   Enters now the highest heav'n. Alleluia!

2. There for him high triumph waits: Alleluia!
   Lift your heads, eternal gates! Alleluia!
   Christ has conquered death and sin; Alleluia!
   Take the King of glory in! Alleluia!

3. See, he lifts his hands above; Alleluia!
   See, he shows the prints of love; Alleluia!
   Though returning to his throne, Alleluia!
   Still he calls mankind his own. Alleluia!

4. Highest heav'n its Lord receives, Alleluia!
   Yet he loves the earth he leaves; Alleluia!
   Hark, his gracious lips bestow, Alleluia!
   Blessings on his church below. Alleluia!

CHARLES WESLEY, 1707–1788, ALT.

96 Hail, Thou Living Bread
87 87

GERMAN CHORALE

1. Hail, thou living Bread from heaven, Sacrament of awful might! I adore thee, I adore thee; Ev'ry moment day and night.
2. Holiest Jesu! Heart of Jesu! O'er me shed thy gifts divine, Holiest Jesu! my Redeemer! All my heart and soul are thine.

VI ADORO OGNI MOMENTO
TR. BY EDWARD CASWALL, 1814–1878

97 Hail to the Lord's Anointed
76 76 D

ELLACOMBE

MAINZER GESANGBUCH, MAINZ, 1833
HARM. BY WILLIAM H. MONK, 1823–1889

1. Hail to the Lord's Anointed, Great David's greater Son!
Hail, in the time appointed, God's reign on earth begun!
Christ comes to break oppression, To set the captive free;
To take away transgression, And rule in equity.

2. He shall come down like showers Upon the fruitful earth,
And joy and hope, like flowers, Spring in his path to birth:
Before him on the mountains Shall peace, the herald, go;
And righteousness in fountains From hill to valley flow.

3. Kings shall bow down before him, And gold and incense bring;
All nations shall adore him, His praise all peoples sing;
To him shall prayer unceasing And daily vows ascend;
His kingdom still increasing, A kingdom without end.

4. O'er ev'ry foe victorious, He on his throne shall rest,
From age to age more glorious, All blessing and all blest.
The tide of time shall never His covenant remove;
His name shall stand forever, That name to us is love.

PSALM 72:1–7, 10–11, 15, 19; JAMES MONTGOMERY, 1771–1854, ALT.

98 Hail to the Lord's Anointed
76 76 D

ES FLOG EIN KLEINS WALDVÖGELEIN   TRADITIONAL GERMAN, 17TH CENT.

1. Hail to the Lord's Anointed, Great David's greater Son!
Hail, in the time appointed, God's reign on earth begun!
Christ comes to break oppression, To set the captive free;
To take away transgression, And rule in equity.

2. He shall come down like showers Upon the fruitful earth,
And joy and hope, like flowers, Spring in his path to birth;
Before him on the mountains Shall peace, the herald, go;
And righteousness in fountains From hill to valley flow.

3. Kings shall bow down before him, And gold and incense bring;
All nations shall adore him, His praise all peoples sing;
To him shall prayer unceasing And daily vows ascend;
His kingdom still increasing, A kingdom without end.

4. O'er ev'ry foe victorious, He on his throne shall rest,
From age to age more glorious, All blessing and all blest.
The tide of time shall never His covenant remove;
His name shall stand forever, That name to us is love.

PSALM 72:1–7, 10–11, 15, 19; JAMES MONTGOMERY, 1771–1854, ALT.

99 Hail, Virgin, Dearest Mary
76 76 D

QUEEN OF MAY

S. M. YENN

1. Hail Virgin, dearest Mary! Our lovely Queen of May!
O spotless, blessed Lady, Our lovely Queen of May.
Thy children, humbly bending, Surround thy shrine so dear;
With heart and voice ascending, Sweet Mary, hear our prayer.

2. Behold earth's blossoms springing In beauteous form and hue.
All nature gladly bringing Her sweetest charms to you.
We'll gather fresh, bright flowers, To bind our fair Queen's brow;
From gay and verdant bowers, We haste to crown thee now.

3. Hail Virgin, dearest Mary! Our lovely Queen of May!
O spotless, blessed Lady, Our lovely Queen of May.
And now, our blessed Mother, Smile on our festal day;
Accept our wreath of flowers, And be our Queen of May.

ANONYMOUS

100 Hark! A Herald Voice Is Sounding
87 87

MERTON
WILLIAM H. MONK, 1823–1889

1. Hark! a herald voice is sounding; "Christ is nigh!" it seems to say; "Cast away the dreams of darkness, O ye children of the day!"

2. Startled at the solemn warning, Let the earth-bound soul arise; Christ her sun, all sloth dispelling, Shines upon the morning skies.

3. Lo! the Lamb so long expected, Comes with pardon down from heav'n; Let us haste, with tears of sorrow, One and all to be forgiv'n.

4. So when next he comes with glory,
   Shrouding all the earth in fear,
   May he then as our defender
   On the clouds of heav'n appear.

5. Honor, glory, virtue, merit,
   To the Father and the Son,
   With the coeternal Spirit
   While eternal ages run.

Vox clara ecce intonat, 5TH CENT.
TR. BY EDWARD CASWALL, 1814–1878, ALT.

101 Hark, My Soul
77 77

SURGE
A. GREGORY MURRAY, O.S.B., 1905-1992

1. Hark, my soul, how ev-'ry-thing Strives to serve our boun-teous King; Each a dou-ble trib-ute pays, Sings its part, and then o-beys.
2. Na-ture's chief and sweet-est choir Him with cheer-ful notes ad-mire; Chant-ing ev-'ry day their lauds, While the grove their song ap-plauds.
3. Though their voic-es low-er be, Streams have too their mel-o-dy; Night and day they war-bling run, Nev-er pause, but still sing on.

4. All the flowers that gild the spring
   Hither their still music bring;
   If heaven bless them, thankful, they
   Smell more sweet, and look more gay.

5. Only we can scarce afford
   This short office to our Lord;
   We, on whom his bounty flows,
   All things gives, and nothing owes.

6. Wake, for shame, my sluggish heart,
   Wake, and gladly sing thy part;
   Learn of birds, and springs, and flowers,
   How to use thy nobler powers.

7. Call whole nature to thy aid;
   Since 'twas he whole nature made;
   Join in one eternal song,
   Who to one God all belong.

JOHN AUSTIN, 1613–1669

102 Hark! The Herald Angels Sing
77 77 D with refrain

MENDELSSOHN

Felix Mendelssohn, 1809–1847
arr. by William H. Cummings, 1831–1915

1. Hark! The herald angels sing, "Glory to the new-born King;
Peace on earth and mercy mild, God and sinners reconciled!"
Joyful, all ye nations, rise, Join the triumph of the skies;
With th' angelic hosts proclaim, "Christ is born in Bethlehem!"

2. Christ, by highest heav'n adored; Christ, the everlasting Lord;
Late in time behold him come, Offspring of a Virgin's womb.
Veiled in flesh the Godhead see; Hail th' incarnate Deity;
Pleased as man with man to dwell; Jesus, our Emmanuel!

3. Hail, the heav'n-born Prince of Peace! Hail, the Sun of Righteousness!
Light and life to all he brings, Ris'n with healing in his wings.
Mild he lays his glory by, Born that man no more may die,
Born to raise the sons of earth, Born to give them second birth!

Refrain: Hark! The herald angels sing, "Glory to the new-born King!"

Charles Wesley, 1707–1788, alt.

103 Hark! The Sound of Holy Voices
87 87 D

MOULTRIE GERARD F. COBB, 1838–1904

1. Hark! The sound of holy voices, Chanting at the crystal sea,
Alleluia! Alleluia! Alleluia! Lord, to thee;
Multitude, which none can number, Like the stars in glory stand
Clothed in white apparel, holding Palms of victory in their hand.

2. Patriarch, and holy prophet, Who prepared the way of Christ;
King, Apostle, saint, confessor, Martyr and evangelist;
Saintly maiden, godly matron, Widows who have watched to prayer,
Joined in holy concert, singing To the Lord of all, are there.

3. Marching with thy cross, their banner, They have triumphed, following
Thee, the Captain of salvation, Thee, their Savior and their King;
Gladly, Lord, with thee they suffered; Gladly, Lord, with thee they died;
And by death to life immortal They were born and glorified.

4. Now they reign in heav'nly glory, Now they walk in golden light,
Now they drink, as from a river, Holy bliss and infinite:
Love and peace they taste forever, And all truth and knowledge see
In the beatific vision Of the blessed Trinity.

CHRISTOPHER WORDSWORTH, 1807–1885

A CATHOLIC BOOK OF HYMNS • 111

104 Hear Thy Children, Gentle Jesus
87 87 D

J. Michael Haydn, 1737–1806
harm. by Nicola A. Montani, 1880–1948

1. Hear thy chil-dren, gen-tle Je-sus, While we breathe our eve-ning prayer,
Save us from all harm and dan-ger, Take us 'neath thy shel-t'ring care.
Save us from the wiles of Sa-tan, 'Mid the lone and sleep-ful night,
Sweet-ly may bright Guard-ian An-gels Keep us 'neath their watch-ful sight.

2. Gen-tle Je-sus, look in pit-y, From thy glo-rious throne a-bove;
All the night thy heart is wake-ful, In thy sac-ra-ment of love.
Shades of e-ven fast are fall-ing, Day is fad-ing in-to gloom.
When the shades of death fall round us, Lead thine ex-iled chil-dren home.

Francis Stanfield, 1835–1914

105 Hear Thy Children, Gentle Jesus
87 87

St. Basil's Hymnal, 1918

1. Hear thy children, gentle Jesus,
While we breathe our evening prayer,
Save us from all harm and danger,
Take us 'neath thy shelt'ring care.

2. Save us from the wiles of Satan,
'Mid the lone and peaceful night,
Sweetly may our Guardian Angels
Keep us 'neath their watchful sight.

3. Gentle Jesus, look in pity,
From thy glorious throne above,
All the night thy heart is wakeful
In thy sacrament of love.

4. Shades of even fast are falling,
Day is fading into gloom;
When the shades of death fall round us,
Lead thine exiled children home.

Francis Stanfield, 1835–1914

106 Heart of Jesus, We Are Grateful
87 87 D with refrain

Theodore A. Metcalf, 1843–1920

1. Heart of Jesus, we are grateful For thy answer to our prayer;
We have sought thee, ever hopeful That thy blessings we might share;
Thou hast heard us interceding, With thy love which is untold,
And in answer to our pleading All thy treasures dost unfold.

2. Heart of Jesus, thou hast taught us How to seek and how to find,
And that lesson now has brought us To thy heart so sweet and kind.
What we ask, with faith believing, Thou hast pledged thy word to give,
And thy word is not deceiving, But the truth by which we live.

3. Heart of Jesus, whilst we waited For the favors now obtained,
Not a moment had we doubted That by prayer they'd be gained.
Thou hadst told us that our treasures Would be found in thy dear heart,
And we knew that without measure Thou dost all thy gifts impart.

Heart of Jesus, we will thank thee, We will love thee more and more;

Heart of Jesus, we will praise thee, And we'll thank thee o'er and o'er.

THEODORE A. METCALF, 1843–1920

107 Help, Lord, the Souls That Thou Hast Made
86 86

REQUIEM   A. GREGORY MURRAY, 1905–1992

1. Help, Lord, the souls that thou hast made, The souls to thee so dear, In prison for the debt unpaid Of sin committed here.
2. These holy souls, they suffer on, Resign'd in heart and will, Until thy high behest is done, And justice has its fill.
3. For daily falls, for pardon'd crime, They joy to undergo The shadow of thy Cross sublime, The remnant of thy woe.

4. Oh, by their patience of delay,
Their hope amid their pain,
Their sacred zeal to burn away
Disfigurement and stain;

5. Oh, by their fire of love, not less
In keenness than the flame;
Oh, by their very helplessness,
Oh, by their own great Name;

6. Good Jesu, help! Sweet Jesu, aid The souls to thee most dear,
In prison for the debt unpaid Of sins committed here.

JOHN HENRY NEWMAN, 1801–1890

108 Holy God, We Praise Thy Name
78 78 77

GROSSER GOTT *ALLGEMEINES KATHOLISCHES GESANGBUCH*, VIENNA, 1774

1 Holy God, we praise thy name; Lord of all, we bow before thee!
All on earth thy scepter claim, All in heav'n above adore thee;
Infinite thy vast domain, Everlasting is thy reign.
Infinite thy vast domain, Everlasting is thy reign.

2 Hark! The loud celestial hymn Angel choirs above are raising,
Cherubim and seraphim, In unceasing chorus praising;
Fill the heav'ns with sweet accord: "Holy, holy, holy Lord."
Fill the heav'ns with sweet accord: "Holy, holy, holy Lord."

3 Holy Father, Holy Son, Holy Spirit, Three we name thee;
While in essence only One, Undivided God we claim thee;
And adoring, bend the knee, While we own the mystery.
And adoring, bend the knee, While we own the mystery.

TE DEUM LAUDAMUS; GERMAN PARAPHRASE ATTR. TO IGNAZ FRANZ, 1719–1790
TR. BY CLARENCE A. WALWORTH, 1820–1900

109 Holy, Holy, Holy
11 12 12 10

NICAEA
JOHN B. DYKES, 1823–1876

1 Ho-ly, ho-ly, ho - ly! Lord God Al-might-y!
Ear-ly in the morn - ing our song shall rise to thee.
Ho-ly, ho-ly, ho - ly, mer-ci-ful and might-y!
God in three Per - sons, bless-ed Trin-i-ty!

2 Ho-ly, ho-ly, ho - ly! All the saints a - dore thee,
Cast-ing down their gold-en crowns a - round the glass-y sea;
Cher-u-bim and ser-a-phim fall-ing down be - fore thee,
Which wert and art, and ev - er - more shalt be.

3 Ho-ly, ho-ly, ho - ly! Though the dark-ness hide thee,
Though the eye of sin-ful man thy glo - ry may not see,
On-ly thou art ho - ly; there is none be-side thee,
Per-fect in pow'r, in love, and pu - ri - ty.

4 Ho-ly, ho-ly, ho - ly! Lord God Al-might-y!
All thy works shall praise thy name in earth and sky and sea.
Ho-ly, ho-ly, ho - ly, mer-ci-ful and might-y!
God in three Per - sons, bless-ed Trin-i-ty!

REGINALD HEBER, 1783–1826

110 Holy, Holy Name of Jesus
87 87 87

RT. REV. MSGR. HENRY TAPPERT, 1855–1929

1. Ho - ly, ho - ly Name of Je - sus, Name of sweet-ness we a - dore;
Lo, through a - ges still un - num-bered Was that Name in Heav-en's store.
Hid - den then in aw - ful si - lence, Now it sounds from shore to shore.

2. Hail! the hour when An - gel's mes - sage Brought that Name to Ma - ry blest;
Hail! the joy that straight from heav - en Filled the Vir - gin Moth - er's breast;
Hail! the light up - on his fea - tures, When his Moth - er him ca - ressed.

3. An - gels' lips can sound none sweet - er Than the sweet-ness of that Name,
Earth - ly ears can list none bet - ter For that Name from Heav - en came.
Let us then with heav'n u - nit - ed Of - fer hom - age still the same.

ANONYMOUS

111 Holy Light on Earth's Horizon
87 87 D

BLAENWERN WILLIAM P. ROWLANDS, 1860–1937

1. Holy light on earth's horizon, Star of hope to fallen man,
Light amid a world of shadows, Dawn of God's redemptive plan.
Chosen from eternal ages, Thou alone, of all our race,
By thy Son's atoning merits Wast conceived in perfect grace.

2. Mother of the world's Redeemer, Promised from the dawn of time:
How could one so highly favored Share the guilt of Adam's crime?
Sun and moon and stars adorn thee, Sinless Eve, triumphant sign;
Thou art she who crushed the serpent, Mary, pledge of life divine.

3. Earth below and highest heaven Praise the splendor of thy state,
Thou who now art crowned in glory Wast conceived immaculate.
Hail, beloved of the Father, Mother of his only Son,
Mystic bride of Love eternal, Hail, thou, fair and spotless one!

ALMA LUX, 17TH CENT.
TR. BY EDWARD CASWALL, 1814–1878

112 Holy Spirit, Lord of Light

777 777

VENI SANCTE SPIRITUS

AN ESSAY ON THE CHURCH PLAIN CHANT, LONDON, 1782
ATTR. TO SAMUEL WEBBE, 1740–1816

1. Holy Spirit, Lord of Light, From thy clear celestial height,
Thy pure beaming radiance give. Come, thou Father of the poor,
Come with treasures which endure; Come, thou Light of all that live.

2. Thou, of all consolers best, Thou, the soul's delight-some guest,
Dost refreshing peace bestow. Thou in toil art comfort sweet;
Pleasant coolness in the heat; Solace in the midst of woe.

3. Light immortal, Light divine, Visit thou these hearts of thine,
And our inmost being fill. If thou take thy grace away,
Nothing pure in man will stay; All his good is turned to ill.

4. Heal our wounds, our strength renew;
On our dryness pour thy dew;
Wash the stains of guilt away.
Bend the stubborn heart and will;
Melt the frozen, warm the chill;
Guide the steps that go astray.

5. Thou, on those who evermore
Thee confess and thee adore,
In thy sev'nfold gifts descend:
Give them comfort when they die;
Give them life with thee on high;
Give them joys that never end.

VENI, SANCTE SPIRITUS; ATTR. TO POPE INNOCENT III, 1161–1216
TR. BY EDWARD CASWALL, 1814–1878

113 How Firm a Foundation

11 11 11 11

FOUNDATION

Joseph Funk's *Genuine Church Music*, Winchester, Va. 1832

1. How firm a foundation, ye saints of the Lord,
Is laid for your faith in his excellent word!
What more can he say than to you he hath said,
To you who for refuge to Jesus have fled?

2. "Fear not, I am with thee, O be not dismayed,
For I am thy God, and will still give thee aid;
I'll strengthen thee, help thee, and cause thee to stand,
Upheld by my righteous, omnipotent hand.

3. "When through the deep waters I call thee to go,
The rivers of sorrow shall not overflow;
For I will be with thee, thy troubles to bless,
And sanctify to thee thy deepest distress.

4. "When through fiery trials thy pathway shall lie,
My grace, all sufficient, shall be thy supply;
The flame shall not hurt thee, I only design
Thy dross to consume, and thy gold to refine.

5. "The soul that on Jesus hath leaned for repose,
I will not, I will not desert to its foes;
That soul, though all hell should endeavor to shake,
I'll never, no, never, no, never forsake!"

1 Cor 3:11; Rippon's *Selection of Hymns*, London, 1787, alt.

114 I Heard the Voice of Jesus Say
86 86 D

KINGSFOLD

TRADITIONAL ENGLISH FOLK SONG
HARM. BY RALPH VAUGHAN WILLIAMS, 1872–1958

1. I heard the voice of Jesus say, "Come unto me and rest;
Lay down, thou weary one, lay down Thy head upon my breast."
I came to Jesus as I was, So weary, worn, and sad;
I found in him a resting place, And he has made me glad.

2. I heard the voice of Jesus say, "Behold, I freely give
The living water; thirsty one, Stoop down, and drink, and live."
I came to Jesus, and I drank Of that life-giving stream;
My thirst was quenched, my soul revived, And now I live in him.

3. I heard the voice of Jesus say, "I am this dark world's light;
Look unto me, thy morn shall rise, And all thy day be bright."
I looked to Jesus, and I found In him my star, my sun;
And in that light of life I'll walk Till trav'ling days are done.

HORATIUS BONAR, 1808–1889

115   I Know That My Redeemer Lives
88 88

DUKE STREET   JOHN WARRINGTON HATTON, 1710–1793

1. I know that my Redeemer lives!
What joy the blest assurance gives!
He lives, he lives, who once was dead;
He lives, my everlasting head!

2. He lives triumphant from the grave;
He lives eternally to save;
He lives in majesty above;
He lives to guide his Church in love.

3. He lives to silence all my fears;
He lives to wipe away my tears;
He lives to calm my troubled heart;
He lives all blessings to impart.

4. He lives, all glory to his name!
He lives, my Savior, still the same;
What joy this blest assurance gives:
I know that my Redeemer lives!

BASED ON JOB 19:23
SAMUEL MEDLEY, 1738–1799, ALT.

116 I Sing the Mighty Power of God
76 76 D

ELLACOMBE

Mainzer Gesangbuch, Mainz, 1833
harm. by William H. Monk, 1823–1889

1. I sing the might-y pow'r of God, That made the moun-tains rise;
That spread the flow-ing seas a-broad, And built the loft-y skies.
I sing the Wis-dom that or-dained The sun to rule the day;
The moon shines full at his com-mand, And all the stars o-bey.

2. I sing the good-ness of the Lord, That filled the earth with food;
He formed the crea-tures with his word, And then pro-nounced them good.
Lord, how thy won-ders are dis-played, Wher-e'er I turn my eye;
If I sur-vey the ground I tread, Or gaze up-on the sky.

3. There's not a plant or flow'r be-low, But makes thy glo-ries known;
And clouds a-rise, and tem-pests blow, By or-der from thy throne;
While all that bor-rows life from thee Is ev-er in thy care,
And ev-'ry-where that man can be, Thou, God art pres-ent there.

Isaac Watts, 1674–1748

117 Immaculate Mary
11 11 WITH REFRAIN

LOURDES HYMN · TRADITIONAL PYRENEAN MELODY

1. Immaculate Mary! Our hearts are on fire;
That title so wondrous Fills all our desire!

2. We pray for God's glory, May his Kingdom come;
We pray for his Vicar, Our Father in Rome.

3. We pray for our Mother, The Church upon earth,
And bless, sweetest Lady, The land of our birth.

4. O Mary! O Mother! Reign o'er us once more:
Be all lands thy "dowry" As in days of yore.

Refrain:
Ave, ave, ave, Maria!
Ave, ave, Maria!

VSS. 1–3, ANON. IN TOZER'S *CATHOLIC CHURCH HYMNAL*, 1906
VS. 4, ANON. IN RONAN'S *JUBILEE HYMNS, BOOK 2*, 1949

118 Immortal, Invisible, God Only Wise
11 11 11 11

ST. DENIO

WELSH MELODY, *CANIADAU Y CYSSEGR*, DENBIGH, 1839
HARM. BY *THE ENGLISH HYMNAL*, LONDON, 1906, ALT.

1. Immortal, invisible, God only wise,
In light inaccessible, hid from our eyes,
Most blessed, most glorious, the Ancient of Days,
Almighty, victorious, thy great name we praise.

2. Unresting, unhasting, and silent as light,
Nor wanting nor wasting, thou rulest in might;
Thy justice like mountains high soaring above,
Thy clouds, which are fountains of goodness and love.

3. To all life thou givest, to both great and small;
In all life thou livest, the true life of all;
We blossom and flourish as leaves on the tree,
And wither and perish, but naught changeth thee.

4. Great Father of glory, pure Father of light,
Thine angels adore thee, all veiling their sight;
All praise we would render: O help us to see
'Tis only the splendor of light hideth thee.

GOD, ALL IN ALL; WALTER C. SMITH, 1824–1908, ALT.

119 In His Temple Now Behold Him
87 87 87

ST. THOMAS (WADE) — JOHN F. WADE, 1711–1786

1. In his temple now behold him, See the long expected Lord;
   Ancient prophets had foretold him; God has now fulfilled his word,
   Now, to praise him, his redeemèd Shall break forth with one accord.

2. In the arms of her who bore him, Virgin pure, behold him lie,
   While his aged saints adore him Ere in faith and hope they die.
   Alleluia! Alleluia! Lo, the Incarnate God most high.

3. Jesus, by your presentation, When they blest you, weak and poor,
   Make us see our great salvation, Seal us with your promise sure,
   And present us in your glory To your Father, cleansed and pure.

4. Prince and author of salvation, Be your boundless love our theme!
   Jesus, praise to you be given, By the world you did redeem,
   With the Father and the Spirit, Lord of majesty supreme.

BASED ON LUKE 2:22–24
VSS. 1–3, HENRY J. PYLE, 1825–1903
VS. 4, WILLIAM COOKE, 1821–1894

120 In the Bleak Midwinter
IRREGULAR

CRANHAM GUSTAV HOLST, 1874–1934

1. In the bleak midwinter, Frosty wind made moan, Earth stood hard as iron, Water like a stone; Snow had fallen, snow on snow, Snow on snow, In the bleak midwinter, Long ago.

2. Our God, heav'n cannot hold him, Nor earth sustain; Heav'n and earth shall flee away When he comes to reign: In the bleak midwinter A stable-place sufficed The Lord God Incarnate, Jesus Christ.

3. Enough for him, whom cherubim Worship night and day, A breastful of milk And a mangerful of hay; Enough for him, whom angels Fall down before, The ox and ass and camel Which adore.

4. Angels and archangels May have gathered there, Cherubim and seraphim Thronged the air; But his mother only, In her maiden bliss, Worshipped the belovèd With a kiss.

5. What can I give him, Poor as I am? If I were a shepherd, I would bring a lamb; If I were a wise man, I would do my part; Yet what I can I give him— Give my heart.

CHRISTINA ROSSETTI, 1830–1894

121   In This Sacrament, Sweet Jesus
87 877

ST. BASIL'S HYMNAL, 1918

1. In this sacrament, sweet Jesus, Thou dost give thy flesh and blood, With thy soul and Godhead also, As our own most precious food, As our own most precious food.

2. Yes, dear Jesus, I believe it, And thy presence I adore; And with all my heart I love thee, May I love thee more and more, May I love thee more and more.

3. Come, sweet Jesus, in thy mercy, Give thy flesh and blood to me; Come to me, O dearest Jesus, Come, my soul's true life to be, Come, my soul's true life to be.

4. Come, that I may live forever,
Thou in me, and I in thee;
Living thus, I shall not perish,
But shall live eternally.

5. Blessèd be the love of Jesus,
Giving us his flesh and blood,
Blessèd be his Mother Mary,
Mother ever kind and good.

6. Blessèd be the great Saint Joseph,
Sing then with devotion true;
Dearest Jesus, Mary, Joseph,
Heart and life I give to you.

ANONYMOUS

122   In This Sacrament, Sweet Jesus
87 87

Sunday School Hymn Book, 1907

1. In this Sacrament, sweet Jesus thou dost give thy flesh and blood, With thy soul and Godhead also As our own most precious food.

2. Yes, dear Jesus, I believe it, And thy presence I adore, And with all my heart I love thee, May I love thee more and more.

3. Come, sweet Jesus, in thy mercy, Give thy flesh and blood to me; Come to me, O dearest Jesus, Come, my soul's true life to be.

4. Come, that I may live forever,
   Thou in me, and I in thee;
   Living thus, I shall not perish,
   But shall live eternally.

5. Blessèd be the love of Jesus,
   Giving us his flesh and blood,
   Blessèd be his Mother Mary,
   Mother ever kind and good.

6. Blessèd be the great Saint Joseph,
   Sing then with devotion true;
   Dearest Jesus, Mary, Joseph,
   Heart and life I give to you.

ANONYMOUS

123 Infant Holy, Infant Lowly
87 87 88 77

W ŻŁOBIE LEŻY · POLISH MELODY

1. Infant holy, Infant lowly, For his bed a cattle stall;
Oxen lowing, little knowing Christ the Babe is Lord of all.
Swift are winging angels singing, Noels ringing, tidings bringing:
Christ the Babe is Lord of all, Christ the Babe is Lord of all.

2. Flocks were sleeping, shepherds keeping Vigil till the morning new
Saw the glory, heard the story, Tidings of a gospel true.
Thus rejoicing, free from sorrow, Praises voicing, greet the morrow:
Christ the Babe was born for you, Christ the Babe was born for you.

W Żłobie leży ktoż pobieży; ATTR. TO PIOTROWI SKARDZE, 1536–1612
TR. BY EDITH M. REED, 1885–1933

124 It Came Upon the Midnight Clear
86 86 D

CAROL RICHARD S. WILLIS, 1819–1900

1. It came up-on the mid-night clear, That glo-rious song of old,
From an-gels bend-ing near the earth To touch their harps of gold:
"Peace on the earth, good will to all, From heav'n's all-gra-cious King."
The world in sol-emn still-ness lay, To hear the an-gels sing.

2. Still through the clo-ven skies they come With peace-ful wings un-furled,
And still their heav'n-ly mu-sic floats O'er all the wear-y world;
A-bove its sad and low-ly plains They bend on hov-'ring wing,
And ev-er o'er its Ba-bel sounds The bless-ed an-gels sing.

3. And ye, be-neath life's crush-ing load, Whose forms are bend-ing low,
Who toil a-long the climb-ing way With pain-ful steps and slow—
Look now, for glad and gold-en hours Come swift-ly on the wing:
O rest be-side the wear-y road, And hear the an-gels sing!

4. For lo, the days are has-t'ning on, By proph-ets seen of old,
When with the ev-er-cir-cling years Comes round the age of gold.
When peace shall o-ver all the earth Its an-cient splen-dors fling,
And all the world give back the song Which now the an-gels sing.

EDMUND H. SEARS, 1810–1876, ALT.

125   It Is a Thing Most Wonderful
88 88

HERONGATE

TRADITIONAL ENGLISH MELODY
HARM. BY RALPH VAUGHAN WILLIAMS, 1872–1958

1. It is a thing most wonderful, Almost too wonderful to be, That God's own Son should come from heav'n, And die to save a child like me.

2. And yet I know that it is true: He chose a poor and humble lot, And wept and toiled and mourned and died For love of those who loved him not.

3. I cannot tell how he could love A child so weak and full of sin; His love must be most wonderful If he could die my love to win.

4. I sometimes think about the cross,
And shut my eyes, and try to see
The cruel nails and crown of thorns,
And Jesus crucified for me.

5. But even could I see him die,
I could but see a little part
Of that great love which, like a fire,
Is always burning in his heart.

6. It is most wonderful to know
His love for me so free and sure;
But 'tis more wonderful to see
My love for him so faint and poor.

7. And yet I want to love thee, Lord;
O light the flame within my heart,
And I will love thee more and more,
Until I see thee as thou art.

WILLIAM WALSHAM HOW, 1823–1897

126 Jerusalem, My Happy Home
86 86

LAND OF REST

TRADITIONAL AMERICAN MELODY
HARM. BY ANNABEL MORRIS BUCHANAN, 1889–1983

1. Jerusalem, my happy home, When shall I come to thee? When shall my sorrows have an end? Thy joys, when shall I see?

2. O happy harbor of the saints, O sweet and pleasant soil! In you no sorrow may be found, No grief, no care, no toil.

3. Your gardens and your gallant walks Continually are green; There grow such sweet and pleasant flow'rs As nowhere else are seen.

4. There, trees forevermore bear fruit
And evermore do spring,
There, evermore the angels sit
And evermore do sing.

5. Jerusalem, Jerusalem,
God grant that I may see
Your endless joy, and of the same
Partaker ever be!

BASED ON AUGUSTINE OF HIPPO, 5TH CENT.
F.B.P., 16TH CENT., IN *SONG OF MARY*, LONDON, 1601

127 Jesu! The Dying Day Hath Left Us Lonely
11 11 11 5

NOCTE SURGENTES

CASSINESE MELODY
ADAPT. BY A. GREGORY MURRAY, 1905–1992

1. Jesu! the dying day hath left us lonely; All fadeth from us; thou remainest only; Earth's light goes out, but thou, true light, art near us, And thou wilt hear us.

2. Bring home the feet that far from thee have wandered, The minds that all but thee all day have pondered; We yield them evermore, awake or sleeping, To thy safe-keeping.

3. O let our souls keep day, though night be round us! So shall the sons of darkness not confound us, But blameless rest delight thy gaze paternal, Un-tired Eternal!

4. White Dove of peace, great God of consolation,
Brood o'er the souls that moan in tribulation,
And with the whisper of serene tomorrows
Soothe all their sorrows.

5. Mother of holy hope, all-blessed Mary,
Whose high-throned mother-love can never vary,
This night, and at out death's deep nightfall aid us,
With him who made us.

JOHN O'CONNOR, 1870–1952

128 Jesus Christ Is Risen Today
77 77 WITH ALLELUIAS

EASTER HYMN
LYRA DAVIDICA, 1708

1. Jesus Christ is ris'n to-day, Alleluia!
Our triumphant holy day, Alleluia!
Who did once upon the cross, Alleluia!
Suffer to redeem our loss. Alleluia!

2. Hymns of praise then let us sing, Alleluia!
Unto Christ, our heav'nly King, Alleluia!
Who endured the cross and grave, Alleluia!
Sinners to redeem and save. Alleluia!

3. But the pains which he endured, Alleluia!
Our salvation have procured; Alleluia!
Now he reigns above as King, Alleluia!
Where the angels ever sing. Alleluia!

4. Sing we to our God above, Alleluia!
Praise eternal as his love; Alleluia!
Praise him, all ye heav'nly host, Alleluia!
Father, Son, and Holy Ghost. Alleluia!

SURREXIT CHRISTUS HODIE; *LYRA DAVIDICA*, 1708, ALT.
THE COMPLEAT PSALMIST, LONDON, 1749; VS. 4, CHARLES WESLEY, 1707–1788, ALT.

129 Jesus Christ Is Risen Today
77 77 WITH ALLELUIAS

EASTER HYMN (MONK)   WILLIAM HENRY MONK, 1823–1889

1. Jesus Christ is ris'n to-day, Alleluia!
   Our triumphant holy day, Alleluia!
   Who did once upon the Cross, Alleluia!
   Suffer to redeem our loss. Alleluia!

2. Hymns of praise then let us sing, Alleluia!
   Unto Christ our heav'nly King, Alleluia!
   Who endured the Cross and grave, Alleluia!
   Sinners to redeem and save. Alleluia!

3. But the pains which he endured, Alleluia!
   Our salvation have procured; Alleluia!
   Now he reigns above as King, Alleluia!
   Where the angels ever sing. Alleluia!

4. Sing we to our God above, Alleluia!
   Praise eternal as his love; Alleluia!
   Praise him, all ye heav'nly host, Alleluia!
   Father, Son, and Holy Ghost. Alleluia!

Surrexit Christus hodie; *Lyra Davidica*, 1708, ALT.
The Compleat Psalmist, LONDON, 1749; vs. 4, CHARLES WESLEY, 1707–1788, ALT.

130 Jesus, Jesus, Come to Me
IRREGULAR

TRADITIONAL MELODY

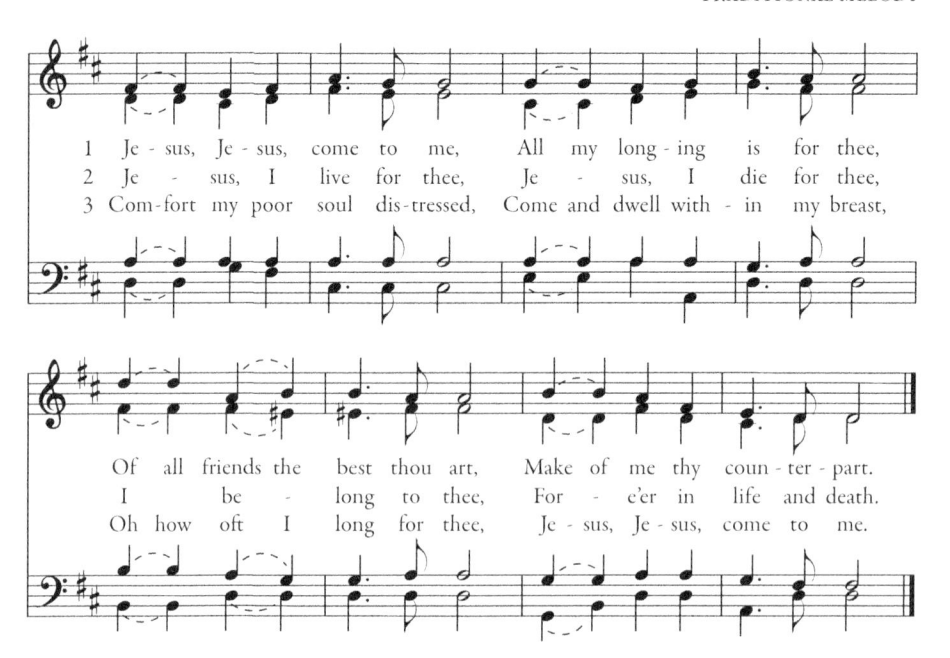

1 Jesus, Jesus, come to me, All my longing is for thee,
Of all friends the best thou art, Make of me thy counter-part.

2 Jesus, I live for thee, Jesus, I die for thee,
I belong to thee, For e'er in life and death.

3 Comfort my poor soul distressed, Come and dwell within my breast,
Oh how oft I long for thee, Jesus, Jesus, come to me.

ANONYMOUS
TR. BY SISTER JEANNE MARIE

131 Jesus, Keep Me Close to Thee
87 87 D

MOTHER MARY ALEXIS DONNELLY, RSM, 1857–1936

1. Thou my ev-er last-ing por-tion, More than friends or life to me,
All a-long my wea-ry jour-ney, Je-sus, keep me close to thee.

2. Not for ease or world-ly pleas-ure, Nor for fame my prayer shall be;
Glad-ly will I toil and suf-fer, On-ly keep me close to thee.

3. Lead me through this vale of sad-ness, Till thine own dear Face I see;
Then the home of life e-ter-nal May I en-ter, Lord, with thee.

All through life and at its clos-ing, Je-sus, keep me close to thee;
All through life and at its clos-ing, Je-sus, keep me close to thee.

FRANCES JANE CROSBY

132   Jesus, My Lord, My God, My All

88 88 WITH REFRAIN

SWEET SACRAMENT   *RÖMISCH-KATHOLISCHES GESANGBÜCHLEIN*, 1826

1. Jesus, my Lord, my God, my all! How can I love thee as I ought? And how revere this wond'rous gift, So far surpassing hope or thought?
2. Had I but Mary's sinless heart, To love thee with, my dearest King; O with what bursts of fervent praise, Thy goodness, Jesus, would I sing!
3. O, see, within a creature's hand, The vast Creator deigns to be, Reposing infant-like, as though On Joseph's arm, or Mary's knee.

Sweet sacrament, we thee adore! O make us love thee

more and more. O make us love thee more and more.

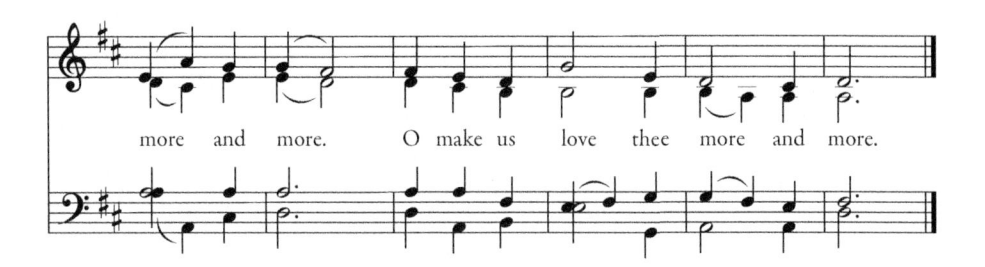

4 Thy body, soul, and Godhead, all,
 O mystery of love divine!
 I cannot compass all I have,
 For all thou hast and art are mine.

5 Sound, sound his praises higher still,
 And come, ye Angels, to our aid;
 'Tis God, 'tis God, the very God,
 Whose pow'r both man and angels made.

FREDERICK W. FABER, 1814–1863

133 Jesus, My Lord, My God, My All

88 88 88 WITH REPEAT

SAWSTON   TRADITIONAL IRISH MELODY

1. Jesus, my Lord, my God, my all! How can I love thee as I ought? And how revere this wondrous gift, So far surpassing hope and thought?
2. Had I but Mary's sinless heart To love thee with, my dearest King, O with what bursts of fervent praise Thy goodness, Jesus, would I sing!
3. Thy body, soul, and Godhead, all, O mystery of love divine! I cannot compass all I have, For all thou hast and art are mine!
4. Sound, sound his praises higher still, And come, ye Angels, to our aid, 'Tis God! 'tis God! the very God, Whose pow'r both man and angels made!

Sweet sacrament, we thee adore! O make us

love thee more and more, O make us love thee more and more.

FREDERICK W. FABER, 1814–1863

134 Jesus, the Very Thought of Thee
86 86

ST. AGNES

JOHN B. DYKES, 1823–1876

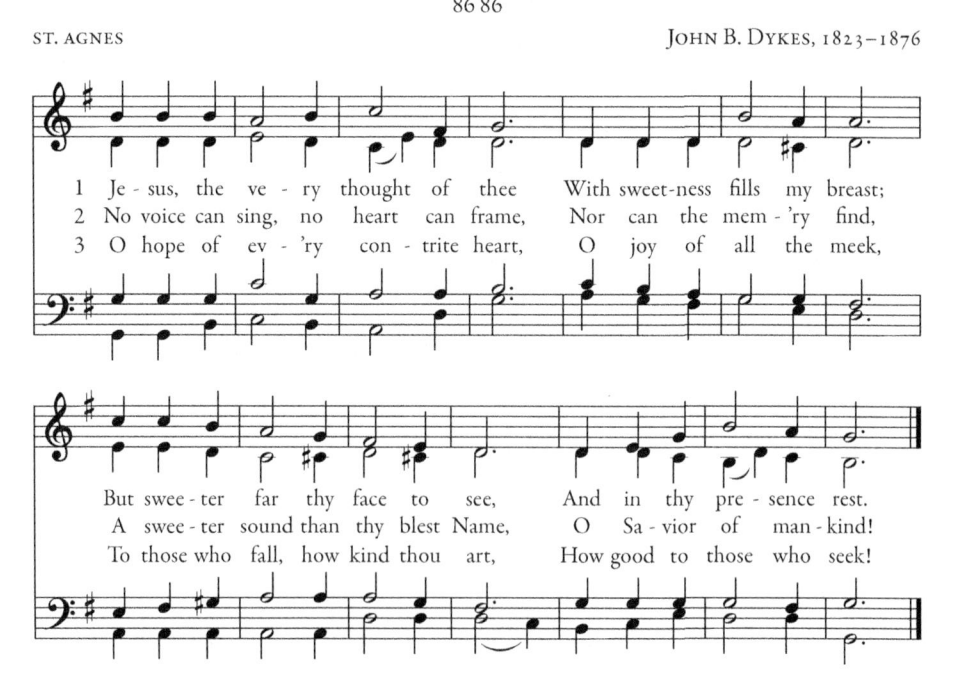

1. Jesus, the very thought of thee With sweetness fills my breast; But sweeter far thy face to see, And in thy presence rest.
2. No voice can sing, no heart can frame, Nor can the mem'ry find, A sweeter sound than thy blest Name, O Savior of mankind!
3. O hope of ev'ry contrite heart, O joy of all the meek, To those who fall, how kind thou art, How good to those who seek!

4. But what to those who find? Ah, this
No tongue nor pen can show;
The love of Jesus, what it is
None but his loved ones know.

5. Jesus, our only joy be thou,
As thou our prize will be;
Jesus, be thou our glory now,
And through eternity.

JESU DULCIS MEMORIA, C. 12TH CENT.
ATTR. TO BERNARD OF CLAIRVAUX, 1091–1153
TR. BY EDWARD CASWALL, 1814–1878

135 Jesus, Thou Art Coming
65 65 D

FROM A SLOVAK HYMNAL

1. Jesus, thou art coming, Holy as thou art,
Thou, the God who made me, To my sinful heart.
Jesus, I believe it On thy only word;
Kneeling, I adore thee As my King and Lord.

2. Who am I, my Jesus, That thou com'st to me?
I have sinned against thee, Often, grievously;
I am very sorry I have caused thee pain;
I will never, never, Wound thy heart again.

3. Put thy kind arms round me, Feeble as I am;
Thou art my Good Shepherd, I, thy little lamb;
Since thou comest, Jesus, Now to be my Guest,
I can trust thee always, Lord, for all the rest.

4. Dearest Lord, I love thee,
With my whole, whole heart,
Not for what thou givest,
But for what thou art.
Come, oh, come, sweet Savior!
Come to me, and stay,
For I want thee, Jesus,
More than I can say.

5. Ah! what gift or present,
Jesus, can I bring?
I have nothing worthy
Of my God and King;
But thou art my Shepherd,
I, thy little lamb;
Take myself, dear Jesus,
All I have and am.

6. Take my body, Jesus,
Eyes, and ears, and tongue;
Never let them, Jesus,
Help to do thee wrong.
Take my heart, and fill it
Full of love for thee;
All I have I give thee,
Give thyself to me.

SISTERS OF NOTRE DAME

136. Jesus, Thou Art Coming
65 65 D

J. FITZPATRICK, SJ

1. Jesus, thou art coming, Holy as thou art,
Thou, the God who made me, To my sinful heart.
Jesus, I believe it On thy only word;
Kneeling, I adore thee As my King and Lord.

2. Who am I, my Jesus, That thou com'st to me?
I have sinned against thee, Often, grievously;
I am very sorry I have caused thee pain;
I will never, never, Wound thy heart again.

3. Put thy kind arms round me, Feeble as I am;
Thou art my Good Shepherd, I, thy little lamb;
Since thou comest, Jesus, Now to be my Guest,
I can trust thee always, Lord, for all the rest.

4. Dearest Lord, I love thee,
With my whole, whole heart,
Not for what thou givest,
But for what thou art.
Come, oh, come, sweet Savior!
Come to me, and stay,
For I want thee, Jesus,
More than I can say.

5. Ah! what gift or present,
Jesus, can I bring?
I have nothing worthy
Of my God and King;
But thou art my Shepherd,
I, thy little lamb;
Take myself, dear Jesus,
All I have and am.

6. Take my body, Jesus,
Eyes, and ears, and tongue;
Never let them, Jesus,
Help to do thee wrong.
Take my heart, and fill it
Full of love for thee;
All I have I give thee,
Give thyself to me.

SISTERS OF NOTRE DAME

137 Joy to the World

86 86 WITH REPEAT

ANTIOCH

GEORGE F. HANDEL, 1685–1759
ARR. BY LOWELL MASON, 1792–1872

1. Joy to the world! The Lord is come: Let earth receive her King; Let ev'ry heart prepare him room, And heav'n and nature sing, And heav'n and nature sing, And heav'n, and heav'n and nature sing.

2. Joy to the world! The Savior reigns: Let men their songs employ, While fields and floods, rocks, hills, and plains, Repeat the sounding joy, Repeat the sounding joy, Repeat, repeat the sounding joy.

3. He rules the world with truth and grace, And makes the nations prove The glories of his righteousness, And wonders of his love, And wonders of his love, And wonders, wonders of his love.

BASED ON PSALM 98; ISSAC WATTS, 1674–1748

138   Joyful, Joyful, We Adore Thee
87 87 D

HYMN TO JOY   LUDWIG VAN BEETHOVEN, 1770–1827
ARR. BY EDWARD HODGES, 1796–1867

1. Joyful, joyful, we adore thee, God of glory, Lord of love;
Hearts unfold like flow'rs before thee, O-p'ning to the sun above.
Melt the clouds of sin and sadness; Drive the dark of doubt away;
Giver of immortal gladness, Fill us with the light of day!

2. All thy works with joy surround thee, Earth and heav'n reflect thy rays,
Stars and angels sing around thee, Center of unbroken praise;
Field and forest, vale and mountain, Flow-'ry meadow, flashing sea,
Chanting bird and flowing fountain, Call us to rejoice in thee.

3. Thou art giving and forgiving, Ever blessing, ever blest,
Well-spring of the joy of living, Ocean-depth of happy rest!
Thou art Father, Christ our brother, All who live in love are thine;
Teach us how to love each other, Lift us to the Joy Divine.

4. Mortals, join the mighty chorus Which the morning stars began;
Father love is reigning o'er us, Brother love binds man to man.
Ever singing, march we onward, Victors in the midst of strife;
Joyful music leads us sunward In the triumph song of life.

HENRY VAN DYKE, 1852–1933, ALT.

139 King of Kings Is He Anointed
86 86 87 85 85

MARGARET LEDDY

1. King of kings is he anointed; Let all men adore him;
   Lord above all lords appointed; Let us bow before him.
   Christ who leads us, Christ who loves us, Christ our ruler from his birth,
   He shall triumph, he shall triumph, Over all the earth.
   King of kings is he anointed Over all the earth.

2. Son of God and yet our Brother, Let all men adore him;
   Son of Mary our sweet Mother, Let us bow before him.
   Christ who made us, Christ who saves us, Christ who can all foes defy,
   He shall triumph, he shall triumph, From his throne on high;
   Son of God and yet our Brother From his throne on high.

CATHERINE MAGUIRE

140 Lead, Kindly Light
10 4 10 4 10 10

SANDON   CHARLES HENRY PURDAY, 1799–1885

1. Lead, kindly Light, amid th'encircling gloom, Lead thou me on; The night is dark, and I am far from home; Lead thou me on. Keep thou my feet; I do not ask to see The distant scene; one step enough for me.

2. I was not ever thus, nor prayed that thou Shouldst lead me on; I loved to choose and see my path; but now Lead thou me on. I loved the garish day, and, spite of fears, Pride ruled my will: remember not past years.

3. So long thy power has blest me, sure it still Will lead me on O'er moor and fen, o'er crag and torrent, till The night is gone; And with the morn those angel faces smile Which I have loved long since, and lost awhile.

FAITH – HEAVENLY LEADINGS; JOHN HENRY NEWMAN, 1801–1890

A CATHOLIC BOOK OF HYMNS • 149

141 Let Thy Blood in Mercy Poured
78 78 77

JESUS MEINE ZUVERSICHT

JOHANN CRÜGER, 1598–1662
HARM. FROM *THE CHORALE BOOK FOR ENGLAND*, 1863

1. Let thy blood in mercy poured, Let thy gracious body broken, Be to me, O gracious Lord, Of thy boundless love the token.
2. Thou didst die that I might live; Blessèd Lord, thou cam'st to save me; All that love of God could give, Jesus by his sorrows gave me.
3. By the thorns that crowned thy brow, By the spear-wound and the nailing, By the pain and death, I now Claim, O Christ, thy love unfailing.
4. Wilt thou own the gift I bring? All my penitence I give thee; Thou art my exalted King, Of thy matchless love forgive me.

Thou didst give thyself for me, Now I give myself to thee.

JOHN BROWNLIE, 1859–1925

142 Lift Up Your Heads
88 88

TRURO

WILLIAMS' *PSALMODIA EVANGELICA II*, 1789
HARM. BY LOWELL MASON, 1792–1827, ALT.

1. Lift up your heads, ye mighty gates; Behold the King of glory waits! The Savior of the world is here.
2. O blest the land, the city blest, Where Christ the ruler is confessed! O happy hearts and happy homes To whom this King of triumph comes!
3. Fling wide the portals of your heart; Make it a temple, set apart From earthly use for heav'n's employ, Adorned with prayer and love and joy.
4. So come, my Sov'reign; enter in! Let new and nobler life begin; Thy Holy Spirit guide us on, Until the glorious crown be won.

BASED ON PSALM 24
MACHT HOCH DIE TÜR; GEORGE WEISSEL, 1590–1635
TR. BY CATHERINE WINKWORTH, 1827–1878, ALT.

143 Light of All Days
88 88

TALLIS' CANON
THOMAS TALLIS, C. 1505–1585

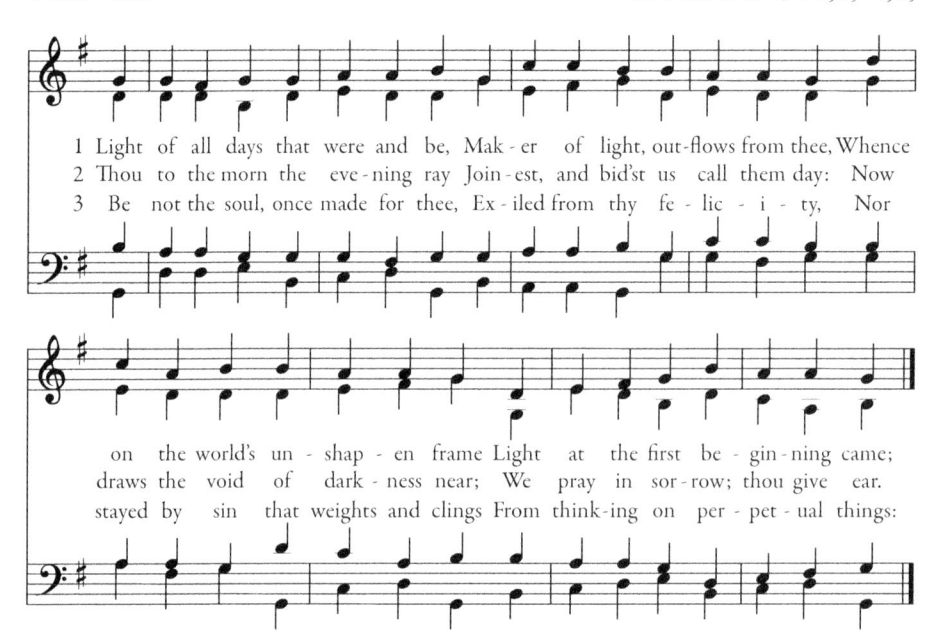

1 Light of all days that were and be, Maker of light, out-flows from thee, Whence on the world's unshapen frame Light at the first beginning came;

2 Thou to the morn the evening ray Joinest, and bid'st us call them day: Now draws the void of darkness near; We pray in sorrow; thou give ear.

3 Be not the soul, once made for thee, Exiled from thy felicity, Nor stayed by sin that weights and clings From thinking on perpetual things:

4 Let it to heav'n's own gate arise,
Knock, and obtain th'eternal prize;
Now and hereafter evil shun,
Repent and purge all evil done.

5 Thou with the Father hear our prayer,
Who dost the Father's glory share,
And thou, proceeding from the twain
In equal everlasting reign.

LUCIS CREATOR OPTIME; ATTR. TO GREGORY THE GREAT, C. 540–604
TR. BY WALTER H. SHEWRING, 1906–1990

144 Lo, He Comes With Clouds Descending
87 87 12 7

HELMSLEY
LOCK HOSPITAL COLLECTION, LONDON, 1765
HARM. BY RALPH VAUGHAN WILLIAMS, 1872–1958, ALT.

1 Lo! He comes with clouds descending, Once for our

2 Ev'ry eye shall now behold him, Robed in dread-

3 Those dear tokens of his passion Still his daz-

4 Yea, amen! Let all adore thee, High on thine

152 • A CATHOLIC BOOK OF HYMNS

salvation slain; Thousand, thousand saints attending
Swell the triumph of his train:
Alleluia! Alleluia! Alleluia!
Christ the Lord returns to reign.

ful majesty; Those who set at nought and sold him,
Pierced, and nailed him to the tree,
Deeply wailing, deeply wailing, deeply wailing,
Shall the true Messiah see.

zling body bears, Cause of endless exultation
To his ransomed worshipers;
With what rapture, with what rapture, with what rapture
Gaze we on those glorious scars!

eternal throne; Savior, take the pow'r and glory;
Claim the kingdom for thine own:
Alleluia! Alleluia! Alleluia!
Thou shalt reign and thou alone.

CHARLES WESLEY, 1707–1788, ALT.

145 Lo, He Comes With Clouds Descending
87 87 87

ST. THOMAS (WADE) JOHN F. WADE, 1711–1786

1. Lo! He comes with clouds descending, Once for our salvation slain; Thousand, thousand saints attending Swell the triumph of his train: Alleluia! Alleluia! Christ the Lord returns to reign.
2. Ev'ry eye shall now behold him, Robed in dreadful majesty; Those who set at nought and sold him, Pierced, and nailed him to the tree, Deeply wailing, deeply wailing, Shall the true Messiah see.
3. Those dear tokens of his passion Still his dazzling body bears, Cause of endless exultation To his ransomed worshipers; With what rapture, with what rapture, Gaze we on those glorious scars!
4. Yea, amen! Let all adore thee, High on thine eternal throne; Savior, take the pow'r and glory; Claim the kingdom for thine own: Alleluia! Alleluia! Thou shalt reign and thou alone.

CHARLES WESLEY, 1707–1788, ALT.

146 Lo, How a Rose E'er Blooming
76 76 676

ES IST EIN' ROS' ENTSPRUNGEN

Speierisches Gesangbuch, Cologne, 1599
Harm. by Michael Praetorius, 1571–1621

1. Lo, how a rose e'er blooming From tender stem hath sprung! Of Jesse's lineage coming As men of old have sung. It came, a flow'r-et bright, Amid the cold of winter, When half-spent was the night.

2. Isaiah 'twas foretold it, The rose I have in mind: With Mary we behold it, The Virgin Mother kind. To show God's love aright, She bore to men a Savior, When half-spent was the night.

Based on Isaiah 11:11
Es ist ein Ros entsprungen; traditional German carol
Tr. by Theodore Baker, 1851–1934

147   Lo! Round the Throne
88 88 WITH ALLELUIAS

ERSCHIENEN IST DER HERRLICH TAG   NIKOLAUS HERMAN, C. 1480–1561

1. Lo! Round the throne, a glorious band, The saints in countless myriads stand, Of every tongue redeemed to God, Arrayed in garments washed in blood. Alleluia!
2. Through tribulation great they came; They bore the cross, despised the shame; From all their labors now they rest, In God's eternal glory blest. Alleluia!
3. They see their Savior face to face, And sing the triumphs of his grace; Him day and night they ceaseless praise, To him the loud thanksgiving raise. Alleluia!

ROWLAND HILL, 1744–1833, ALT.

148   Long Live the Pope!
86 86 D WITH REPEAT

PAPAL HYMN   HENRY GEORGE GANSS, 1855–1912

1. Long live the Pope! His praises sound Again and yet again:
2. Beleaguered by the foes of earth, Beset by hosts of hell,
3. His signet is the Fisherman's; No scepter does he bear;
4. Then raise the chant, with heart and voice, In church and school and home:

His rule is o-ver space and time; His throne the hearts of men:
He guards the loy-al flock of Christ, A watch-ful sen-ti-nel:
In meek and low-ly maj-es-ty He rules from Pe-ter's Chair:
"Long live the Shep-herd of the flock! Long live the Pope of Rome!"

All hail! the Shep-herd-King of Rome, The theme of lov-ing song:
And yet, a-mid the din and strife, The clash of mace and sword,
And yet from ev-'ry tribe and tongue, From ev-'ry clime and zone,
Al-might-y Fa-ther, bless his work, Pro-tect him in his ways,

Let all the earth his glo-ry sing, And heav'n the strain pro-long.
He bears a-lone the shep-herd staff, This cham-pion of the Lord.
Three hun-dred mil-lion voic-es sing The glo-ry of his throne.
Re-ceive his prayers, ful-fill his hopes, And grant him "length of days."

Let all the earth his glo-ry sing, And heav'n the strain pro-long.
He bears a-lone the shep-herd staff, This cham-pion of the Lord.
Three hun-dred mil-lion voic-es sing The glo-ry of his throne.
Re-ceive his prayers, ful-fill his hopes, And grant him "length of days."

Hugh T. Henry, 1862–1946

149 Look, Ye Saints! The Sight Is Glorious
87 87 444 77

BRYN CALFARIA WILLIAM OWEN, 1814–1893

1. Look, ye saints! the sight is glorious: See the Man of Sorrows now;
From the fight returned victorious, Ev'ry knee to him shall bow;
Crown him, crown him, Crown him, crown him, Crown him, crown him.
Crowns become the Victor's brow, Crowns become the Victor's brow.

2. Crown the Savior! angels, crown him; Rich the trophies Jesus brings;
In the seat of pow'r enthrone him, While the vault of heaven rings;
Crown him, crown him, Crown him, crown him, Crown him, crown him.
Crown the Savior King of kings, Crown the Savior King of kings.

3. Sinners in derision crowned him, Mocking thus the Savior's claim;
Saints and angels crowd around him, Own his title, praise his name:
Crown him, crown him, Crown him, crown him, Crown him, crown him.
Spread abroad the Victor's fame, Spread abroad the Victor's fame.

4. Hark, those bursts of acclamation! Hark, those loud triumphant chords!
Jesus takes the highest station; O what joy the sight affords!
Crown him, crown him, Crown him, crown him, Crown him, crown him.
King of kings, and Lord of lords! King of kings, and Lord of lords!

THOMAS KELLY, 1769–1855

150. Lord, Accept the Gifts We Offer

87 87 87

BRYNTIRION
ATTR. TO HEINRICH ROTH, 1802–1899

1. Lord, accept the gifts we offer At this Eucharistic feast, Bread and wine to be transformed now, Through the action of thy priest, Take us too, Lord, and transform us, May thy grace in us increase.

2. May our souls be pure and spotless, As the host of wheat so fine, May all stain of sin be crushed out Like the grape that forms the wine, As we too become partakers In this sacrifice of love.

3. Take our gifts, Almighty Father, Living God, eternal true, Which we give through Christ, our Savior, Pleading here for us anew; Grant salvation to us present And our faith and love renew.

ANONYMOUS

A CATHOLIC BOOK OF HYMNS • 159

151 Lord, Enthroned in Heavenly Splendor
87 87 87

ST. HELEN GEORGE CLEMENT MARTIN, 1844–1916

1. Lord, enthroned in heav'nly splendor, First-begotten from the dead,
Thou alone, our strong defender, Liftest up thy people's head.
Alleluia, alleluia, Jesu, true and living bread.

2. Here our humblest homage pay we, Here in loving rev-'rence bow;
Here for faith's discernment pray we, Lest we fail to know thee now.
Alleluia, alleluia, Thou art here, we ask not how.

3. Though the lowliest form doth veil thee As of old in Bethlehem,
Here as there thine angels hail thee, Branch and Flow'r of Jesse's Stem.
Alleluia, alleluia, We in worship join with them.

4. Paschal Lamb, thine off'ring, finished
Once for all when thou wast slain,
In its fullness undiminished
Shall for evermore remain.
Alleluia, alleluia,
Cleansing souls from ev'ry stain.

5. Life-imparting heav'nly manna,
Stricken rock with streaming side,
Heav'n and earth with loud hosanna
Worship thee, the Lamb who died.
Alleluia, alleluia,
Ris'n, ascended, glorified!

GEORGE HUGH BOURNE, 1840–1925

152 Lord, for Tomorrow and Its Needs
84 84

PROVIDENCE
RICHARD R. TERRY, 1865–1938

1. Lord, for tomorrow and its needs I do not pray;
   Keep me, my God, from stain of sin, Just for today.

2. Let me both diligently work And duly pray;
   Let me be kind in word and deed, Just for today.

3. Let me be slow to do my will, Prompt to obey;
   Help me to mortify my flesh, Just for today.

4. Let me no wrong or idle word
   Unthinking say;
   Set thou a seal upon my lips,
   Just for today.

5. Let me in season, Lord, be grave,
   In season, gay;
   Let me be faithful to thy grace,
   Just for today.

6. And if today my tide of life
   Should ebb away,
   Give me thy sacraments divine,
   Sweet Lord, today.

7. In Purgatory's cleansing fires
   Brief be my stay;
   Oh, bid me, if today I die,
   Go home today.

8. So for tomorrow and its needs
   I do not pray;
   But keep me, guide me, love me, Lord,
   Just for today.

SISTER MARY XAVIER PARTRIDGE, SND, 1856–1917

153 Lord Jesus, Think on Me
66 86

SOUTHWELL

WILLIAM DAMAN, C. 1540–1591
THE PSALMES OF DAVID IN ENGLISH METRE, LONDON, 1579

1. Lord Jesus, think on me,
And purge away my sin;
From earth-born passions set me free,
And make me pure within.

2. Lord Jesus, think on me,
With care and woe oppressed;
Let me thy loving servant be,
And taste thy promised rest.

3. Lord Jesus, think on me,
Amid the battle's strife;
In all my pain and misery
Be thou my health and life.

4. Lord Jesus, think on me,
Nor let me go astray;
Through darkness and perplexity
Point thou the heav'nly way.

5. Lord Jesus, think on me,
That, when the flood is past,
I may th'eternal brightness see,
And share thy joy at last.

6. Lord Jesus, think on me,
That I may sing above
To Father, Spirit, and to thee
The strains of praise and love.

μνώεο Χριστέ (MNŌEO CHRISTE); SYNESIUS OF CYRENE, C. 375–430
TR. BY ALLEN W. CHATFIELD, 1808–1896, ALT.

154 Lord Jesus, When I Think of Thee
88 88

WORD OF FIRE

NOEL JONES, 1947–

1. Lord Jesus, when I think of thee, And look upon thy cross aright, Thy body stained with blood I see, Lord, pierce my heart with that sad sight!
2. Jesus, true love I owe to thee Who on the cross didst show that tide, The crown of thorns, the sharp nails three, The cruel spear that pierced thy side.
3. Jesus, love made thy tears to fall, 'Twas love that made thy blood to flow, For love was scourged and smitten all, For love thy life thou didst forgo.
4. Mary, I pray, as thou art free, A part of this thy grief I'll bear, That I may sorrow here with thee, And bliss with thee hereafter share!

RICHARD ROLLE, C. 1300–1349

155 Lord, Who at Cana's Wedding Feast
86 86 D

JOHN LEWIS BROWNE, 1866–1933

1. Lord, who at Cana's wedding feast Didst as a guest appear, Thou, dearer far than earthly guest, Vouchsafe thy presence here; For holy thou indeed dost prove The marriage vow to be, Pro-

2. The holiest vow that man can make, The golden thread in life, The bond that none may dare to break, That bindeth man and wife; Which blest by thee, what e'er betides, No evil shall destroy, Through

3. On those who at thine altar kneel, O Lord, thy blessing pour, That each may wake the other's zeal To love thee more and more: O grant them here in peace to live, In purity and love, And,

164 • A CATHOLIC BOOK OF HYMNS

claim - ing it a type of love Be - tween the Church and thee.
care - worn days each care di - vides, And dou - bles ev - 'ry joy.
this world leav - ing, to re - ceive A crown of life a - bove!

A - men.
A - men.
A - men.

ADELAIDE THRUPP, 1831–1908

156 Lord, Who at Thy First Eucharist
10 10 10 10 10 10

UNDE ET MEMORES

WILLIAM H. MONK, 1823–1889, ALT.

1 Lord, who at thy first Eucharist didst pray
That all thy Church might be for-ev-er one,
Grant us at ev-'ry Eucharist to say
With long-ing heart and soul, "Thy will be done."

2 For all thy Church, O Lord, we in-ter-cede;
Make thou our sad di-vi-sions soon to cease;
Draw us the near-er each to each, we plead,
By draw-ing all to thee, O Prince of peace;

3 We pray thee, too, for wan-d'rers from thy fold;
O bring them back, Good Shep-herd of the sheep,
Back to the faith which saints be-lieved of old,
Back to the Church which still that faith doth keep;

4 So, Lord, at length when sac-ra-ments shall cease,
May we be one with all thy Church a-bove,
One with thy saints in one un-bro-ken peace,
One with thy saints in one un-bound-ed love;

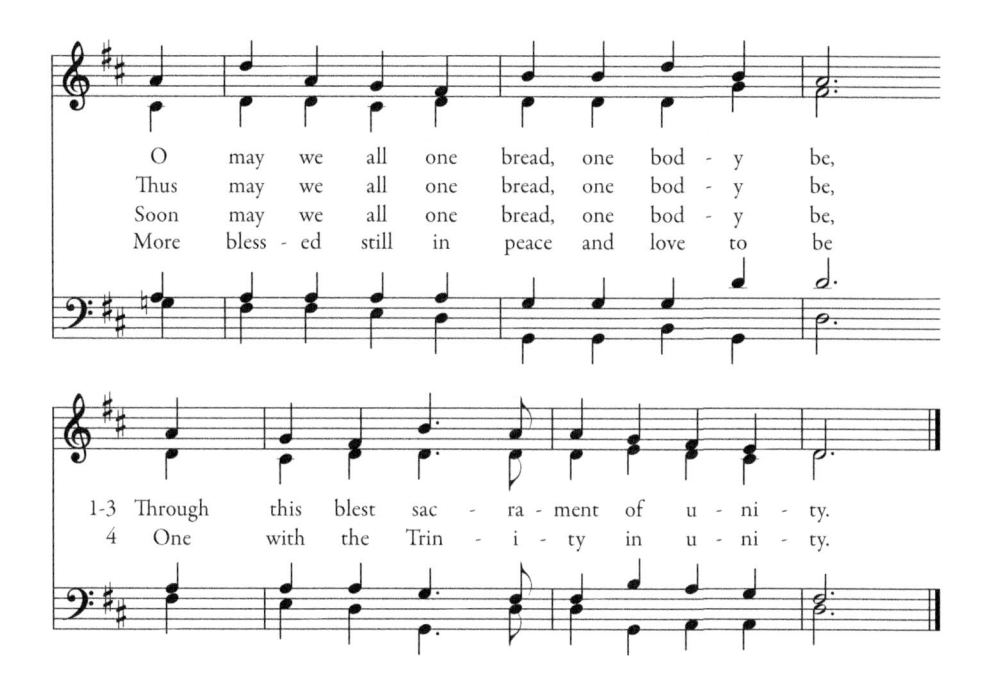

O may we all one bread, one body be,
Thus may we all one bread, one body be,
Soon may we all one bread, one body be,
More blessed still in peace and love to be

1-3 Through this blest sacrament of unity.
4 One with the Trinity in unity.

WILLIAM H. TURTON, 1856–1938

157 Lord, Who Throughout These Forty Days
86 86

ST. FLAVIAN

THE WHOLE BOOK OF PSALMES IN FOURE PARTES, 1563
ADAPT. BY RICHARD REDHEAD, 1820–1901
HARM. FROM *HYMNS ANCIENT AND MODERN*, 1875, ALT.

1. Lord, who through-out these for-ty days For us didst fast and pray,
2. As thou with Sa-tan didst con-tend, And didst the vic-t'ry win,
3. As thou didst hun-ger bear and thirst, So teach us, gra-cious Lord,

Teach us with thee to mourn our sins, And close by thee to stay.
O give us strength in thee to fight, In thee to con-quer sin.
To die to self, and ev-er live By thy most ho-ly word.

4. And through these days of penitence,
And through thy Passiontide,
Forevermore, in life and death,
O Lord, with us abide.

5. Abide with us that when this life
Of suffering is past,
An Easter of unending joy
We may attain at last!

CLAUDIA F. HERNAMAN, 1838–1898, ALT.

158 Love Divine, All Loves Excelling
87 87 D

BLAENWERN

WILLIAM PENFRO ROWLANDS, 1860–1937

1. Love di-vine, all loves ex-cel-ling, Joy of heav'n to
2. Come, al-might-y to de-liv-er, Let us all thy
3. Fin-ish then thy new cre-a-tion, Pure and spot-less

1. earth come down, Fix in us thy humble dwelling, All thy faithful mercies crown. Jesus, thou art all compassion, Pure unbounded love thou art; Visit us with thy salvation; Enter ev'ry trembling heart.

2. life receive; Suddenly return and never, Nevermore thy temples leave. Thee we would be always blessing, Serve thee as thy hosts above, Pray, and praise thee without ceasing, Glory in thy perfect love.

3. let us be; Let us see thy great salvation Perfectly restored in thee: Changed from glory into glory, Till in heav'n we take our place, Till we cast our crowns before thee, Lost in wonder, love, and praise.

CHARLES WESLEY, 1707–1788, ALT.

159 Love Divine, All Loves Excelling
87 87 D

HYFRYDOL ROWLAND H. PRITCHARD, 1811–1887

1. Love, divine, all loves excelling, Joy of heav'n to earth come down, Fix in us thy humble dwelling, All thy faithful mercies crown. Jesus, thou art all compassion, Pure un-
2. Come, almighty to deliver, Let us all thy life receive; Suddenly return and never, Nevermore thy temples leave. Thee we would be always blessing, Serve thee
3. Finish then thy new creation, Pure and spotless let us be; Let us see thy great salvation Perfectly restored in thee: Changed from glory into glory, Till in

bound - ed	love	thou	art;	Vis - it	us	with
as	thy	hosts	a - bove,	Pray,	and	praise	thee
heav'n	we	take	our	place,	Till	we	cast	our

thy	sal - va - tion;	En - ter	ev - 'ry	trem - bling	heart.
with - out	ceas - ing,	Glo - ry	in	thy per - fect	love.
crowns	be - fore	thee,	Lost	in won - der,	love,	and	praise.

CHARLES WESLEY, 1707–1788, ALT.

160 Maiden Mother, Meek and Mild
77 77

ORIENTIS PARTIBUS
PIERRE DE CORBEIL, C. 1190–1222

1. Maiden Mother, meek and mild, Take, oh, take me for thy child, All my life, oh, let it be My best joy to think of thee, *Virgo María!*

2. Teach me, when the sunbeam bright, Calls me with its golden light, How my waking thoughts may be, Turned to Jesus and to thee, *Virgo María!*

3. Teach me also through the day Oft to raise my heart and say, "Maiden Mother, meek and mild, Guard, oh, guard thy faithful child!" *Virgo María!*

4. When my eyes are closed in sleep, Through the night my slumbers keep, Make my latest thought to be How to love thy Son and thee, *Virgo María!*

5. Thus, sweet Mother, day and night Thou shalt guide my steps aright; And my dying words shall be "Virgin Mother, pray for me!" *Virgo María!*

CECILIA MARY CADDELL, 1814–1877

161 Michael, Prince of Highest Heaven
87 87 WITH REFRAIN

JULES BRAZIL, fl. 1910–1925

Michael, Prince of highest heav'n, Noblest of celestial ranks,
Lowly singing in thine honor, Bring we now our meed of thanks,
Bring we now our meed of thanks.

1. Mighty victor all resplendent, Next to Mary thou dost reign;
Come and bless us with thy presence, Bring with thee thy heav'nly train.

2. Gabriel, silver-tongued and glorious, Raphael, healer of our woes,
Blessed angels, gentle guardians, Be our aid, repel our foes.

3. Breathe into our hearts your sweetness, Fill our souls with love divine,
May your gracious presence ever Round your charge protecting shine.

ANONYMOUS

162 Mother Dear, O Pray for Me

87 87 WITH REFRAIN

CATHOLIC HARP

ISAAC B. WOODBURY, 1819–1858

1. Mother dear, O pray for me! Whilst far from heav'n and thee
I wander in a fragile bark O'er life's tempestuous sea,
O Virgin Mother, from thy throne, So bright in bliss above,
Protect thy child and cheer my path With thy sweet smile of love.

2. Mother dear, O pray for me! Should pleasure's siren lay,
E'er tempt thy child to wander far From Virtue's path away.
When thorns beset life's devious way, And darkling waters flow,
Then, Mary, aid thy weeping child, Thyself a mother show.

3. Mother dear, O pray for me! When all looks bright and fair,
That I may all my danger see, For surely then 'tis near.
A mother's pray'r how much we need If pros-p'rous be the ray
That paints with gold the flow'ry mead, Which blossoms in our way.

174 • A CATHOLIC BOOK OF HYMNS

Mother dear, remember me, And never cease thy care,
Till in heav'n eternally, Thy love and bliss I share.

ISAAC B. WOODBURY, 1819–1858

163 Mother Dearest, Mother Fairest
87 87 WITH REFRAIN

Wreath of Mary, 1883

1. Mother dearest, Mother fairest, Help of all who call on thee,
Virgin purest, brightest rarest, Help us, help, we cry to thee.

2. Lady, help in pain and sorrow, Soothe those rack'd on beds of pain,
May the golden light of morrow, Bring them health and joy again.

3. Help our priests, our virgins holy, Help our Pope, long may he reign,
Pray that we who sing thy praises, May in heav'n all meet again.

Refrain:
Mary, help us, help we pray, Mary, help us, help we pray,
Help us in all care and sorrow: Mary, help us, help we pray.

4. Lady, help the wounded soldier,
Set the pining captive free,
Help the sailor in mid-ocean,
Help those in their agony.

5. Lady, help the absent loved ones,
How we miss their presence here,
May the hand of thy protection
Guide and guard them far and near.

ANONYMOUS

164 Mother of Christ
IRREGULAR

MOTHER OF CHRIST — SISTERS OF NOTRE DAME DE NAMUR, ENGLAND

1. Moth-er of Christ, Moth-er of Christ, What shall I ask of thee? I do not sigh for the wealth of earth, For the joys that fade and flee; But, Moth-er of Christ, Moth-er of Christ, This do I long to see, The bliss un-told which thine arms en-fold, The treas-ure up-on thy knee.

2. Moth-er of Christ, Moth-er of Christ, What shall I do for thee? I will love thy Son with the whole of my strength, My on-ly King shall he be. Yes, Moth-er of Christ, Moth-er of Christ, This will I do for thee, Of all that are dear or cher-ished here, None shall be dear as he.

3. Moth-er of Christ, Moth-er of Christ, I toss on a storm-y sea, O lift thy Child as a bea-con light To the port where I fain would be. And, Moth-er of Christ, Moth-er of Christ, This do I ask of thee, When the voy-age is o'er, O stand on the shore, And show him at last to me.

SISTERS OF NOTRE DAME DE NAMUR, ENGLAND

165 My God, Accept My Heart This Day
86 86

NICOLA A. MONTANI, 1880–1948

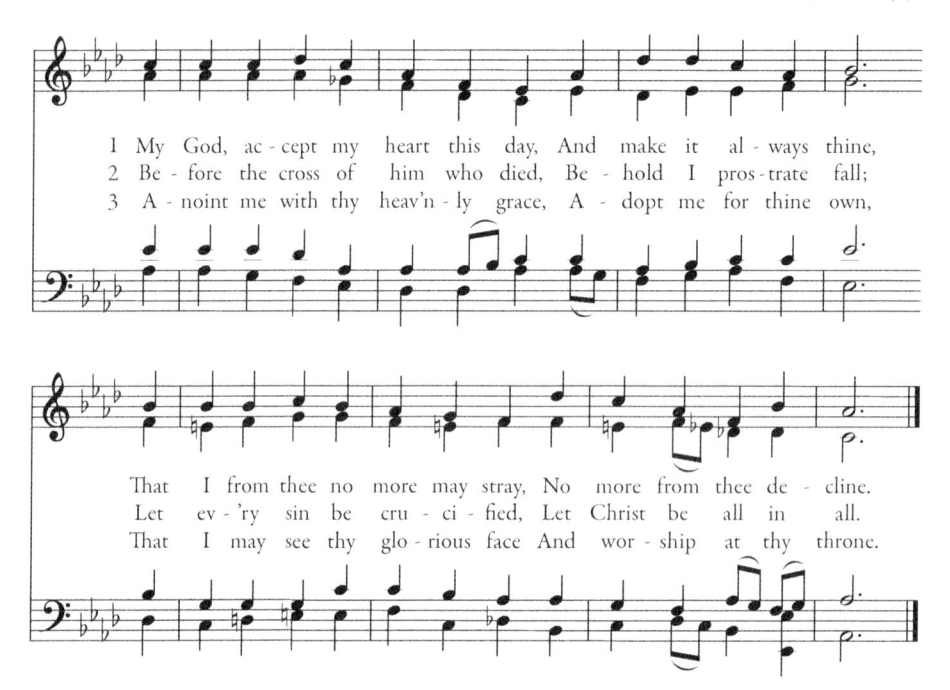

1. My God, accept my heart this day, And make it always thine,
That I from thee no more may stray, No more from thee decline.

2. Before the cross of him who died, Behold I prostrate fall;
Let ev'ry sin be crucified, Let Christ be all in all.

3. Anoint me with thy heav'nly grace, Adopt me for thine own,
That I may see thy glorious face And worship at thy throne.

4. May the dear blood, once shed for me,
My best atonement prove;
That I from first to last may be
The purchase of thy love!

5. Let every thought, and work, and word,
To thee be ever giv'n
Then life shall be thy service, Lord,
And death the gate of heaven!

MATTHEW BRIDGES, 1800–1894

166 My Song Is Love Unknown
66 66 88

LOVE UNKNOWN
JOHN IRELAND, 1879–1962

1. My song is love unknown, My Savior's love to me, Love to the loveless shown, That they might lovely be. O who am I, that for my sake My Lord should take frail flesh and die?

2. He came from his blest throne, Salvation to bestow; But men cared not, and none The longed-for Christ would know. But oh, my Friend, my Friend indeed, Who at my need his life did spend!

3. Sometimes they strew his way, And his sweet praises sing; Resounding all the day Hosannas to their King. Then "Crucify!" is all their breath, And for his death they thirst and cry.

4. Why, what hath my Lord done?
   What makes this rage and spite?
   He made the lame to run,
   He gave the blind their sight.
   Sweet injuries! Yet all his deeds
   Their hatred feeds; they 'gainst him rise.

5. They rise, and needs will have
   My dear Lord sent away;
   A murderer they save,
   The Prince of Life they slay.
   Yet willing he to suff'ring goes,
   That he his foes from thence might free.

6. In life, no house, no home
   My Lord on earth might have;
   In death, no friendly tomb
   But what a stranger gave.
   What may I say? Heav'n was his home,
   But mine the tomb wherein he lay.

7. Here might I stay and sing,
   No story so divine;
   Never was love, dear King,
   Never was grief like thine.
   This is my Friend, in whose sweet praise
   I all my days could gladly spend.

SAMUEL CROSSMAN, 1624–1683

167 My Soul Doth Long for Thee
66 86 D

MOTHER MARY ALEXIS DONNELLY, RSM, 1857–1936
HARM. COMPOSITE

1. My soul doth long for thee, To dwell within my breast, Unworthy though, O Lord, I be, Of so Divine a Guest, Of so Divine a Guest, Unworthy though I be, Yet hath my longing heart no rest, Until it come to thee.

2. Until it come to thee, In vain I look around; In all I have, in all I see No rest is to be found, No rest is to be found, But in thy sweet embrace; Oh! when I have my Jesus Lord, Naught else can take his place.

3. Naught else can take his place, My soul longs more and more To see my Jesus face to face When this short life is o'er, When this short life is o'er, And weary strife shall cease; O may I dwell forevermore, In everlasting peace.

VSS. 1–2, JOHN BYROM
VS. 3, SISTERS OF MERCY

168 Now, My Tongue, the Mystery Telling
87 87 87

DOWLING NOEL JONES, 1947–

1. Now, my tongue, the mys-t'ry tell-ing, Of the glo-rious bo-dy sing, And the blood, all price ex-cel-ling, Which the na-tions' Lord and King, Once on earth a-mong us dwell-ing, Shed for this world's ran-som-ing.
2. Giv'n for us, and con-des-cend-ing To be born for us be-low, He, with us in con-verse blend-ing, Dwelt the seed of truth to sow, Till he closed with won-drous end-ing His most pa-tient life of woe.
3. That last night, at sup-per ly-ing With the twelve, his cho-sen band, Je-sus, with the law com-ply-ing, Keeps the feast its rites de-mand; Then, more pre-cious food sup-ply-ing, Gives him-self with his own hand.

4. Word made flesh, by word he maketh
Very bread his flesh to be,
Wine his blood for whoso taketh;
And if senses fail to see,
Faith alone the true heart waketh
To behold the mystery.

5. Therefore we, before him bending,
This great sacrament revere;
Types and shadows have their ending,
For the newer rite is here;
Faith, our outward sense befriending,
Makes our inward vision clear.

6. Glory let us give, and blessing,
To the Father and the Son;
Honor, thanks, and praise addressing
While eternal ages run,
And the Spirit's power confessing,
Who from both with both is one.

Pange lingua gloriosi; ATTR. TO THOMAS AQUINAS, C. 1225–1274
TR. BY EDWARD CASWALL, 1814–1878, ALT.

169 Now, My Tongue, the Mystery Telling
87 87 87

GRAFTON *Chants Ordinaires de l'Office Divin*, Paris, 1881

1 Now, my tongue, the myst'ry tell-ing Of the glo-rious bo-dy sing,
And the blood, all price ex-cell-ing, Which the na-tions' Lord and King,
Once on earth a-mong us dwell-ing, Shed for this world's ran-som-ing.

2 Giv'n for us, and con-de-scend-ing To be born for us be-low,
He with us in con-verse blend-ing, Dwelt the seed of truth to sow,
Till he closed with won-drous end-ing His most pa-tient life of woe.

3 That last night, at sup-per ly-ing With the twelve, his cho-sen band,
Je-sus, with the law com-ply-ing, Keeps the feast its rites de-mand;
Then, more pre-cious food sup-ply-ing, Gives him-self with his own hand.

4 Word made flesh, by word he maketh
Very bread his flesh to be,
Wine his blood for whoso taketh;
And if senses fail to see,
Faith alone the true heart waketh
To behold the mystery.

5 Therefore we, before him bending,
This great sacrament revere;
Types and shadows have their ending,
For the newer rite is here;
Faith, our outward sense befriending,
Makes our inward vision clear.

6 Glory let us give, and blessing,
To the Father and the Son;
Honor, thanks, and praise addressing
While eternal ages run,
And the Spirit's power confessing,
Who from both with both is one.

Pange lingua gloriosi; attr. to Thomas Aquinas, c. 1225–1274
tr. by Edward Caswall, 1814–1878, alt.

170 Now Thank We All Our God
67 67 66 66

NUN DANKET

JOHANN CRÜGER, 1598–1662
HARM. BY FELIX MENDELSSOHN, 1809–1847

1. Now thank we all our God With hearts and hands and voices,
Who won-drous things hath done, In whom his world re-joices;
Who from our moth-ers' arms, Hath blessed us on our way
With count-less gifts of love, And still is ours to-day.

2. O may this gra-cious God Through all our life be near us,
With ev-er joy-ful hearts And bless-ed peace to cheer us;
Pre-serve us in his grace, And guide us in dis-tress,
And free us from all sin, Till heav-en we pos-sess.

3. All praise and thanks to God The Fa-ther now be giv-en,
The Son, and him who reigns With them in high-est heav-en,
E-ter-nal, Tri-une God, Whom earth and heav'n a-dore;
For thus it was, is now, And shall be ev-er-more.

BASED ON SIRACH 50:22–24
NUN DANKET ALLE GOTT; MARTIN RINCKART, 1586–1649
TR. BY CATHERINE WINKWORTH, 1827–1878, ALT.

171 Now That the Day-Star Glimmers Bright
86 86

FARRANT
RICHARD FARRANT, 1525–1580

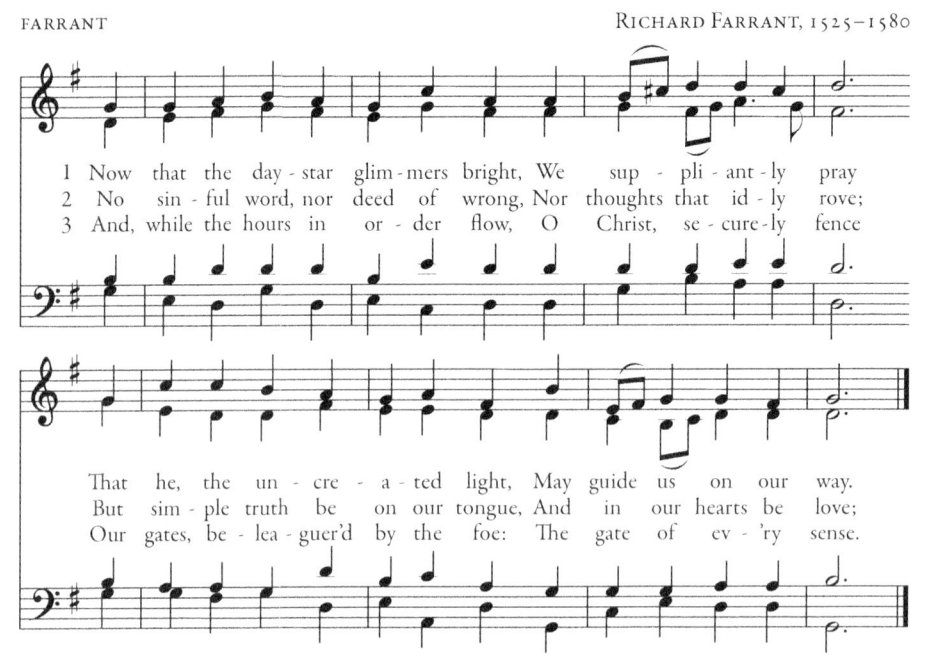

1. Now that the day-star glimmers bright, We suppliantly pray
   That he, the uncreated light, May guide us on our way.

2. No sinful word, nor deed of wrong, Nor thoughts that idly rove;
   But simple truth be on our tongue, And in our hearts be love.

3. And, while the hours in order flow, O Christ, securely fence
   Our gates, beleaguer'd by the foe: The gate of ev'ry sense.

4. And grant that to thine honor, Lord,
   Our daily toil may tend;
   That we begin it at thy word,
   And in thy blessing end;

5. And, lest the flesh in its excess
   Should lord it o'er the soul,
   Let taming abstinence repress
   The rebel, and control.

6. To God the Father glory be,
   And to his only Son,
   And to the Spirit, One and Three,
   While endless ages run.

IAM LUCIS ORTO SIDERE, 6TH CENT.
TR. BY JOHN HENRY NEWMAN, 1801–1890

172 O Blessed Saint Joseph
11 11 11 11

MARIA ZU LIEBEN
MELODY FROM THE *TRIER GESANGBUCH*, 1872
HARM. AFTER *ST. GREGORY HYMNAL AND CATHOLIC CHOIR BOOK*, 1920

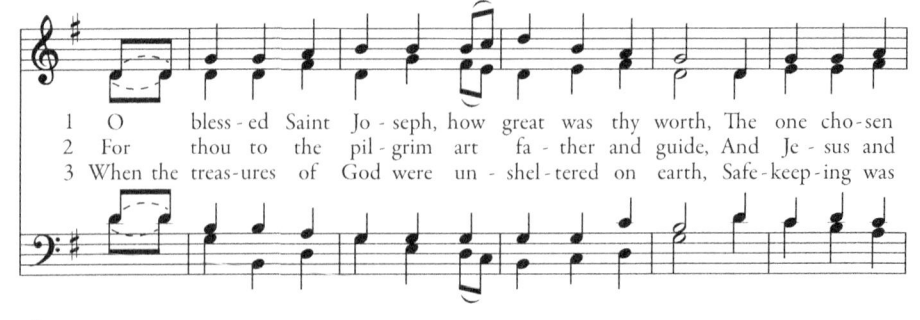

1. O blessed Saint Joseph, how great was thy worth, The one chosen
2. For thou to the pilgrim art father and guide, And Jesus and
3. When the treasures of God were unsheltered on earth, Safe-keeping was

184 • A CATHOLIC BOOK OF HYMNS

shad - ow of God up - on earth, The fa - ther of Je - sus!— Ah,
Ma - ry felt safe by thy side; Ah, bless - ed Saint Jo - seph, how
found for them both in thy worth; O fa - ther of Je - sus, be

then, wilt thou be, Sweet spouse of our La-dy! a fa - ther to me?
safe I should be, Sweet spouse of our La-dy! if thou wert with me!
fa - ther to me, Sweet spouse of our La-dy! and I will love thee.

FREDERICK W. FABER, 1814–1863

173   O Breathe on Me, O Breath of God
86 86

ST. COLUMBA (IRISH)

TRADITIONAL IRISH MELODY
HARM. BY CHARLES V. STANFORD, 1852–1924, ALT.

1. O breathe on me, O Breath of God, Fill me with life a - new,
2. O breathe on me, O Breath of God, Un - til my heart is pure;
3. O breathe on me, O Breath of God, So shall I ne - ver die,

That I may love the things you love, And do what you would do.
Un - til my will is one with yours, To do and to en - dure.
But live with you the per - fect life For all e - ter - ni - ty.

EDWIN HATCH, 1835–1889, ALT.

174   O Christ, Our Hope
86 86 with repeat

LOBT GOTT, IHR CHRISTEN   Nikolaus Herman, c. 1480–1561

1. O Christ, our hope, our hearts' desire, Redemption's only spring; Creator of the world art thou, Its Savior and its King, Its Savior and its King.

2. How vast the mercy and the love Which laid our sins on thee, And led thee to the cross to die To set thy people free, To set thy people free.

3. But now the bands of death are burst, The ransom has been paid; And thou art on thy Father's throne In majesty arrayed, In majesty arrayed.

4. O may thy mighty love prevail Our sinful souls to spare;
   O may we come before thy throne And find acceptance there, And find acceptance there!

5. Christ Jesus, be our present joy, Our future great reward;
   Our only glory may it be To glory in the Lord, To glory in the Lord!

6. All praise to thee, ascended Lord; All glory ever be
   To Father, Son and Holy Ghost Through all eternity, Through all eternity.

Jesu, nostra redemptio, c. 8th cent.
tr. by John Chandler, 1806–1876

175 O Christ, the Heavens' Eternal King
88 88

CHURCH TRIUMPHANT JAMES WILLIAM ELLIOTT, 1833–1915

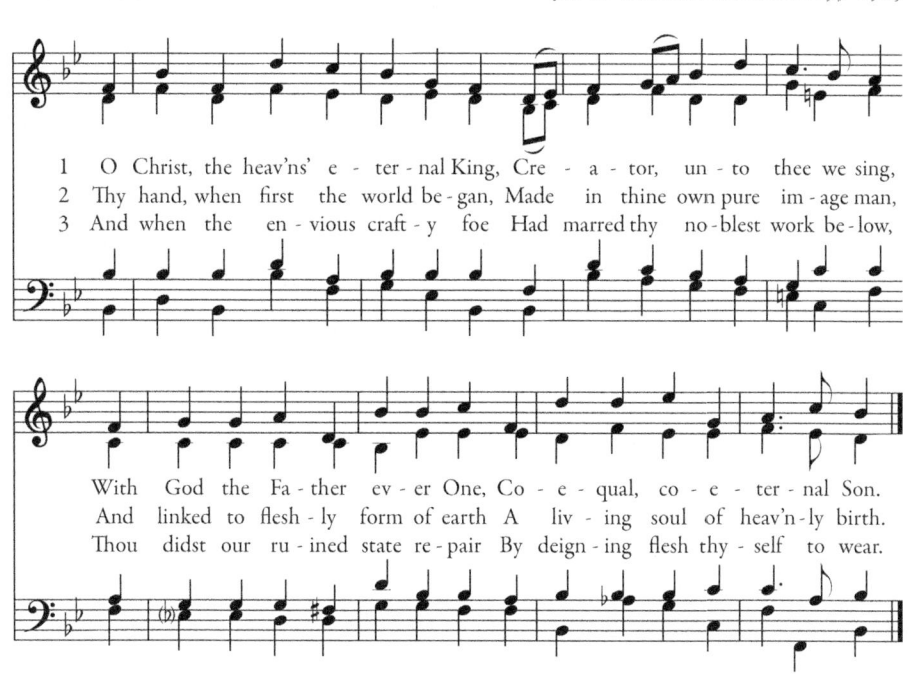

1. O Christ, the heav'ns' eternal King, Creator, unto thee we sing,
With God the Father ever One, Co-equal, co-eternal Son.

2. Thy hand, when first the world began, Made in thine own pure image man,
And linked to fleshly form of earth A living soul of heav'nly birth.

3. And when the envious crafty foe Had marred thy noblest work below,
Thou didst our ruined state repair By deigning flesh thyself to wear.

4. Once of a virgin born to save,
And now new born from death's dark grave,
O Christ, thou bidd'st us rise with thee
From death to immortality.

5. Eternal Shepherd, thou art wont
To cleanse thy sheep within the font,
That mystic bath, that grave of sin,
Where ransomed souls new life begin.

6. Divine Redeemer, thou didst deign
To bear for us the cross of pain,
And freely pay the precious price
Of all thy blood in sacrifice.

7. Jesu, do thou to every heart
Unceasing Paschal joy impart;
From death of sin and guilty strife
Set free the new born sons of life.

8. All praise be thine, O risen Lord,
From death to endless life restored;
All praise to God the Father be
And Holy Ghost eternally.

Rex Æterne Domine, 6TH CENT.
TR. BY THE COMPILERS OF *Hymns Ancient and Modern*, 1861

176 — O Come, All Ye Faithful

IRREGULAR
ADESTE FIDELES
JOHN F. WADE, 1711–1786

1. O come, all ye faithful, joyful and triumphant;
2. God of God, Light of Light,
3. Sing, choirs of angels, sing in exultation;
4. Yea, Lord we greet thee, Born this happy morning,

1. Adéste, fidéles, laéti, triumphántes;
2. Deum de Deo, Lumen de Lúmine,
3. Cantet nunc io chorus angelórum.
4. Ergo qui natus die hodiérna,

O come ye, O come ye to Bethlehem.
Lo! he abhors not the Virgin's womb:
Sing, all ye citizens of heav'n above!
Jesus, to thee be all glory giv'n;

Veníte, veníte in Béthlehem.
Gestant puéllae víscera,
Cantet nunc aula caeléstium.
Jesu, tibi sit glória.

Come and behold him, born the King of angels;
Very God, begotten, not created;
Glory to God, glory in the highest;
Word of the Father, now in flesh appearing;

Natum vidéte Regem angelórum.
Deum verum, Génitum, non factum.
Glória, glória in excélsis Deo.
Patris aetérni Verbum caro factum.

O come, let us adore him, O come, let us adore him,
Veníte, adorémus, Veníte, adorémus,

188 • A CATHOLIC BOOK OF HYMNS

O come, let us adore him, Christ the Lord.
Veníte, adorémus Dóminum.

Adeste Fideles, attr. to John F. Wade, 1711–1786
tr. by Frederick Oakeley, 1802–1880, alt.

177 O Come and Mourn With Me Awhile
88 88

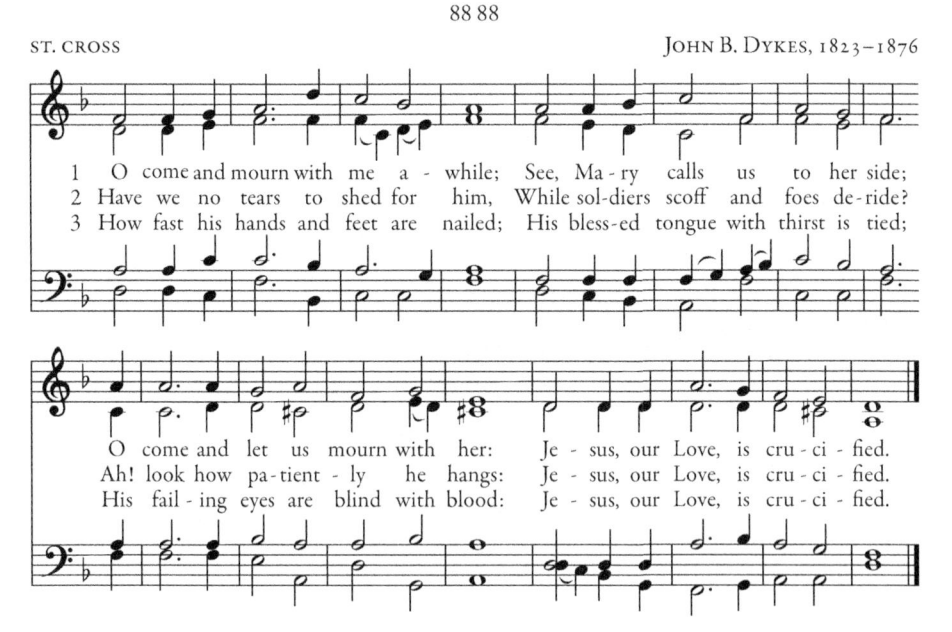

ST. CROSS   John B. Dykes, 1823–1876

1. O come and mourn with me awhile; See, Mary calls us to her side;
O come and let us mourn with her: Jesus, our Love, is crucified.

2. Have we no tears to shed for him, While soldiers scoff and foes deride?
Ah! look how patiently he hangs: Jesus, our Love, is crucified.

3. How fast his hands and feet are nailed; His blessed tongue with thirst is tied;
His failing eyes are blind with blood: Jesus, our Love, is crucified.

4. His Mother cannot reach his face;
She stands in helplessness beside;
Her heart is martyred with her Son's:
Jesus, our Love, is crucified.

5. Sev'n times he spoke, sev'n words of love;
And all three hours his silence cried
For mercy on the souls of men:
Jesus, our Love, is crucified.

6. O break, O break, hard heart of mine!
Thy weak self-love and guilty pride
His Pilate and his Judas were:
Jesus, our Love, is crucified.

7. A broken heart, a fount of tears;
Ask, and they will not be denied;
A broken heart love's cradle is:
Jesus, our Love, is crucified.

8. O Love of God! O sin of man!
In this dread act your strength is tried;
And victory remains with love:
For he, our Love, is crucified.

Jesus Crucified; Frederick W. Faber, 1814–1863

178 O Come and Mourn With Me Awhile
88 88

NICOLA A. MONTANI, 1880–1948

1. O come and mourn with me awhile! See,
Mary calls us to her side; O come and let us
mourn with her; Jesus, our Love, is crucified!

2. Have we no tears to shed for him, While
soldiers scoff and foes deride? Ah! look how patiently
he hangs; Jesus, our Love, is crucified!

3. How fast his hands and feet are nailed: His
blessed tongue with thirst is tied; His failing eyes are
blind with blood; Jesus, our Love, is crucified!

4. His Mother cannot reach his face;
She stands in helplessness beside;
Her heart is martyred with her Son's:
Jesus, our Love, is crucified.

5. Sev'n times he spoke, sev'n words of love;
And all three hours his silence cried
For mercy on the souls of men:
Jesus, our Love, is crucified.

6. O break, O break, hard heart of mine!
Thy weak self-love and guilty pride
His Pilate and his Judas were:
Jesus, our Love, is crucified.

7. A broken heart, a fount of tears;
Ask, and they will not be denied;
A broken heart love's cradle is:
Jesus, our Love, is crucified.

8. O Love of God! O sin of man!
In this dread act your strength is tried;
And victory remains with love:
For he, our Love, is crucified.

JESUS CRUCIFIED; FREDERICK W. FABER, 1814–1863

179   O Come and Mourn With Me Awhile
88 88

St. Cecilia Hymnal, 1935

1. O come and mourn with me awhile; See, Mary calls us to her side; O come and let us mourn with her: Jesus, our Love, is crucified, Jesus, our Love, is crucified.

2. Have we no tears to shed for him, While soldiers scoff and foes deride? Ah! look how patiently he hangs: Jesus, our Love, is crucified, Jesus, our Love, is crucified.

3. How fast his hands and feet are nailed; His blessed tongue with thirst is tied; His failing eyes are blind with blood: Jesus, our Love, is crucified, Jesus, our Love, is crucified.

4. His Mother cannot reach his face;
She stands in helplessness beside;
Her heart is martyred with her Son's:
Jesus, our Love, is crucified.

5. Sev'n times he spoke, sev'n words of love;
And all three hours his silence cried
For mercy on the souls of men:
Jesus, our Love, is crucified.

6. O break, O break, hard heart of mine!
Thy weak self-love and guilty pride
His Pilate and his Judas were:
Jesus, our Love, is crucified.

7. A broken heart, a fount of tears;
Ask, and they will not be denied;
A broken heart love's cradle is:
Jesus, our Love, is crucified.

8. O Love of God! O sin of man!
In this dread act your strength is tried;
And victory remains with love:
For he, our Love, is crucified.

Jesus Crucified; Frederick W. Faber, 1814–1863

180   O Come, Divine Messiah
IRREGULAR

VENEZ, DIVIN MESSIE   FRENCH CAROL, 16TH CENT.

1. O come, divine Messiah! The world in silence waits the day When hope shall sing its triumph, And sadness flee away. Dear Savior, haste; Come, come to earth, Dispel the

2. O thou, whom nations sighed for, Whom priests and prophets long foretold, Wilt break the captive fetters, Redeem the long-lost fold.

3. Shalt come, in peace and meekness, And lowly will thy cradle be; All clothed in human weakness Shall we thy Godhead see.

night and show thy face, And bid us hail the dawn of grace. O come, divine Messiah; The world in silence waits the day When hope shall sing its triumph and sadness flee away.

VENEZ, DIVIN MESSIE; SIMON-JOSEPH PELLEGRIN, 1663–1745
TR. BY SISTER MARY OF ST. PHILIP, 1825–1904

181 O Come, Little Children
11 11 11 11

IHR KINDERLEIN, KOMMET

JOHANN A. P. SCHULTZ, 1747–1800
HARM. BY J. ALFRED SCHEHL, 1882–1959

1. O, come, little children, O, come, one and all,
To Bethlehem's stable, in Bethlehem's stall,
And see with rejoicing this glorious sight
Our Father in heaven has sent us this night.

2. O, see in the manger, in hallowed light
A star throws its beam on this holiest sight.
In clean swaddling clothes lies the heavenly Child,
More lovely than angels, this Baby so mild.

3. O, there lies the Christ Child, on hay and on straw;
The shepherds are kneeling before him with awe.
And Mary and Joseph smile on him with love,
While angels are singing sweet songs from above.

1. Ihr Kinderlein, kommet, O kommet doch all!
Zur Krippe her kommet in Bethlehems Stall,
Und seht, was in dieser hochheiligen Nacht
Der Vater im Himmel für Freude uns macht.

IHR KINDERLEIN, KOMMET; JOHANN C. VON SCHMID, 1768–1854
TR. ANONYMOUS

182 O Come, O Come, Emmanuel
88 88 88

VENI EMMANUEL   ADAPT. BY THOMAS HELMORE, 1811–1890

1. O come, O come, Emmanuel, And ransom captive Israel
That mourns in lonely exile here Until the Son of God appear.
Rejoice! Rejoice! Emmanuel Shall come to you, O Israel.

2. O come, O Wisdom from on high, Who ordered all things mightily;
To us the path of knowledge show And teach us in its ways to go.

3. O come, O come, great Lord of might, Who to your tribes on Sinai's height
In ancient times did give the law In cloud and majesty and awe.

4. O come, O Branch of Jesse's stem,
Unto your own and rescue them!
From depths of hell your people save,
And give them vict'ry o'er the grave.

5. O come, O Key of David, come
And open wide our heav'nly home.
Make safe for us the heav'nward road
And bar the way to death's abode.

6. O come, O Bright and Morning Star,
And bring us comfort from afar!
Dispel the shadows of the night
And turn our darkness into light.

7. O come, O King of nations, bind
In one the hearts of all mankind.
Bid all our sad divisions cease
And be yourself our King of Peace.

VENI, VENI EMMANUEL; PARA. OF THE ANCIENT ANTIPHONS, 12TH CENT.
TR. BY JOHN M. NEALE, 1818–1866

183 O Day of Rest and Gladness
76 76 D

ES FLOG EIN KLEINS WALDVÖGELEIN TRADITIONAL GERMAN, 17TH CENT.

1. O day of rest and gladness, O day of joy and light,
O balm of care and sadness, Most beautiful, most bright:
On thee, the high and lowly, Through ages joined in tune,
Sing holy, holy, holy, To the great God Triune.

2. On thee, at the creation, The light first had its birth;
On thee, for our salvation, Christ rose from depths of earth;
On thee, our Lord victorious, The Spirit sent from heaven,
And thus on thee, most glorious, A triple light was given.

3. Thou art a holy ladder, Where angels go and come;
Each Sunday finds us gladder, Nearer to heaven, our home;
A day of sweet reflection, Thou art a day of love,
A day of resurrection From earth to things above.

4. New graces ever gaining From this our day of rest,
We reach the rest remaining To spirits of the blessed.
To Holy Ghost be praises, To Father, and to Son,
The Church her voice upraises To thee, blessed Three in One.

CHRISTOPHER WORDSWORTH, 1807–1885, ALT.

184 O Food to Pilgrims Given
776 776

INNSBRUCK

HEINRICH ISAAC, C. 1450–1517
HARM. BY JOHANN SEBASTIAN BACH, 1685–1750

1. O Food to pilgrims given, Bread of the hosts of Heaven, Thou Manna of the sky! Feed with the blessed sweetness, Of thy divine completeness The hearts that for thee sigh.

2. O Fountain ruby glowing, O Stream of love outflowing From Jesus' piercèd Side! This thought alone shall bless us, This one desire possess us, To drink of thy sweet tide.

3. We love thee, Jesu tender, Who hid'st thine awful splendor Beneath these veils of grace: O let the veils be riven, And our clear eye in heaven Behold thee face to face.

O ESCA VIATORUM, 17TH CENT.
TR. BY HUGH T. HENRY, 1862–1946

185   O for a Thousand Tongues to Sing
86 86

AZMON

CARL G. GLÄSER, 1784–1829
HARM. BY LOWELL MASON, 1792–1872

1. O for a thousand tongues to sing My great Redeemer's praise, The glories of my God and King, The triumphs of his grace!
2. Jesus, the Name that charms our fears, And bids our sorrows cease; 'Tis music in the sinner's ears, 'Tis life and health and peace.
3. He speaks; and, list'ning to his voice, New life the dead receive, The mournful broken hearts rejoice, The humble poor believe.

4. Hear him, ye deaf; his praise, ye dumb,
   Your loosened tongues employ;
   Ye blind, behold, your Savior come;
   And leap, ye lame, for joy!

5. My gracious Master and my God,
   Assist me to proclaim
   And spread through all the earth abroad
   The honors of thy Name.

EXHORTING AND BESEECHING TO RETURN TO GOD;
CHARLES WESLEY, 1707–1788, ALT.

186   O God, Our Help in Ages Past
86 86

ST. ANNE   WILLIAM CROFT, 1678–1727

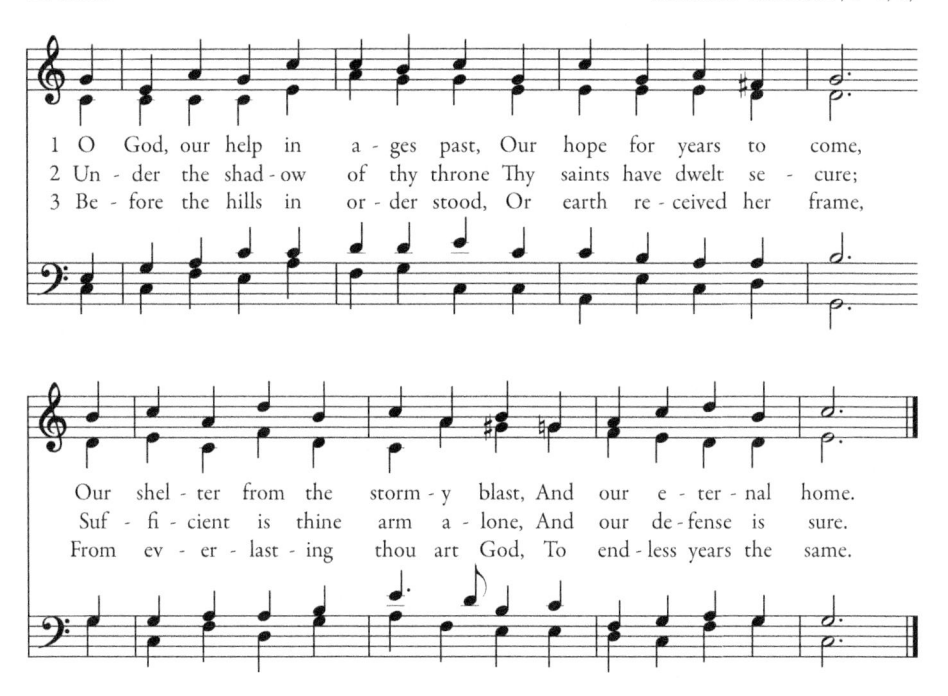

1. O God, our help in ages past, Our hope for years to come,
Our shelter from the stormy blast, And our eternal home.

2. Under the shadow of thy throne Thy saints have dwelt secure;
Sufficient is thine arm alone, And our defense is sure.

3. Before the hills in order stood, Or earth received her frame,
From everlasting thou art God, To endless years the same.

4. A thousand ages in thy sight
Are like an evening gone,
Short as the watch that ends the night
Before the rising sun.

5. Time, like an ever-rolling stream,
Bears all its sons away;
They fly, forgotten, as a dream
Dies at the op'ning day.

6. O God, our help in ages past,
Our hope for years to come,
Be thou our guard while troubles last,
And our eternal home.

PSALM 90:1–2, 4–6, 12
ISAAC WATTS, 1674–1748, ALT.

187 O Godhead Hid, Devoutly I Adore Thee
11 11 11 11

AQUINAS RICHARD R. TERRY, 1865–1938

1. O Godhead hid, devoutly I adore thee, Who truly art within the forms before me; To thee my heart I bow with bended knee, As failing quite in contemplating thee.

2. Sight, touch, and taste in thee are each deceived; The ear alone most safely is believed. I believe all the Son of God has spoken: Than Truth's own word there is no truer token.

3. God only on the Cross lay hid from view, But here lies hid at once the manhood too: And I, in both professing my belief, Make the same prayer as the repentant thief.

4. Thy wounds, as Thomas saw, I do not see; Yet thee confess my Lord and God to be. Make me believe thee ever more and more, In thee my hope, in thee my love to store.

5. O thou, memorial of our Lord's own dying! O living bread, to mortals life supplying! Make thou my soul henceforth on thee to live; Ever a taste of heavenly sweetness give.

6. O loving Pelican! O Jesu, Lord! Unclean I am, but cleanse me in thy blood: Of which a single drop, for sinners spilt, Can purge the entire world from all its guilt.

7. Jesu! whom for the present veiled I see, What I so thirst for, oh, vouchsafe to me: That I may see thy countenance unfolding, And may be blest thy glory in beholding. Amen.

ADÓRO TE DEVOTE; THOMAS AQUINAS, 1225–1274
TR. BY EDWARD CASWALL, 1814–1878

188   O Jesus Christ, Remember
76 76 D

AURELIA   SAMUEL S. WESLEY, 1810–1876

1. O Jesus Christ, remember, When thou shalt come again, Upon the clouds of heaven With all thy shining train; When ev'ry eye shall see thee In Deity revealed, Who now upon this altar In silence art concealed.

2. Remember, then, O Savior, I supplicate of thee, That here I bowed before thee, Upon my bended knee; That here I owned thy presence, And did not thee deny; And glorified thy greatness, Though hid from human eye.

3. Accept, divine Redeemer, The homage of my praise, Be thou the light and honor And glory of my days. Be thou my consolation When death is drawing nigh; Be thou my only treasure, Through all eternity.

PRAYER TO JESUS IN THE BLESSED SACRAMENT; EDWARD CASWALL, 1814–1878

189 O Jesus Christ, Remember
76 76 D

"Burns" traditional melody
St. Basil's Hymnal, 1918

1. O Jesus Christ, remember, When thou shalt come again,
Upon the clouds of heaven With all thy shining train;
When ev-'ry eye shall see thee In Deity revealed,
Who now upon this altar In silence art concealed.

2. Remember, then, O Savior, I supplicate of thee,
That here I bowed before thee, Upon my bended knee;
That here I owned thy presence, And did not thee deny;
And glorify thy greatness, Though hid from human eye.

3. Accept, divine Redeemer, The homage of my praise,
Be thou the light and honor And glory of my days.
Be thou my consolation When death is drawing nigh;
Be thou my only treasure, Through all eternity.

Prayer to Jesus in the Blessed Sacrament; Edward Caswall, 1814–1878

190 O Jesus, King Most Wonderful
86 86

ST. ANNE
WILLIAM CROFT, 1678–1727

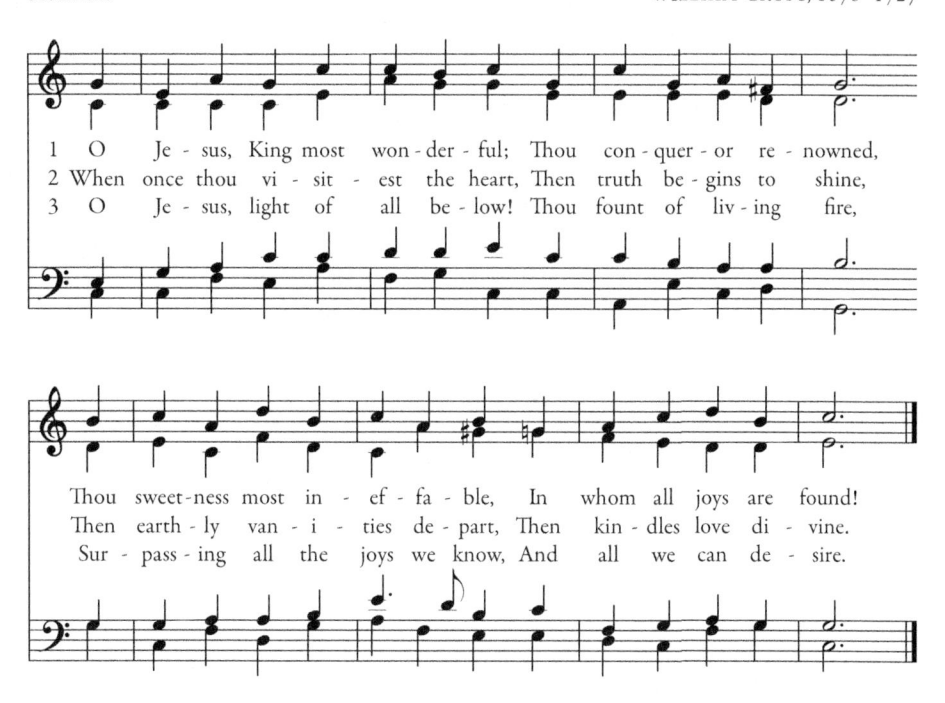

1. O Jesus, King most wonderful; Thou conqueror renowned,
Thou sweetness most ineffable, In whom all joys are found!

2. When once thou visitest the heart, Then truth begins to shine,
Then earthly vanities depart, Then kindles love divine.

3. O Jesus, light of all below! Thou fount of living fire,
Surpassing all the joys we know, And all we can desire.

4. Jesus, may all confess thy name,
   Thy wondrous love adore;
   And, seeking thee, themselves inflame
   To seek thee more and more.

5. Thee may our tongues for ever bless,
   Thee may we love alone,
   And ever in our lives express
   The image of thine own.

6. Abide with us, and let thy light
   Shine, Lord, on every heart;
   Dispel the darkness of our night,
   And joy to all impart.

7. Jesus, our love and joy, to thee,
   The Father's only Son,
   All might, and praise, and glory be,
   While endless ages run.

JESU REX ADMIRABILIS; BERNARD OF CLAIRVAUX, 1091–1153
TR. BY EDWARD CASWALL, 1814–1878, ALT.

191 O Kind Creator, Bow Thine Ear
88 88

TALLIS' CANON
THOMAS TALLIS, C. 1505–1585

1. O kind Creator, bow thine ear To mark the cry, to know the tear Before thy throne of mercy spent In this thy holy fast of Lent.

2. Our hearts are open, Lord, to thee; Thou knowest our infirmity; Pour out on all who seek thy face Abundance of thy pard'ning grace.

3. Our sins are many, this we know; Spare us, good Lord, thy mercy show; And for the honor of thy name Our fainting souls to life reclaim.

4. Give us the self-control that springs
   From discipline of outward things,
   That fasting inward secretly
   The soul may purely dwell with thee.

5. We pray thee, Holy Trinity,
   One God, unchanging Unity,
   That we from this our abstinence
   May reap the fruits of penitence.

AUDI, BENIGNE CONDITOR; ATTR. TO GREGORY THE GREAT, C. 540–604
TR. BY THOMAS A. LACEY, 1853–1931

192   O Little Town of Bethlehem
86 86 76 86

FOREST GREEN   TRADITIONAL ENGLISH MELODY
HARM. BY RALPH VAUGHAN WILLIAMS, 1872–1958

1. O little town of Bethlehem, How still we see thee lie!
Above thy deep and dreamless sleep The silent stars go by.
Yet in thy dark streets shineth The everlasting light;
The hopes and fears of all the years Are met in thee tonight.

2. For Christ is born of Mary, And gathered all above,
While mortals sleep, the angels keep Their watch of wond'ring love.
O morning stars, together Proclaim the holy birth,
And praises sing to God the King, And peace to men on earth.

3. How silently, how silently, The wondrous gift is giv'n!
So God imparts to human hearts The blessings of his heav'n.
No ear may hear his coming, But in this world of sin,
Where meek souls will receive him, still The dear Christ enters in.

PHILLIPS BROOKS, 1835–1893

193 O Little Town of Bethlehem

86 86 76 86

ST. LOUIS
LEWIS H. REDNER, 1831–1908

1. O little town of Bethlehem, How still we see thee lie!
2. For Christ is born of Mary, And gathered all above,
3. How silently, how silently, The wondrous gift is giv'n!
4. O holy Child of Bethlehem! Descend to us, we pray;

Above thy deep and dreamless sleep The silent stars go by;
While mortals sleep, the angels keep Their watch of wond'ring love.
So God imparts to human hearts The blessings of his heav'n.
Cast out our sin and enter in, Be born in us today.

Yet in thy dark streets shineth The everlasting Light;
O morning stars, together Proclaim the holy birth!
No ear may hear his coming, But in this world of sin,
We hear the Christmas angels The great glad tidings tell;

The hopes and fears of all the years Are met in thee tonight.
And praises sing to God the King, And peace to men on earth.
Where meek souls will receive him, still The dear Christ enters in.
O come to us, abide with us, Our Lord Emmanuel!

PHILLIPS BROOKS, 1835–1893

194   O Lord, I Am Not Worthy
7676

NON DIGNUS   CATHOLIC YOUTH HYMNAL, 1871

1. O Lord, I am not worthy That thou should'st come to me; But speak the words of comfort, My spirit healed shall be.

2. And humbly I'll receive thee, The bridegroom of my soul, No more by sin to grieve thee, Or fly thy sweet control.

3. Eternal Holy Spirit, Unworthy though I be, Prepare me to receive him, And trust the Word to me.

4. Increase my faith, dear Jesus,
   In thy real presence here,
   And make me feel most deeply
   That thou to me art near.

5. O Sacrament most holy!
   O Sacrament divine!
   All praise and all thanksgiving
   Be ev'ry moment thine!

BASED ON MATTHEW 8:8
O HERR, ICH BIN NICHT WÜRDIG; LANDSHUTER GESANGBUCH, 1777
TR. ANONYMOUS

195 O Praise Ye the Lord

10 10 11 11

LAUDATE DOMINUM
CHARLES HUBERT H. PARRY, 1848–1918

1. O praise ye the Lord! prepare a new song;
And let all his saints in full concert join:
With voices united the anthem prolong,
And show forth his praises with music divine.

2. Let praise to the Lord, who made us, ascend;
Let each grateful heart be glad in its King;
For God, whom we worship, our songs will attend,
And view with complacence the off'ring we bring.

3. Be joyful, ye saints, sustain'd by his might,
And let your glad songs awake with each morn:
For those who obey him are still his delight;
His hand with salvation the meek will adorn.

4. Then praise ye the Lord! prepare a glad song;
And let all his saints in full concert join;
With voices united the anthem prolong,
And shew forth his praises with music divine.

PHILIP DODDRIDGE, 1702–1751

196   O Purest of Creatures
11 11 11 11

MARIA ZU LIEBEN   THE WESTMINSTER HYMNAL, 1912

1. O purest of creatures! sweet Mother! sweet Maid! The one spotless womb wherein Jesus was laid! Dark night hath come down on us, Mother! and we Look out for thy shining, sweet Star of the Sea!
2. Deep night hath come down on this rough-spoken world, And the banners of darkness are boldly unfurled: And the tempest-tossed Church— all her eyes are on thee, They look to thy shining, sweet Star of the Sea!
3. He gazed on thy soul; it was spotless and fair; For the empire of sin— it had never been there; None had ever owned thee, dear Mother, but he, And he blessed thy clear shining, sweet Star of the Sea!
4. Earth gave him one lodging; 'twas deep in thy breast, And God found a home where the sinner finds rest; His home and his hiding-place both were in thee, He was won by thy shining, sweet Star of the Sea!

THE IMMACULATE CONCEPTION; FREDERICK W. FABER, 1814–1863

197 O Queen of the Holy Rosary
96 76 76 76

ACH GOTT VOM HIMMELREICHE

MICHAEL PRAETORIUS, 1571–1621
ALT. AND HARM. BY J. ALFRED SCHEHL, 1882–1959

1. O Queen of the Holy Rosary! Oh, bless us, as we pray,
And offer thee our roses, In garlands day by day;
While from our Father's garden, With loving hearts and bold,
We gather to thine honor, Buds white and red and gold.

2. O Queen of the Holy Rosary! Christ's mission blends with thine;
And so each bead I finger Is rich with grace divine;
Each Ave, nectar laden, Brings sweetness to my soul,
Thy prayer, Heav'nly Maiden, Will lead me to my goal.

EMILY M. C. SHAPCOTE, 1828–1909
REVISED BY REV. HENRY MEYER

198 O Queen of the Holy Rosary
96 76 76 76

ELLACOMBE

MAINZER GESANGBUCH, MAINZ, 1833
HARM. AFTER *ST. BASIL'S HYMNAL*, 1918

1. O Queen of the Holy Rosary! Oh, bless us as we pray,
And offer thee our roses In garlands day by day,
While from our Father's garden With loving hearts and bold,
We gather to thine honor Buds white and red and gold.

2. O Queen of the Holy Rosary! Each myst'ry blends with thine
The sacred life of Jesus In ev'ry step divine,
Thy soul was his fair garden, Thy virgin breast his throne,
Thy thoughts his faithful mirror, Reflecting him above.

3. Sweet Lady of the Rosary, White roses let us bring,
And lay them round thy footstool Before our Infant King.
For nestling in thy bosom God's Son was fain to be,
The Child of thy obedience And spotless purity.

4. Dear Lady of the Rosary, Red roses cast we down,
But let thy fingers weave them Into a worthy crown.
For how can we poor sinners Do aught but weep with thee,
When in thy train we follow Our God to Calvary?

EMILY M. C. SHAPCOTE, 1828–1909

199   O Sacrament Most Holy
76 76

O SACRAMENT MOST HOLY   TRADITIONAL

O Sacrament most Holy, O Sacrament Divine,
All praise and all thanksgiving Be ev'ry moment thine.

ANONYMOUS

200   O Sacred Head, Surrounded
76 76 D

PASSION CHORALE   HANS L. HASSLER, 1564–1612
        HARM. BY JOHANN SEBASTIAN BACH, 1685–1750

1. O Sacred Head, surrounded By crown of piercing thorn!
2. I see thy strength and vigor All fading in the strife,
3. In this, thy bitter passion, Good Shepherd, think of me

O bleed-ing Head, so wound-ed, Re-viled and put to scorn!
And death with cru-el rig-or, Be-reav-ing thee of life;
With thy most sweet com-pas-sion, Un-wor-thy though I be:

Death's pal-lid hue comes o'er thee, The glow of life de-cays,
O ag-o-ny and dy-ing! O love to sin-ners free!
Be-neath thy cross a-bid-ing For-ev-er would I rest,

Yet an-gel hosts a-dore thee, And trem-ble as they gaze.
Je-sus, all grace sup-ply-ing, O turn thy face on me.
In thy dear love con-fid-ing, And with thy pres-ence blest.

SALVE CAPUT CRUENTATUM; ATTR. TO BERNARD OF CLAIRVAUX, 1091–1153
TR. BY HENRY BAKER, 1821–1877

201 O Sacred Heart
4 6 8 8 4

LAURENCE
RICHARD R. TERRY, 1865–1938

1. O Sacred Heart, Our home lies deep in thee;
On earth thou art an exile's rest,
In heav'n the glory of the blest,
O Sacred Heart.

2. O Sacred Heart, Thou fount of contrite tears;
Where'er those living waters flow,
New life to sinners they bestow,
O Sacred Heart.

3. O Sacred Heart, Bless our dear native land;
May all her sons in truth e'er stand,
With faith's bright banner still in hand,
O Sacred Heart.

4. O Sacred Heart, Our trust is all in thee;
For though earth's night be dark and drear,
Thou breathest rest where thou art near,
O Sacred Heart.

5. O Sacred Heart,
When shades of death shall fall,
Receive us 'neath thy gentle care,
And save us from the tempter's snare,
O Sacred Heart.

6. O Sacred Heart,
Lead exiled children home,
Where we may ever rest near thee,
In peace and joy eternally,
O Sacred Heart.

FRANCIS STANFIELD, 1835–1914, ALT.

202   O Sacred Heart, O Love Divine

86 86 WITH REFRAIN

THEODORE A. METCALF, 1843–1920

1. O Sacred Heart, O Love Divine! Do keep us near to thee; And make our love so like to thine That we may holy be.
2. O Temple pure! O House of gold! Our heaven here below! What sweet delights, what wealth untold, From thee do ever flow.
3. O wounded Heart, O Font of tears! O Throne of grief and pain! Whereon for the eternal years, Thy love for man does reign.
4. Ungrateful hearts, forgetful hearts, The hearts of men have been, To wound thy side with cruel darts Which they have made by sin.

Refrain:
Heart of Jesus, hear! O Heart of Love Divine! Listen to our prayer; Make us always thine.

THEODORE A. METCALF, 1843–1920

203 O Sacred Heart, What Shall I Render Thee

10 10 10 10 WITH REFRAIN

NOTRE DAME HYMN TUNE BOOK, 1905

1. O Sacred Heart, what shall I render thee, For all the gifts thou hast bestowed on me? O Heart of God, thou seem'st but to implore, That I should love thee daily more and more.
2. O Heart of Jesus, come and live in me, That with thy love my heart consumed may be; O Sacred Heart of Jesus, I implore, That I may love thee daily more and more.
3. O Sacred Heart, be this our life's one aim, To labor for the glory of thy name; O dearest Heart, this grace we thee implore, That all the world may know and love thee more.

Then I will love thee, then I will love thee, then I will love thee daily more and more.

ANONYMOUS

204 O Salutaris Hostia
88 88

DUGUET — DIEUDONNÉ DUGUET, 1794–1849

1. O salutáris hóstia, Quae caeli pandis óstium: Bella premunt hostília, Da robur, fer auxílium.
2. Uni trinóque Dómino Sit sempitérna glória, Qui vitam sine término Nobis donet in pátria. Amen.

Verbum supernum prodiens; THOMAS AQUINAS, 1225–1274

205 O Salutaris Hostia
88 88

WERNER — ANTHONY WERNER, fl. 1863

1. O salutáris hóstia, Quae caeli pandis óstium: Bella premunt hostília, Da robur, fer auxílium.
2. Uni trinóque Dómino Sit sempitérna glória, Qui vitam sine término Nobis donet in pátria. Amen.

Verbum supernum prodiens; THOMAS AQUINAS, 1225–1274

206 O Sanctissima
557 557

SICILIAN MARINERS
TRADITIONAL SICILIAN MELODY, 18TH CENT.

1. O sanctíssima, O piíssima, Dulcis Virgo María! Mater amáta, Intemeráta, Ora, ora pro nobis!
2. Tu, solátium Et refúgium, Virgo Mater María! Quidquid optámus, Per te sperámus; Ora, ora pro nobis!
3. Ecce débiles, Perquam flébiles, Salva nos, María! Tolle languores, Sana dolores, Ora, ora pro nobis!
4. Virgo, réspice, Mater, áspice, Audi nos, María! Tu medicínam, Portas divínam; Ora, ora pro nobis!

LATIN HYMN, 18TH CENT.

207 O Saving Victim
88 88

DUGUET — DIEUDONNÉ DUGUET, 1794-1849

1. O saving Victim, o-p'ning wide The gate of Heav'n to man below; Our foes press on from ev'ry side; Thine aid supply, thy strength bestow.
2. To thy great Name be endless praise; Immortal Godhead, One in Three; O grant us endless length of days, In our true native land with thee. A-men.

O SALUTÁRIS HÓSTIA; THOMAS AQUINAS, 1225–1274
TR. BY EDWARD CASWALL, 1814–1878

208 O Saving Victim
88 88

HERR JESU CHRIST

CANTICUM GERMANICUM, 1628
ADAPT. AND HARM. BY JOHANN SEBASTIAN BACH, 1685–1750

1. O saving Victim, opening wide
The gate of heaven to us below;
Our foes press on from every side;
Thine aid supply, thy strength bestow.

2. All praise and thanks to thee ascend
For evermore, blest One in Three;
O grant us life that shall not end
In our true native land with thee.

O SALUTÁRIS HÓSTIA; THOMAS AQUINAS, 1225–1274
TR. BY EDWARD CASWALL, 1814–1878, ALT.

209 O Saving Victim
88 88

WERNER
ANTHONY WERNER, fl. 1863

1. O saving Victim, op'ning wide The gate of Heav'n to man below; Our foes press on from ev'ry side; Thine aid supply, thy strength bestow.
2. To thy great Name be endless praise; Immortal Godhead, One in Three; O grant us endless length of days, In our true native land with thee. A-men.

O SALUTÁRIS HÓSTIA; THOMAS AQUINAS, 1225–1274
TR. BY EDWARD CASWALL, 1814–1878

210   O Splendor of God's Glory Bright
88 88

PUER NOBIS NASCITUR

TRIER MANUSCRIPT, 15TH CENT.
ADAPT. BY MICHAEL PRAETORIUS, 1571–1621

1. O splendor of God's glory bright, O thou that bringest light from light, O Light of Light, light's living spring, O Day, all days illumining.

2. O thou true Sun, on us thy glance Let fall in royal radiance, The Spirit's sanctifying beam Upon our earthly senses stream.

3. The Father, too, our prayers implore, Father of glory evermore; The Father of all grace and might, To banish sin from our delight.

4. To guide whate'er we nobly do, With love all envy to subdue, To make ill fortune turn to fair, And give us grace our wrongs to bear.

5. Our mind be in his keeping placed,
Our body true to him and chaste,
Where only faith her fire shall feed
To burn the tares of Satan's seed.

6. And Christ to us for food shall be,
From him our drink that welleth free,
The Spirit's wine, that maketh whole,
And mocking not, exalts the soul.

7. Rejoicing may this day go hence,
Like virgin dawn our innocence,
Like fiery noon our faith appear,
Nor know the gloom of twilight drear.

8. Morn in her rosy car is borne:
Let him come forth our Perfect Morn,
The Word in God the Father One,
The Father perfect in the Son.   Amen.

SPLENDOR PATERNAE GLORIAE; AMBROSE OF MILAN, C. 340–397
TR. BY ROBERT BRIDGES, 1844–1930

211   O Star, for Whose Pure Light
10 10 10 10

FARLEY CASTLE   HENRY LAWES, 1596–1662
ADAPT. BY A. GREGORY MURRAY, 1905–1992

1. O star, for whose pure light the heav'n makes room, Hope of the world thy death redeemed and won, Though veiled thy rising in a Virgin's womb, Before time was, the Father's Word and Son;

2. Strengthen the wav'rer; let thy Church below, Still lifting unreprovèd hands to heav'n, In worthier strains thy deathless glory shew, And those free mercies count, thy grace hath giv'n.

3. Now doth the day-star, ush'ring in the dawn, Salute this meaner sun's returning ray; Fades the wan mist, from silver skies withdrawn; Shine in our hearts, more pure, more welcome Day.

4. Sustain our weakness, light our path obscure,
Pierce the dull shades of this dark night beneath;
Arm our frail thoughts against the dazzling lure
Of those deceitful loves whose fruit is death.

5. Mysterious Trinity, be endless praise,
Father, and Son, and Holy Spirit, thine,
Long as time's star this twilight world displays,
And when outwearied suns no more shall shine.

ASTRE QUE L'OLYMPE REVÈRE; BASED ON *AETERNA CAELI GLORIA*
JEAN-BAPTISTE RACINE, 1639–1699
TR. BY RONALD KNOX, 1888–1957

212 O Strength and Stay

11 10 11 10

STRENGTH AND STAY

JOHN B. DYKES, 1823–1876

1. O Strength and Stay upholding all creation,
Who ever dost thyself unmoved abide,
Yet day by day the light in due gradation
From hour to hour through all its changes guide.

2. Grant to life's day a calm unclouded ending,
An eve untouched by shadows of decay,
The brightness of a holy death-bed blending
With glories of the eternal day.

3. Hear us, O Father, gracious and forgiving,
Through Jesus Christ thy co-eternal Word,
Who, with the Holy Ghost, by all things living
Now and to endless ages art adored.

Rerum Deus tenax vigor; ATTR. TO AMBROSE OF MILAN, 340–397
TR. BY JOHN ELLERTON, 1826–1893 & FENTON J. A. HORT, 1828–1892

213   O Trinity of Blessed Light
88 88

BROMLEY   FRANZ JOSEPH HAYDN, 1732–1809, ALT.

1. O Trinity of blessed light,
   O Unity of princely might,
   The fiery sun now goes his way;
   Shed thou within our hearts thy ray.

2. To thee our morning song of praise,
   To thee our evening prayer we raise;
   O grant us with thy saints on high
   To praise thee through eternity.

3. All laud to God the Father be,
   All praise, eternal Son, to thee;
   All glory, as is ever meet,
   To God the holy Paraclete.

O LUX BEATA TRINITAS; ATTR. TO AMBROSE OF MILAN, C. 340–397
TR. BY JOHN M. NEALE, 1818–1866, ALT.

214   O Trinity of Blessed Light
88 88

DANBY

PARKER'S *WHOLE PSALTER*, C. 1561
HARM. BY RALPH VAUGHAN WILLIAMS, 1872–1958

1. O Trinity of blessed light,
   O Unity of princely might,
   The fiery sun now goes his way;
   Shed thou within our hearts thy ray.

2. To thee our morning song of praise,
   To thee our evening prayer we raise;
   O grant us with thy saints on high
   To praise thee through eternity.

3. All laud to God the Father be;
   All praise, eternal Son, to thee;
   All glory, as is ever meet,
   To God the holy Paraclete.

O LUX BEATA TRINITAS; ATTR. TO AMBROSE OF MILAN, C. 340–397
TR. BY JOHN M. NEALE, 1818–1866, ALT.

215 O What Their Joy and Their Glory Must Be
10 10 10 10

O QUANTA QUALIA   *Paris Antiphoner*, 1681

1. O what their joy and their glory must be, Those endless Sabbaths the blessed ones see; Crowns for the valiant, to weary ones rest: God shall be All, and in all ever blest.

2. Truly, "Jerusalem" name we that shore, City of peace that brings joy evermore; Wish and fulfillment are not severed there, Nor do things prayed for come short of the prayer.

3. There, where no troubles distraction can bring, We the sweet anthems of Zion shall sing; While for thy grace, Lord, their voices of praise Thy blessed people eternally raise.

4. Now, in the meantime, with hearts raised on high, We for that country must yearn and must sigh, Seeking Jerusalem, dear native Land, Through our long exile on Babylon's strand.

5. Low before him with our praises we fall, Of whom and in whom and through whom are all; Of whom, the Father; and in whom, the Son; Through whom, the Spirit, with them ever One.

O QUANTA QUALIA SUNT ILLA SABBATA; Peter Abelard, 1079-1142
tr. by John M. Neale, 1818–1866, alt.

216 O Wondrous Sight! O Vision Fair
88 88

WAREHAM WILLIAM KNAPP, 1698–1768

1. O wondrous sight! O vision fair
Of glory that the Church shall share,
Which Christ upon the mountain shows,
Where brighter than the sun he glows!

2. From age to age the tale declares
How with the three disciples there
Where Moses and Elijah meet,
The Lord holds converse high and sweet.

3. The law and prophets there have place,
Two chosen witnesses of grace;
The Father's voice from out the cloud
Proclaims his only Son aloud.

4. With shining face and bright array,
Christ deigns to manifest that day
What glory shall be theirs above
Who joy in God with perfect love.

5. And faithful hearts are raised on high
By this great vision's mystery;
For which in joyful strains we raise
The voice of prayer, the hymn of praise.

COELESTIS FORMAM GLORIAE, 15TH CENT.
TR. BY JOHN M. NEALE, 1818–1866, ALT.

217 O Word of God Incarnate

76 76 D

MUNICH

Neuvermehrtes Meiningisches Gesangbuch, 1613
adapt. by Felix Mendelssohn, 1809–1847

1. O Word of God incarnate, O Wisdom from on high,
O Truth unchanged, unchanging, O Light of our dark sky:
We praise you for the radiance That from the hallowed page,
A lantern to our footsteps, Shines on from age to age.

2. The Church from you, dear Savior, Received this gift divine;
And still that light is lifted On all the earth to shine.
It is the chart and compass That, all life's voyage through,
Amid the rocks and quicksands Still guides, O Christ, to you.

3. O make your Church, dear Savior, A lamp of purest gold
To bear before the nations Your true light, as of old;
O teach your wand'ring pilgrims By this our path to trace,
Till, clouds and storms thus ended, We see you face to face.

William Walsham How, 1823–1897, alt.

218   O Worship the King
10 10 11 11

HANOVER   WILLIAM CROFT, 1678–1727

1. O worship the King, all glorious above! O gratefully sing his power and his love! Our shield and defender, the Ancient of Days, Pavilioned in splendor, and girded with praise.

2. O tell of his might! O sing of his grace! Whose robe is the light, whose canopy space. His chariots of wrath the deep thunderclouds form, And dark is his path on the wings of the storm.

3. The earth, with its store of wonders untold, Almighty thy power hath founded of old, Hath stablished it fast by a changeless decree, And round it hath cast, like a mantle, the sea.

4. Thy bountiful care, what tongue can recite?
It breathes in the air; it shines in the light;
It streams from the hills, it descends to the plain,
And sweetly distills in the dew and the rain.

5. Frail children of dust, and feeble as frail,
In thee do we trust, nor find thee to fail;
Thy mercies how tender! how firm to the end!
Our Maker, Defender, Redeemer, and Friend!

ROBERT GRANT, 1779–1838

219 On Jordan's Bank

88 88

WINCHESTER NEW

MUSICALISCHES HANDBUCH, HAMBURG, 1690
HARM. BY WILLIAM H. MONK, 1823–1889

1. On Jordan's bank the Baptist's cry Announces that the Lord is nigh; Awake and hearken, for he brings Glad tidings of the King of kings.

2. Then cleansed be ev'ry heart from sin; Make straight the way for God within, And let each heart prepare a home Where such a mighty guest may come.

3. For thou art our salvation, Lord, Our refuge and our great reward; Without thy grace we waste away Like flow'rs that wither and decay.

4. To heal the sick, stretch out thine hand, And bid the fallen sinner stand; Shine forth and let thy light restore Earth's own true loveliness once more.

5. All praise, eternal Son, to thee, Whose advent doth thy people free; Whom with the Father we adore, And Holy Ghost forevermore.

JORDANIS ORAS PRÆVIA; CHARLES COFFIN, 1676–1749
TR. BY JOHN CHANDLER, 1806–1876, ALT.

220   On This Day, O Beautiful Mother
77 77 WITH REFRAIN

BEAUTIFUL MOTHER   LOUIS LAMBILLOTTE, 1796–1855

On this day, O beautiful Mother, On this day we give thee our love. Near thee, Madonna, fondly we hover, Trusting thy gentle care to prove.

Fine

1. On this day we ask to share, Dearest Mother, thy sweet care;
   Aid us ere our feet astray Wander from thy guiding way.
2. Queen of angels, deign to hear Humble children's tender prayer;
   Young hearts gain, O Virgin pure, Jesus' love for them assure.

D.C. al Fine

FAVORITE CATHOLIC MELODIES, BOSTON, 1854

221 On This Day, the First of Days

77 77

LÜBECK

Freylinghausen's *Geistreiches Gesangbuch*, Halle, 1704
harm. by William H. Havergal, 1793–1870

1. On this day, the first of days, God the Father's name we praise; Who, creation's Lord and spring, Did the world from darkness bring.
2. On this day, th'eternal Son Over death his triumph won; On this day the Spirit came With his gifts of living flame.
3. Father, who didst fashion man God-like in thy loving plan, Fill us with that love divine, And conform our wills to thine.

4. Word-made-flesh, all hail to thee!
Thou from sin hast set us free;
And with thee, we die and rise
Unto God in sacrifice.

5. Thou who dost all gifts impart,
Shine, blest Spirit, in each heart;
Give us light and grace, we pray,
Fill our hearts this holy day.

6. God, the blessed Three-in-One,
May thy holy will be done;
In thy word our souls are free,
And we rest this day with thee.

Die parente temporum; *Carcasonne Breviary*, 1745
tr. by Henry W. Baker, 1821–1877, alt.

222 — Once in Royal David's City

87 87 77

IRBY
HENRY J. GAUNTLETT, 1805–1876

1. Once in royal David's city Stood a lowly cattle shed, Where a mother laid her baby In a manger for his bed: Mary was that mother mild, Jesus Christ, her little child.

2. He came down to earth from heaven, Who is God and Lord of all; And his shelter was a stable And his cradle was a stall: With the poor, the scorned, the lowly, Lived on earth our Savior holy.

3. For he is our life-long pattern; Daily, when on earth he grew; He was tempted, scorned, rejected, Tears and smiles like us he knew: Thus he feels for all our sadness, And he shares in all our gladness.

4. And our eyes at last shall see him, Through his own redeeming love, For that child who seemed so helpless Is our Lord in heav'n above: And he leads his children on To the place where he is gone.

5. Not in that poor lowly stable, With the oxen standing round, We shall see him, but in heaven, Where his saints his throne surround: Christ, revealed to faithful eye, Set at God's right hand on high.

6. We, like Mary, rest confounded That a stable should display Heaven's Word, the world's creator, Cradled there on Christmas Day! Yet this child, our Lord and brother, Brought us love for one another.

WHO WAS CONCEIVED BY THE HOLY GHOST BORN OF THE VIRGIN MARY;
CECIL F. ALEXANDER, 1818–1895, ALT.

223 Only-Begotten, Word of God Eternal
11 11 11 5

ISTE CONFESSOR
ANTIPHONER, POITIERS, 1746

1. Only-begotten, Word of God eternal, Lord of creation, merciful and mighty; Hear us, your servants, as our tuneful voices Rise in your presence.

2. Holy this temple where our Lord is dwelling; This is none other than the gate of heaven. Ever your children, year by year rejoicing, Chant in your temple.

3. Hear us, O Father, as we throng your temple. By your past blessings, by your present bounty, Smile on your children, and in grace and mercy Hear our petition.

4. God in three persons, Father everlasting, Son co-eternal, ever blessèd Spirit: To you be praises, thanks, and adoration, Glory forever.

CHRISTE CUNCTORUM DOMINATOR ALME, 9TH CENT.
TR. BY MAXWELL J. BLACKER, 1822–1888, ALT.

224 Panis Angelicus
12 12 12 8

SACRIS SOLEMNIIS — LOUIS LAMBILLOTTE, 1796–1885

1. Panis angélicus fit panis hóminum,
   Dat panis cǽlicus figúris términum;
   O res mirábilis! mandúcat Dóminum
   Pauper, servus et húmilis.

2. Te trina Déitas únaque póscimus,
   Sic nos tu vísita, sicut te cólimus;
   Per tuas sémitas duc nos quo téndimus
   Ad lucem quam inhábitas.

THOMAS AQUINAS, 1225–1274

225 Praise God! Who in His Grace

86 86 8

MELODY AS USED IN OBERAMMERGAU PASSION PLAY
HARM. BY J. ALFRED SCHEHL, 1882–1959

1. Praise God! Praise God! Who in his grace, Now comes to bless this holy place. Hark, Cherubim and Seraphim! With Angel voices welcome him! Hosannas raise! To God be praise!

2. O great Jehovah, God of Might, Here too is now thy throne of light. Here is our rest, our strength, our food; Here is thy living flesh and blood, Here is thy new Jerusalem.

REV. HENRY MEYER

226   Praise, My Soul, the King of Heaven
87 87 87

LAUDA ANIMA   JOHN GOSS, 1800–1880

1. Praise, my soul, the King of heaven; To his feet thy tribute bring; Ransomed, healed, restored, forgiven, Evermore his praises sing. Alleluia! Alleluia! Praise the everlasting King.

2. Praise him for his grace and favor To our fathers in distress; Praise him still the same as ever, Slow to chide and swift to bless. Alleluia! Alleluia! Glorious in his faithfulness.

3. Father-like he tends and spares us; Well our feeble frame he knows; In his hands he gently bears us, Rescues us from all our foes. Alleluia! Alleluia! Widely yet his mercy flows.

4. Frail as summer's flow'r we flourish;
Blows the wind and it is gone.
But while mortals rise and perish,
God endures unchanging on.
Alleluia! Alleluia!
Praise the high eternal one.

5. Angels, help us to adore him;
Ye behold him face to face;
Sun and moon, bow down before him,
Dwellers all in time and space.
Alleluia! Alleluia!
Praise with us the God of grace.

HENRY F. LYTE, 1793–1847, ALT.

227 Praise to the Holiest in the Height

86 86

BILLING RICHARD R. TERRY, 1865–1938

1. Praise to the holiest in the height,
And in the depth be praise;
In all his words most wonderful,
Most sure in all his ways!

2. O loving wisdom of our God!
When all was sin and shame,
A second Adam to the fight
And to the rescue came.

3. O wisest love! that flesh and blood,
Which did in Adam fail,
Should strive afresh against the foe,
Should strive, and should prevail;

4. And that a higher gift than grace
Should flesh and blood refine:
God's presence and his very self,
And essence all-divine.

5. And in the garden secretly,
And on the cross on high,
Should teach his brethren, and inspire
To suffer and to die.

6. Praise to the holiest in the height,
And in the depth be praise;
In all his words most wonderful,
Most sure in all his ways!

JOHN HENRY NEWMAN, 1801–1890

228   Praise to the Lord
14 14 4 7 8

LOBE DEN HERREN

ERNEUERTES GESANGBUCH, STRALSUND, 1665
HARM. FROM *THE CHORALE BOOK FOR ENGLAND*, LONDON, 1863

1. Praise to the Lord, the Almighty, the King of creation; O my soul, praise him, for he is thy health and salvation. All ye who hear, Now to his altar draw near, Joining in glad adoration.
2. Praise to the Lord, who doth prosper thy work and defend thee; Surely his goodness and mercy here daily attend thee. Ponder anew What the Almighty can do, Who with his love doth befriend thee.
3. Praise to the Lord, who o'er all things so wondrously reigneth, Shelters thee under his wings, yea, so gently sustaineth. Hast thou not seen All that is needful hath been Granted in what he ordaineth?
4. Praise to the Lord, O let all that is in me adore him! All that hath life and breath come now with praises before him! Let the Amen Sound from his people again, Now as we worship before him.

LOBE DEN HERREN DEN MÄCHTIGEN KÖNIG; JOACHIM NEANDER, 1650–1680
TR. BY CATHERINE WINKWORTH, 1827–1878, ALT.

229 Raise Your Voices, Vales and Mountains
88 87 WITH REFRAIN

OLD ENGLISH HYMNAL

1. Raise your voices, vales and mountains, Flow'ry meadows, streams and fountains, Praise, O praise the loveliest maiden Ever the Creator made.
2. Murm'ring brooks your tribute bringing, Little birds with joyful singing, Come with mirthful praises laden To your Queen be homage paid.
3. Say, sweet Virgin, we implore thee, Say what beauty God sheds o'er thee; Praise and thanks to him be given, Who in love created thee.

Refrain:
Laudate, Laudate, Laudate Mariam;
Laudate, Laudate, Laudate Mariam.

CAUSA NOSTRA LAETITIAE; ALPHONSUS M. DE LIGUORI, 1696–1787
TR. BY EDMUND VAUGHAN, C.SS.R., 1827–1908

230 Rejoice, Rejoice, Believers
76 76 D

LLANGLOFFAN

TRADITIONAL WELSH MELODY

1. Rejoice! rejoice, believers, And let your lights appear!
The evening is advancing, And darker night is near.
The Bridegroom is arising, And soon he will draw nigh;
Up, watch in expectation! At midnight comes the cry.

2. See that your lamps are burning, Replenish them with oil;
Look now for your salvation, The end of sin and toil.
The marriage-feast is waiting, The gates wide open stand;
Rise up, ye heirs of glory; The Bridegroom is at hand!

3. Our hope and expectation, O Jesus, now appear;
Arise, thou Sun so longed for, Above this darkened sphere!
With hearts and hands uplifted, We plead, O Lord, to see
The day of earth's redemption, And ever be with thee!

Ermuntert euch, ihr Frommen; Laurentius Laurenti, 1660–1722
Tr. by Sarah Laurie Findlater, 1823-1907, ALT.

231 Rejoice, the Lord Is King
66 66 88

DARWALL'S 148TH JOHN DARWALL, 1731–1789

1 Re - joice, the Lord is King: Your Lord and King a - dore!
2 Je - sus, the Sav - ior reigns, The God of truth and love;
3 His king - dom can - not fail, He rules o'er earth and heav'n;
4 Re - joice in glo - rious hope! Our Lord and judge shall come

Re - joice, give thanks and sing, And tri - umph ev - er - more.
When he had purged our stains, He took his seat a - bove;
The keys of death and hell Are to our Je - sus giv'n:
And take his ser - vants up To their e - ter - nal home:

Lift up your heart, Lift up your voice,

Re - joice, a - gain, I say, re - joice!

ON THE RESURRECTION; CHARLES WESLEY, 1707–1788, ALT.

232 Ride On, Ride On in Majesty
88 88

WINCHESTER NEW

MUSICALISCHES HANDBUCH, HAMBURG, 1690
HARM. BY WILLIAM H. MONK, 1823–1889

1. Ride on, ride on in majesty! Hark! All the tribes hosanna cry; Thy humble beast pursues his road With palms and scattered garments strowed.

2. Ride on, ride on in majesty! In lowly pomp ride on to die; O Christ, thy triumphs now begin O'er captive death and conquered sin.

3. Ride on, ride on in majesty! The angel armies of the sky Look down with sad and wond'ring eyes To see the approaching sacrifice.

4. Ride on, ride on in majesty!
Thy last and fiercest strife is nigh;
The Father on his sapphire throne
Expects his own anointed Son.

5. Ride on, ride on in majesty!
In lowly pomp ride on to die;
Bow thy meek head to mortal pain,
Then take, O God, thy pow'r and reign.

PALM SUNDAY; HENRY H. MILMAN, 1791–1868, ALT.

233 Round the Lord in Glory Seated

87 87 D

RUSTINGTON

CHARLES HUBERT H. PARRY, 1848–1918

1. Round the Lord in glory seated, Cherubim and seraphim
Filled his temple, and repeated Each to each th'alternate hymn:
"Lord, thy glory fills the heaven, Earth is with thy fullness stored;
Unto thee be glory given, Holy, holy, holy Lord."

2. Heav'n is still with glory ringing; Earth takes up the angels' cry,
"Holy, holy, holy," singing, "Lord of Hosts, the Lord Most High!"
"Lord, thy glory fills the heaven, Earth is with thy fullness stored;
Unto thee be glory given, Holy, holy, holy Lord."

3. With his seraph train before him, With his holy Church below,
Thus conspire we to adore him, Bid we thus our anthem flow:
"Lord, thy glory fills the heaven, Earth is with thy fullness stored;
Unto thee be glory given, Holy, holy, holy Lord."

4. Thus thy glorious name confessing, With thine angel hosts we cry,
"Holy, holy, holy," blessing Thee, the Lord of Hosts Most High.
"Lord, thy glory fills the heaven, Earth is with thy fullness stored;
Unto thee be glory given, Holy, holy, holy Lord."

TE DEUM LAUDAMUS; RICHARD MANT, 1776–1848

234 Savior of the Nations, Come
77 77

NUN KOMM DER HEIDEN HEILAND   *GEYSTLICHE GESANGK BUCHLEYN*, WITTENBERG, 1524
HARM. BY MELCHIOR VULPIUS, C. 1560–1615

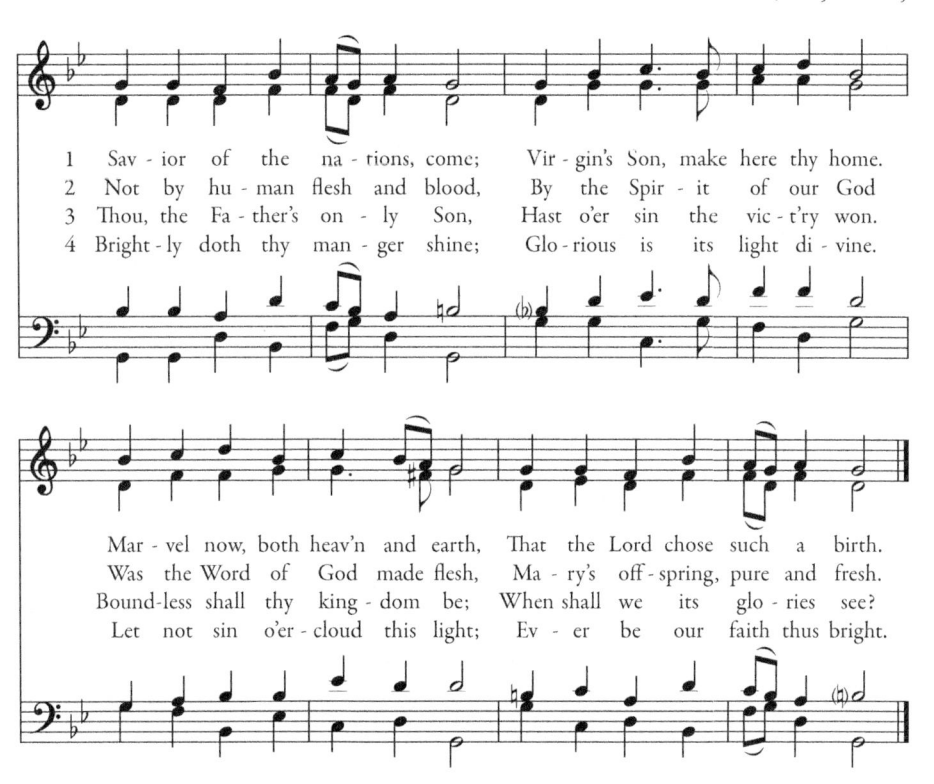

1. Savior of the nations, come; Virgin's Son, make here thy home.
Marvel now, both heav'n and earth, That the Lord chose such a birth.

2. Not by human flesh and blood, By the Spirit of our God
Was the Word of God made flesh, Mary's offspring, pure and fresh.

3. Thou, the Father's only Son, Hast o'er sin the vict'ry won.
Boundless shall thy kingdom be; When shall we its glories see?

4. Brightly doth thy manger shine; Glorious is its light divine.
Let not sin o'er-cloud this light; Ever be our faith thus bright.

VENI REDEMPTOR GENTIUM; AMBROSE OF MILAN, C. 340–397
PARA. BY MARTIN LUTHER, 1483–1546: *NUN KOMM, DER HEIDEN HEILAND*
TR. BY WILLIAM M. REYNOLDS, 1812–1876, ALT.

A CATHOLIC BOOK OF HYMNS • 247

235   See, Amid the Winter's Snow
77 77 D

CHRISTMAS MORN   TRADITIONAL MELODY

1. See, amid the winter's snow, Born for us on earth below; See, the tender lamb appears, Promised from eternal years! Hail! thou ever-blessed morn! Hail, redemption's happy dawn! Sing through all Jerusalem, Christ is born in Bethlehem!

2. Lo, within a manger lies He who built the starry skies; He, who throned in height sublime, Sits amid the Cherubim!

3. Teach, O teach us, holy Child, By thy face so meek and mild; Teach us to resemble thee, In thy sweet humility.

4. Sacred Infant, all Divine, What a tender love was thine; Thus to come from highest bliss, Down to such a world as this!

Hymn for Christmas; Edward Caswall, 1814–1878, abr.

236   See, Amid the Winter's Snow
77 77 D

St. Basil's Hymnal, 1918

1. See! a-mid the win-ter's snow Born for us on earth be-low, See the ten-der lamb ap-pears, Prom-ised from e-ter-nal years. Hail! thou ev-er bless-ed morn, Hail! re-demp-tion's hap-py dawn; Sing through all Je-ru-sa-lem, Christ is born in Beth-le-hem.

2. Lo! with-in a man-ger lies He who built the star-ry skies, He who throned in height sub-lime Sits a-mid the cher-ub-im. Hail! thou ev-er bless-ed morn, Hail! re-demp-tion's hap-py dawn; Sing through all Je-ru-sa-lem, Christ is born in Beth-le-hem.

3. Say, ye ho-ly shep-herds, say What your joy-ful news to-day; Where-fore have ye left your sheep On the lone-ly moun-tain steep? Hail! thou ev-er bless-ed morn, Hail! re-demp-tion's hap-py dawn; Sing through all Je-ru-sa-lem, Christ is born in Beth-le-hem.

4. "As we watch'd at dead of night, Lo, we saw a won-drous light; An-gels sing-ing peace on earth, Told us of the Sav-ior's birth." Hail! thou ev-er bless-ed morn, Hail! re-demp-tion's hap-py dawn; Sing through all Je-ru-sa-lem, Christ is born in Beth-le-hem.

Hymn for Christmas; Edward Caswall, 1814–1878, abr.

237 See the Conqueror Mounts in Triumph
87 87 D

REX GLORIAE HENRY SMART, 1813–1879

1. See the Conqueror mounts in triumph, See the King in royal state,
Riding on the clouds his chariot To his heav'nly palace gate!
Hark! the choir of angel voices Joyful alleluias sing,
And the portals high are lifted To receive their heav'nly King.

2. Who is this that comes in glory With the trump of jubilee?
Lord of battles, God of armies, He has gained the victory!
He who on the Cross did suffer, He who from the grave arose,
He has vanquished sin and Satan, He by death has spoiled his foes.

3. He has raised our human nature On the clouds to God's right hand;
There we sit in heav'nly places, There with thee in glory stand;
Jesus reigns, adored by angels; Man with God is on the throne;
Mighty Lord, in thine Ascension We by faith behold our own.

4. Glory be to God the Father; Glory be to God the Son,
Dying, ris'n, ascending for us, Who the heav'nly realm has won;
Glory to the Holy Spirit; To One God, in Persons Three;
Glory both in earth and heaven, Glory, endless glory, be.

CHRISTOPHER WORDSWORTH, 1807–1885

238 Silent Night
IRREGULAR

STILLE NACHT

FRANZ GRÜBER, 1787–1863

1. Silent night, holy night, All is calm, all is bright Round yon Virgin Mother and Child, Holy Infant, so tender and mild, Sleep in heavenly peace, Sleep in heavenly peace.
2. Silent night, holy night, Shepherds quake at the sight; Glories stream from heaven afar, Heav'nly hosts sing alleluia; Christ, the Savior, is born! Christ, the Savior, is born!
3. Silent night, holy night, Son of God, love's pure light Radiant beams from thy holy face, With the dawn of redeeming grace, Jesus, Lord, at thy birth, Jesus, Lord, at thy birth.

1. Stille Nacht, heilige Nacht! Alles schläft, einsam wacht Nur das traute hochheilige Paar. Holder Knabe im lockigen Haar, Schlaf in himmlischer Ruh, Schlaf in himmlischer Ruh.

STILLE NACHT, HEILIGE NACHT; JOSEPH MOHR, 1792–1848
TR. BY JOHN F. YOUNG, 1820–1885

239 Sing, My Soul, His Wondrous Love
77 77

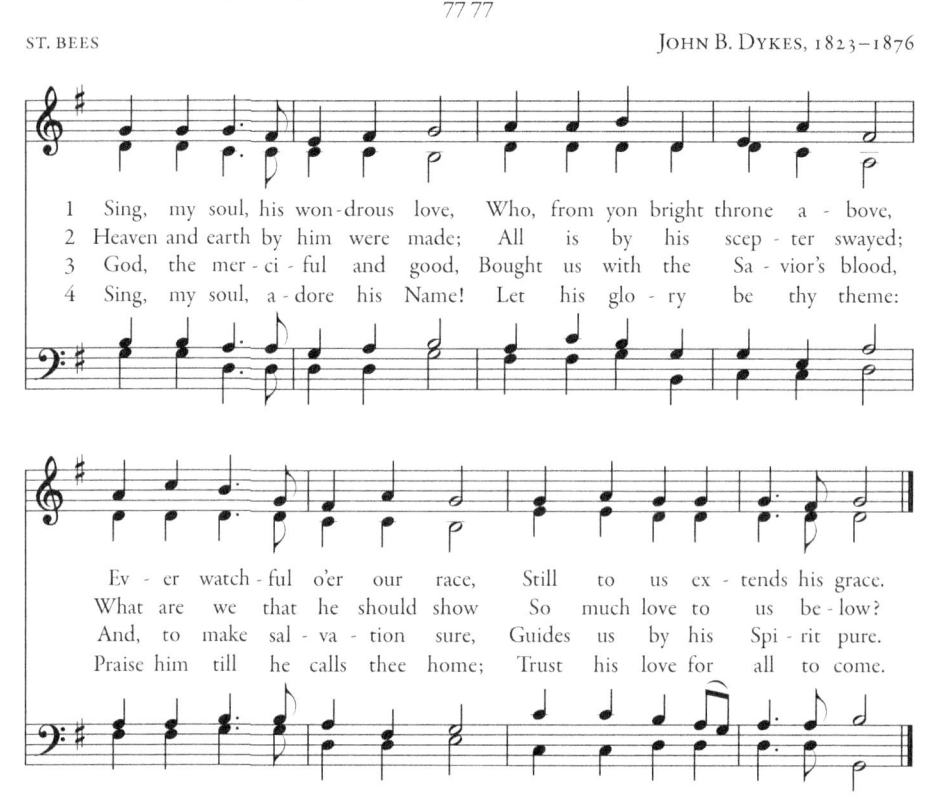

ST. BEES
JOHN B. DYKES, 1823–1876

1. Sing, my soul, his wondrous love, Who, from yon bright throne above,
Ever watchful o'er our race, Still to us extends his grace.

2. Heaven and earth by him were made; All is by his scepter swayed;
What are we that he should show So much love to us below?

3. God, the merciful and good, Bought us with the Savior's blood,
And, to make salvation sure, Guides us by his Spirit pure.

4. Sing, my soul, adore his Name! Let his glory be thy theme:
Praise him till he calls thee home; Trust his love for all to come.

ANONYMOUS, 19TH CENT.

240 Sing Praise to God Who Reigns Above
87 87 887

MIT FREUDEN ZART
BOHEMIAN *BRETHREN'S KIRCHENGESANG*, IVANČICE, 1566
HARM. *THE ENGLISH HYMNAL*, LONDON, 1906

1. Sing praise to God who reigns above, The
2. What God's almighty pow'r has made, His
3. Then all my toilsome way along, I
4. Let all who name Christ's holy name Give

1. God of all creation, The God of pow'r, the God of love, The God of our salvation; With healing balm my soul he fills, And ev'ry faithless murmur stills: To God all praise and glory.

2. gracious mercy keeping; By morning glow or evening shade His watchful eye ne'er sleeping; Within the kingdom of his might, Lo! all is just and all is right: To God all praise and glory.

3. Sing aloud your praises, That all may hear the grateful song My voice unwearied raises; Be joyful in the Lord, my heart, Both soul and body sing your part: To God all praise and glory.

4. God all praise and glory; All you who own his pow'r proclaim Aloud the wondrous story! He reigns triumphant on his throne; The Lord is God, and he alone: To God all praise and glory.

BASED ON PS 95:1–7; JOHANN J. SCHÜTZ, 1640–1690
TR. BY FRANCES A. COX, 1812–1897, ALT.

241 Sing Praise to the Lord
10 10 11 11

LAUDATE DOMINUM CHARLES HUBERT H. PARRY, 1840–1918

1. Sing praise to the Lord! praise God in the height;
Rejoice in his word, you angels of light;
O heavens, adore him by whom you were made,
And worship before him in brightness arrayed.

2. Sing praise to the Lord! praise God upon earth,
In tuneful accord, all men of new birth;
Praise him who has brought you his grace from above,
Praise him who has taught you to sing of his love.

3. Sing praise to the Lord! all things that give sound;
Each jubilant chord, re-echo around;
Loud organs, his glory tell forth in deep tone,
And trumpets, the story of what God has done.

4. Sing praise to the Lord! thanksgiving and song
To him be outpoured all ages along;
For love in creation, for heaven restored,
For grace of salvation, sing praise to the Lord!

HENRY W. BAKER, 1821–1877, ALT.

254 • A CATHOLIC BOOK OF HYMNS

242 Sing We Triumphant Hymns of Praise
88 88 WITH ALLELUIAS

LASST UNS ERFREUEN

GEISTLICHE KIRCHENGESÄNGE, COLOGNE, 1623
HARM. BY RALPH VAUGHAN WILLIAMS, 1872–1958

1 Sing we tri-um-phant hymns of praise To greet our Lord these fes-tive days, Al-le-lu-ia, Al-le-lu-ia! Who by a road be-fore un-trod As-cend-ed to the throne of God, Al-le-lu-ia, al-le-lu-ia, al-le-lu-ia, al-le-lu-ia, al-le-lu-ia!

2 In won-d'ring awe his faith-ful band Up-on the Mount of O-lives stand, Al-le-lu-ia, Al-le-lu-ia! And with the Vir-gin Moth-er see Their Lord as-scend in maj-es-ty.

3 O ris-en Christ, as-cend-ed Lord, All praise to you let earth ac-cord, Al-le-lu-ia, Al-le-lu-ia! Who are, while end-less a-ges run, With Fa-ther and with Spir-it, One.

HYMNUM CANAMUS GLORIAE; BEDE THE VENERABLE, 673–735
VSS. 1–2: TR. BY JOHN D. CHAMBERS, 1805–1893, ALT.
VS. 3: TR. BY BENJAMIN WEBB, 1819–1885

243 Sing With All the Saints in Glory
87 87 D

RUSTINGTON
CHARLES HUBERT H. PARRY, 1848–1918

1. Sing with all the saints in glory, Sing the res‑ur‑rec‑tion song!
Death and sor‑row, earth's dark sto‑ry, To the form‑er days be‑long.
All a‑round the clouds are break‑ing, Soon the storms of time shall cease;
In God's like‑ness we a‑wak‑en, Know‑ing ev‑er‑last‑ing peace.

2. O what glo‑ry, far ex‑ceed‑ing All that eye has yet per‑ceived!
Ho‑liest hearts, for a‑ges plead‑ing, Nev‑er that full joy con‑ceived.
God has prom‑ised, Christ pre‑pares it, There on high our wel‑come waits.
Ev‑'ry hum‑ble spir‑it shares it; Christ has passed th'e‑ter‑nal gates.

3. Life e‑ter‑nal! heav'n re‑joic‑es: Je‑sus lives who once was dead.
Shout with joy, O death‑less voic‑es! Child of God, lift up your head!
Pa‑tri‑archs from dis‑tant a‑ges, Saints all long‑ing for their heav'n,
Proph‑ets, psalm‑ists, seers, and sag‑es, All a‑wait the glo‑ry giv'n.

4. Life e‑ter‑nal! O what won‑ders Crowd on faith; what joy un‑known,
When, a‑mid earth's clos‑ing thun‑ders, Saints shall stand be‑fore the throne!
O, to en‑ter that bright port‑al, See that glow‑ing fir‑ma‑ment,
Know, with you, O God im‑mor‑tal, Je‑sus Christ whom you have sent!

WILLIAM J. IRONS, 1812–1883, ALT.

244 Songs of Thankfulness and Praise
77 77 D

SALZBURG
Jakob Hintze, 1622–1702
harm. by Johann Sebastian Bach, 1685–1750

1. Songs of thankfulness and praise, Jesus, Lord, to thee we raise,
Manifested by the star To the sages from afar;
Branch of royal David's stem In thy birth at Bethlehem;
Anthems be to thee addressed, God in man made manifest.

2. Manifest at Jordan's stream, Prophet, Priest, and King supreme;
And, at Cana, wedding guest In thy Godhead manifest;
Manifest in pow'r divine, Changing water into wine;
Anthems be to thee addressed, God in man made manifest.

3. Manifest in making whole Palsied limbs and fainting soul;
Manifest in valiant fight, Quelling all the devil's might;
Manifest in gracious will, Ever bringing good from ill;
Anthems be to thee addressed, God in man made manifest.

4. Grant us grace to see thee, Lord, Mirrored in thy holy word;
May we imitate thee now, And be pure, as pure art thou;
That we like to thee may be At thy great epiphany;
And may praise thee, ever blest, God in man made manifest.

Christopher Wordsworth, 1807–1885

245 Soul of My Savior
10 10 10 10

ANIMA CHRISTI
WILLIAM J. MAHER, 1823–1877

1. Soul of my Savior, sancti-fy my breast;
Body of Christ, be thou my saving guest;
Blood of my Savior, bathe me in thy tide;
Wash me with water flowing from thy side.

2. Strength and protection may thy passion be;
O blessed Jesus, hear and answer me;
Deep in thy wounds, Lord, hide and shelter me;
So shall I never, never part from thee.

3. Guard and defend me from the foe malign;
In death's drear moments make me only thine;
Call me and bid me come to thee on high,
Where I may praise thee with thy saints for aye.

ANIMA CHRISTI; ATTR. TO POPE JOHN XXII, 1249–1334
TR. BY EDWARD CASWALL, 1814–1878

246 Soul of My Savior
10 10 10 10

LORENZO DOBICI

1. Soul of my Savior, sanctify my breast;
Body of Christ, be thou my saving guest;
Blood of my Savior, bathe me in thy tide;
Wash me with water flowing from thy side.

2. Strength and protection may thy passion be;
O blessed Jesus, hear and answer me;
Deep in thy wounds, Lord, hide and shelter me;
So shall I never, never part from thee.

3. Guard and defend me from the foe malign;
In death's drear moments make me only thine;
Call me and bid me come to thee on high,
Where I may praise thee with thy saints for aye.

Anima Christi; attr. to Pope John XXII, 1249–1334
tr. by Edward Caswall, 1814–1878

247 Sweet Heart of Jesus

11 10 11 10 WITH REFRAIN

HOLY GHOST HYMNAL, IRELAND, 1954

1. Sweet Heart of Jesus! fount of love and mercy,
Today we come thy blessing to implore;
Oh, touch our hearts, so cold and so ungrateful,
And make them, Lord, thine own for evermore.

2. Sweet Heart of Jesus! make us know and love thee,
Unfold to us the treasures of thy grace,
That so our hearts, from things of earth uplifted,
May long alone to gaze upon thy face.

3. Sweet Heart of Jesus! make us pure and gentle,
And teach us how to do thy blessed will,
To follow close the prints of thy dear footsteps,
And when we fall— Sweet Heart, oh love us still.

4. Sweet Heart of Jesus! bless all hearts that love thee,
And may thine own Heart ever blessed be.
Bless us, dear Lord, and bless the friends we cherish,
And keep us true to Mary and to thee.

Sweet Heart of Jesus! we implore,
Oh, make us love thee more and more.

ANONYMOUS

248 Sweet Sacrament Divine
66 66 88 66

DIVINE MYSTERIES   FRANCIS STANFIELD, 1835–1914

1. Sweet sacrament divine, Hid in thy earthly home,
Lo, round thy lowly shrine, With suppliant hearts we come;
Jesus, to thee our voice we raise, In songs of love and heartful praise,
Sweet sacrament divine, Sweet sacrament divine.

2. Sweet sacrament of peace, Dear home of ev'ry heart,
Where restless yearnings cease, And sorrows all depart,
There in thine ear all trustfully We tell our tale of misery,
Sweet sacrament of peace, Sweet sacrament of peace.

3. Sweet sacrament of rest, Ark from the ocean's roar,
Within thy shelter blest Soon may we reach the shore;
Save us, for still the tempest raves; Save, lest we sink beneath the waves,
Sweet sacrament of rest, Sweet sacrament of rest.

4. Sweet sacrament divine, Earth's light and jubilee,
In thy far depths doth shine Thy Godhead's majesty;
Sweet light, so shine on us, we pray, That earthly joys may fade away,
Sweet sacrament divine, Sweet sacrament divine.

FRANCIS STANFIELD, 1835–1914, ALT.

249   Sweet Savior, Bless Us Ere We Go
88 88 88

SUNSET   GEORGE HERBERT, 1817–1906

1. Sweet Savior, bless us ere we go; Thy word into our minds instill; And make our lukewarm hearts to glow With lowly love and fervent will.
2. The day is done; its hours have run; And thou hast taken count of all, The scanty triumphs grace has won, The broken vow, the frequent fall.
3. Grant us, dear Lord, from evil ways True absolution and release; And bless us more than in past days With purity and inward peace.

Through life's long day and death's dark night, O gentle Jesus, be our light.

4. Do more than pardon; give us joy, Sweet fear and sober liberty, And loving hearts without alloy, That only long to be like thee.

5. Labor is sweet, for thou hast toiled, And care is light, for thou hast cared; Let not our works with self be soiled, Nor in unsimple ways ensnared.

6. For all we love— the poor, the sad, The sinful— unto thee we call; O let thy mercy make us glad; Thou art our Jesus and our all.

FREDERICK W. FABER, 1814–1863

250 Take Up Your Cross
88 88 88

BRESLAU *As Hymnodus Sacer*, Leipzig, 1625

1. "Take up your cross," the Savior said, "If you would my disciple be; Take up your cross with willing heart, And humbly follow after me."

2. Take up your cross, let not its weight Fill your weak spirit with alarm; Christ's strength shall bear your spirit up, And brace your heart, and nerve your arm.

3. Take up your cross, heed not the shame, And let your foolish heart be still; The Lord for you accepted death Upon the cross, on Cal'vry's hill.

4. Take up your cross, then, in Christ's strength,
   And calmly ev'ry danger brave:
   It guides you to abundant life
   And leads to vict'ry o'er the grave.

5. Take up your cross, and follow Christ,
   Nor think till death to lay it down;
   For only those who bear the cross
   May hope to wear the glorious crown.

CHARLES W. EVEREST, 1814–1877, ALT.

251 Take Up Your Cross

88 88 88

ERHALT UNS, HERR

J. KLUG'S *GEISTLICHE LIEDER*, WITTENBERG, 1543
HARM. BY JOHANN SEBASTIAN BACH, 1685–1750

1. "Take up your cross," the Savior said, "If you would my disciple be; Take up your cross with willing heart, And humbly follow after me."

2. Take up your cross; let not its weight Fill your weak spirit with alarm; Christ's strength shall bear your spirit up And brace your heart and nerve your arm.

3. Take up your cross, heed not the shame, And let your foolish heart be still; The Lord for you accepted death Upon the cross, on Calv'ry's hill.

4. Take up your cross, then, in Christ's strength,
   And calmly ev'ry danger brave:
   It guides you to abundant life
   And leads to vict'ry o'er the grave.

5. Take up your cross, and follow Christ,
   Nor think till death to lay it down;
   For only those who bear the cross
   May hope to wear the glorious crown.

CHARLES W. EVEREST, 1814–1877, ALT.

252 Tantum Ergo
87 87 87

ST. THOMAS (WADE)
JOHN F. WADE, 1711–1786

1. Tantum ergo Sacraméntum Venerémur cérnui: Et antíquum documéntum Novo cedat rítui: Praestet fides suppleméntum Sénsuum deféctui.
2. Genitóri Genitóque Laus et jubilátio, Salus, honor, virtus quoque Sit et benedíctio: Procedénti ab utróque Cómpar sit laudátio. Amen.

THOMAS AQUINAS, 1225–1274

253 Tantum Ergo
87 87 87

UNSER HERRSCHER
JOACHIM NEANDER, 1650–1680

1. Tantum ergo Sacraméntum Venerémur cérnui: Et antíquum documéntum Novo cedat rítui: Praestet fides suppleméntum Sénsuum deféctui.
2. Genitóri Genitóque Laus et jubilátio, Salus, honor, virtus quoque Sit et benedíctio. Procedénti ab utróque Cómpar sit laudátio. A-men.

THOMAS AQUINAS, 1225–1274

254   The Advent of Our King
66 86

ST. THOMAS (WILLIAMS)   AARON WILLIAMS, 1731–1776

1. The advent of our King Our prayers must now employ,
And we must hymns of welcome sing In strains of holy joy.

2. The everlasting Son Incarnate deigns to be:
Himself a servant's form puts on To set his servants free.

3. O Zion's Daughter, rise To meet thy lowly King,
Nor let thy faithless heart despise The peace he comes to bring.

4. As Judge on clouds of light, He soon will come again
And his true members all unite With him in heav'n to reign.

5. Before the dawning day Let sin's dark deeds be gone,
The old man all be put away, The new man all put on.

6. All glory to the Son, Who comes to set us free,
With Father, Spirit, ever One, Through all eternity.

INSTANTIS ADVENTUM DEI; CHARLES COFFIN, 1676–1749
TR. BY ROBERT CAMPBELL, 1814–1866, ALT.

255 The Angel Gabriel
10 10 12 10

GABRIEL'S MESSAGE

TRADITIONAL BASQUE CAROL
HARM. BY CHARLES EDGAR PETTMAN, 1866-1943

1. The angel Gabriel from heaven came,
His wings as drifted snow, his eyes as flame;
"All hail," said he, "O lowly maiden Mary,"
"Most highly favored lady!" Gloria!

2. "For know a blessed Mother you shall be,
All generations praise continually,
Your Son shall be Emmanuel, by seers foretold."
"Most highly favored lady!" Gloria!

3. Then gentle Mary meekly bowed her head;
"To me be as it pleases God!" she said.
"My soul shall laud and magnify his holy name."
"Most highly favored lady!" Gloria!

4. Of her, Emmanuel, the Christ, was born
In Bethlehem, all on a Christmas morn;
And Christian folk throughout the world will ever say:
"Most highly favored lady!" Gloria!

BIRJINA GAZTETTOBAT ZEGOEN; TRADITIONAL BASQUE CAROL
TR. BY SABINE BARING-GOULD, 1834-1924

256 The Church's One Foundation
76 76 D

AURELIA — SAMUEL S. WESLEY, 1810–1876

1. The Church's one foundation Is Jesus Christ, her Lord;
She is his new creation By water and the Word:
From heav'n he came and sought her To be his holy bride;
With his own blood he bought her, And for her life he died.

2. Elect from ev'ry nation, Yet one o'er all the earth,
Her charter of salvation, One Lord, one faith, one birth;
One holy name she blesses, Partakes one holy food,
And to one hope she presses, With ev'ry grace endued.

3. Though with a scornful wonder Men see her sore oppressed,
By schisms rent asunder, By heresies distressed,
Yet saints their watch are keeping, Their cry goes up, "How long?"
And soon the night of weeping Shall be the morn of song.

4 The Church shall never perish!
   Her dear Lord to defend,
   To guide, sustain, and cherish,
   Is with her to the end;
   Though there be those that hate her,
   And false sons in her pale,
   Against both foe and traitor
   She ever shall prevail.

5 'Mid toil and tribulation,
   And tumult of her war,
   She waits the consummation
   Of peace forevermore;
   Till with the vision glorious
   Her longing eyes are blest,
   And the great Church victorious
   Shall be the Church at rest.

6 Yet she on earth hath union
   With God the Three in One,
   And mystic sweet communion
   With those whose rest is won:
   O happy ones and holy!
   Lord, give us grace that we,
   Like them, the meek and lowly,
   On high may dwell with thee.

The Holy Catholic Church: The Communion of Saints;
Samuel J. Stone, 1839–1900

257 The Day of Resurrection
76 76 D

CHARTRES

TRADITIONAL FRENCH MELODY
HARM. BY J. ALFRED SCHEHL, 1882–1959

1. The day of Resurrection: Earth, tell it out abroad! The Passover of gladness, The Passover of God! From death to life eternal, From earth unto the sky, Our Christ hath brought us over With hymns of victory.

2. Our hearts be pure from evil, That we may see aright The Lord in rays eternal Of Resurrection-light: And, list'ning to his accents, May hear so calm and plain His own "All hail!" and, hearing, May raise the victor strain.

3. Now let the heav'ns be joyful! Let earth her song begin! The round world keep high triumph, And all that is therein! Let all things seen and unseen Their notes of gladness blend, For Christ the Lord is risen, Our joy that hath no end.

Ἀναστάσεως ἡμέρα (ANASTASEOS IMERA); JOHN OF DAMASCUS, c. 675–749
TR. BY JOHN M. NEALE, 1818–1866

258 The Day of Resurrection
76 76 D

ELLACOMBE

MAINZER GESANGBUCH, MAINZ, 1833
HARM. BY WILLIAM H. MONK, 1823–1889

1. The day of resurrection! Earth, tell it out abroad;
The Passover of gladness, The Passover of God.
From death to life eternal, From earth unto the sky,
Our Christ hath brought us over, With hymns of victory.

2. Our hearts be pure from evil, That we may see aright
The Lord in rays eternal Of resurrection light;
And list'ning to his accents, May hear so calm and plain
His own "All hail!" and, hearing, May raise the victor strain.

3. Now let the heav'ns be joyful! Let earth her song begin!
The round world keep high triumph, And all that is therein!
Let all things seen and unseen Their notes in gladness blend,
For Christ the Lord is risen, Our joy that hath no end.

Ἀναστάσεως ἡμέρα (ANASTASEOS IMERA); JOHN OF DAMASCUS, c. 675–749
TR. BY JOHN M. NEALE, 1818–1866

259 The Day of Resurrection
76 76 D

LANCASHIRE
HENRY T. SMART, 1813–1879

1. The day of resurrection! Earth, tell it out abroad;
The Passover of gladness, The Passover of God.
From death to life eternal, From earth unto the sky,
Our Christ hath brought us over, With hymns of victory.

2. Our hearts be pure from evil, That we may see aright
The Lord in rays eternal Of resurrection light;
And list'ning to his accents, May hear so calm and plain
His own "All hail!" and, hearing, May raise the victor strain.

3. Now let the heav'ns be joyful! Let earth her song begin!
The round world keep high triumph, And all that is therein!
Let all things seen and unseen Their notes in gladness blend,
For Christ the Lord is risen, Our joy that hath no end.

Ἀναστάσεως ἡμέρα (ANASTASEOS IMERA); JOHN OF DAMASCUS, C. 675–749
TR. BY JOHN M. NEALE, 1818–1866

260   The Fiery Sun Now Rolls Away
88 88

ANGELUS   GEORG JOSEPH, 1630–1668

1. The fiery sun now rolls away, And hastens to close of the day; Thy brightness beams, O Lord, impart, And rise in our benighted heart.
2. To us the praises of thy name Are morning-song and evening-theme; Thus may we sing ourselves to rest Amidst the music of the blest.
3. To God the Father and the Son, And Holy Spirit, Three in One, Be endless glory, as before The world began, so evermore.

IAM SOL RECEDIT IGNEUS; ATTR. TO AMBROSE OF MILAN, 340–397
TR. PRIMER, 1706

261 The First Noël

IRREGULAR

THE FIRST NOWELL

ENGLISH CAROL, 17TH CENT.

1 The first Noël the angels did say, Was to certain poor shepherds in fields as they lay, In fields where they lay keeping their sheep, On a cold winter's night that was so deep.
2 They looked up and saw a star Shining in the east beyond them far, And to the earth it gave great light, And so it continued both day and night.
3 And by the light of that same star, Three wise men came from country far, To seek for a King was their intent, And to follow the star wherever it went.

Refrain: Noël, Noël, Noël, Noël, Born is the King of Israel!

4 This star drew nigh to the northwest, O'er Bethlehem it took its rest,
And there it did both stop and stay Right over the place where Jesus lay.

5 Then entered in those wise men three Full rev'rently upon their knee,
And offered there in his presence Their gold, and myrrh, and frankincense.

6 Then let us all with one accord Sing praises to our heav'nly Lord;
That hath made heav'n and earth of nought, And with his blood mankind hath bought.

ENGLISH CAROL, 17TH CENT.

262 The Glory of These Forty Days
88 88

ERHALT UNS, HERR

J. KLUG'S *GEISTLICHE LIEDER*, WITTENBERG, 1543
HARM. BY JOHANN SEBASTIAN BACH, 1685–1750

1. The glory of these forty days
We celebrate with songs of praise:
For Christ, by whom all things were made,
Himself hath fasted and hath prayed.

2. Alone and fasting Moses saw
The loving God who gave the law;
And to Elijah, fasting, came
The steeds and chariots of flame.

3. So Daniel trained his mystic sight,
Deliver'd from the lion's might;
And John, the Bridegroom's friend, became
The herald of Messiah's name.

4. Then grant us, Lord, like them to be
Full oft in fast and prayer with thee;
Our spirits strengthen with thy grace,
And give us joy to see thy face.

5. O Father, Son, and Spirit blest,
To thee be ev'ry prayer addrest;
Who art in three-fold Name adored,
From age to age the only Lord.

CLARUM DECUS JEJUNII; ATTR. TO GREGORY THE GREAT, C. 540–604
TR. BY MAURICE F. BELL, 1862–1947

263 The God of Abraham Praise
66 84 D

LEONI

Hebrew melody
adapt. by Meyer Lyon, 1751–1797

1. The God of Abraham praise, Who reigns enthroned above;
Ancient of everlasting days, And God of love;
The Lord, the great I AM, By earth and heaven confessed:
We bow and bless the sacred Name For ever blest.

2. He by himself hath sworn: We on his oath depend;
We shall, on eagle-wings upborne, To heaven ascend:
We shall behold his face, We shall his power adore,
And sing the wonders of his grace For evermore.

3. There dwells the Lord, our King, The Lord, our Righteousness,
Triumphant o'er the world and sin, The Prince of Peace;
On Zion's sacred heights His kingdom he maintains,
And, glorious with his saints in light, For ever reigns.

278 • A CATHOLIC BOOK OF HYMNS

4 The God who reigns on high
　The great archangels sing,
　And "Holy, holy, holy," cry,
　"Almighty King!
　Who was, and is, the same,
　And evermore shall be:
　Eternal Father, great I AM,
　We worship thee."

5 The whole triumphant host
　Give thanks to God on high;
　"Hail, Father, Son, and Holy Ghost!"
　They ever cry;
　Hail, Abraham's Lord divine!
　With heaven our songs we raise;
　All might and majesty are thine,
　And endless praise.

BASED ON THE JEWISH *YIGDAL ELOHIM HAI*;
ATTR. TO DANIEL BEN JUDAH, C. 14TH CENT.
THOMAS OLIVERS, 1725–1799

264 The King of Love
87 87

ST. COLUMBA (IRISH)

TRADITIONAL IRISH MELODY
HARM. BY CHARLES V. STANFORD, 1824–1924, ALT.

1. The King of love my shepherd is, Whose goodness faileth never; I nothing lack if I am his, And he is mine forever.

2. Where streams of living water flow My ransomed soul he leadeth, And where the verdant pastures grow With food celestial feedeth.

3. Perverse and foolish oft I strayed, But yet in love he sought me, And on his shoulder gently laid, And home, rejoicing, brought me.

4. In death's dark vale I fear no ill With thee, dear Lord, beside me; Thy rod and staff my comfort still, Thy cross before to guide me.

5. Thou spread'st a table in my sight, Thy unction grace bestoweth; And oh, what transport of delight From thy pure chalice floweth!

6. And so through all the length of days Thy goodness faileth never, Good Shepherd, may I sing thy praise Within thy house forever.

BASED ON PSALM 23
HENRY W. BAKER, 1821–1877

265 The Strife Is O'er

888 WITH ALLELUIAS

VICTORY

GIOVANNI PIERLUIGI DA PALESTRINA, 1525–1594
ADAPT. BY WILLIAM H. MONK, 1823–1889

Alleluia! Alleluia! Alleluia!

1. The strife is o'er, the battle done; Now is the Victor's triumph won; O let the song of praise be sung: Alleluia!
2. Death's mightiest pow'rs have done their worst, And Jesus hath his foes dispersed; Let shouts of praise and joy outburst: Alleluia!
3. He closed the yawning gates of hell; The bars from heav'n's high portals fell; Let hymns of praise his triumph tell: Alleluia!

4. On the third morn he rose again,
   Glorious in majesty to reign;
   O let us swell the joyful strain:
   Alleluia!

5. Lord, by the stripes that wounded thee,
   From death's dread sting thy servants free,
   That we may live and sing to thee:
   Alleluia!

FINITA JAM SUN PROELIA IN *SYMPHONIA SIRENUM SELECTARUM*, COLOGNE, 1695
TR. BY FRANCIS POTT, 1832–1909, ALT.

266 The Sun Is Shining Brightly

76 76 D WITH REFRAIN

THE PAROCHIAL HYMN BOOK, LONDON, 1883

1. The sun is shining brightly, The trees are clothed with green,
The beauteous bloom of flowers On ev'ry side is seen;
The fields are gold and em'rald, And all the world is gay;
For 'tis the month of Mary, The lovely month of May.

2. There's music in the heavens, For birds are singing there,
And nature's songs and praises Are sounding through the air;
And we with hearts o'erflowing With joy will sing today;
For 'tis the month of Mary, The lovely month of May.

3. And when night closes o'er us, And twinkling stars appear;
The chaste moon calmly reigneth, In skies so bright and clear.
Oh! how that sight reminds us Of heaven far away,
Where reigns, o'er saints and angels, Our lovely Queen of May.

282 • A CATHOLIC BOOK OF HYMNS

O Mary, dear Mother, We sing a hymn to thee; Thou art the Queen of heaven, Thou too the Queen shall be, O rule us and guide us Unto eternity.

ATTR. TO SISTERS OF NOTRE DAME DE NAMUR

267 The Sun Is Sinking Fast
64 66

ST. COLUMBA (IRONS) — HERBERT STEPHEN IRONS, 1834-1905

1. The sun is sinking fast, The daylight dies;
   Let love awake, and pay Her evening sacrifice.

2. As Christ upon the Cross, In death reclined,
   Into his Father's hands His parting soul resigned.

3. So now herself my soul Would wholly give
   Into his sacred charge In whom all spirits live;

4. So now beneath his eye
   Would calmly rest,
   Without a wish or thought
   Abiding in the breast,

5. Save that his will be done,
   Whate'er betide,
   Dead to herself, and dead
   In him to all aside.

6. Thus would I live; yet now
   Not I, but he
   In all his power and love
   Henceforth alive in me—

7. One sacred Trinity,
   One Lord divine,
   Myself for ever his
   And he for ever mine!

Sol praeceps rapitur, 18TH CENT.
TR. BY EDWARD CASWALL, 1814–1878

268. There Is a Green Hill Far Away

86 86

HORSLEY — WILLIAM HORSLEY, 1774–1858

1. There is a green hill far away, With-out a city wall,
Where the dear Lord was cru-ci-fied, Who died to save us all.

2. We may not know, we cannot tell What pains he had to bear,
But we believe it was for us He hung and suffered there.

3. He died that we might be forgiv'n, He died to make us good,
That we might go at last to heav'n, Saved by his precious blood.

4. There was no other good enough
To pay the price of sin;
He only could unlock the gate
Of heav'n, and let us in.

5. O dearly, dearly has he loved,
And we must love him too,
And trust in his redeeming blood,
And try his works to do.

CECIL FRANCES ALEXANDER, 1818–1895

269 There's a Wideness in God's Mercy
87 87

GOTT WILL'S MACHEN   JOHANN LUDWIG STEINER, 1688–1761

1. There's a wideness in God's mercy
Like the wideness of the sea;
There's a kindness in his justice
Which is more than liberty.

2. There is no place where earth's sorrows
Are more felt than up in heav'n;
There is no place where earth's failings
Have such kindly judgment giv'n.

3. There is plentiful redemption
In the blood that has been shed;
There is joy for all the members
In the sorrows of the Head.

4. Souls of men! why will ye scatter
Like a crowd of frightened sheep?
Foolish hearts! why will ye wander
From a love so true and deep?

5. For the love of God is broader
Than the measures of man's mind,
And the heart of the Eternal
Is most wonderfully kind.

COME TO JESUS; FREDERICK W. FABER, 1814–1863

270 There's a Wideness in God's Mercy
87 87

IN BABILONE   TRADITIONAL DUTCH MELODY

1. There's a wideness in God's mercy Like the wideness of the sea;
There's a kindness in his justice Which is more than liberty.
There is plentiful redemption In the blood that has been shed;
There is joy for all the members In the sorrows of the Head.

2. For the love of God is broader Than the measures of man's mind,
And the heart of the Eternal Is most wonderfully kind.
If our love were but more simple We should take him at his word,
And our lives would be all sunshine In the sweetness of our Lord.

3. Souls of men! why will ye scatter Like a crowd of frightened sheep?
Foolish hearts! why will ye wander From a love so true and deep?
There is welcome for the sinner And more graces for the good;
There is mercy with the Savior, There is healing in his blood.

Come to Jesus; FREDERICK W. FABER, 1814–1863

271 Through the Red Sea

7 4 7 4 6 7 4

STRAF MICH NICHT ATTR. TO JOHANN ROSENMÜLLER, C. 1619–1684

1. Through the Red Sea brought at last, Alleluia!
Egypt's chains behind we cast, Alleluia!
Deep and wide flows the tide,
Sev'ring us from bondage past, Alleluia!

2. Like the cloud that overhead, Alleluia!
Through the billows Israel led, Alleluia!
By his tomb Christ makes room,
Souls restoring from the dead, Alleluia!

3. In that cloud and in that sea, Alleluia!
Buried and baptized were we, Alleluia!
Earthly night brought us light,
Which is ours eternally, Alleluia!

RONALD A. KNOX, 1888–1957

272 'Tis Good, Lord, to Be Here
66 86

SWABIA

JOHANN M. SPEISS, 1715–1772
ADAPT. BY WILLIAM A. HAVERGAL, 1793–1870

1. 'Tis good, Lord, to be here! Thy glory fills the night; Thy face and garments, like the sun, Shine with un-bor-rowed light.
2. 'Tis good, Lord, to be here, Thy beauty to behold, Where Moses and Elijah stand, Thy messengers of old.
3. Fulfiller of the past! Promise of things to be! We hail thy body glorified, And our redemption see.

4. Before we taste of death,
We see thy kingdom come;
We fain would hold the vision bright,
And make this hill our home.

5. 'Tis good, Lord, to be here!
Yet we may not remain;
But since thou bidst us leave the mount,
Come with us to the plain.

BASED ON LUKE 9:32–33
JOSEPH A. ROBINSON, 1858–1933

273 'Tis the Month of Our Mother

78 78 WITH REFRAIN

LOUIS LAMBILLOTTE SJ, 1796–1855

1. 'Tis the month of our Mother, The blessed and beautiful days,
   When our lips and our spirits Are glowing with love and with praise.
2. Oh! what peace to her children, 'Mid sorrows and trials to know
   That the love of their Mother Hath ever a solace for woe.
3. And what joy to the erring, The sinful and sorrowful soul;
   That a trust in her guidance Will lead to a glorious goal.
4. Let us sing, then, rejoicing, That God hath so honored our race,
   As to clothe with our nature Sweet Mary, the Mother of grace.

Refrain:
All hail! to dear Mary, The guardian of our way,
To the fairest of Queens, Be the fairest of seasons, sweet May.

BASED ON *C'EST LE MOIS DE MARIE*, FROM LAMBILLOTTE'S *CHOIX DE CANTIQUES*, 1867

274 To Jesus' Heart All Burning

76 76 WITH REFRAIN

COR JESU

WILLIAM J. MAHER, 1823–1877

1. To Jesus' heart all burning With fervent love for men,
My heart with fondest yearning Shall raise the joyful strain.

2. O heart for me on fire With love no man can speak,
My yet untold desire God gives me for thy sake.

3. Too true, I have forsaken Thy love for wilful sin,
Yet now let me be taken Back by thy grace again.

4. As thou art meek and lowly, And ever pure at heart,
So may my heart be wholly Of thine the counterpart.

Refrain:
While ages course along, Blest be with loudest song
The Sacred Heart of Jesus By ev'ry heart and tongue,
The Sacred Heart of Jesus By ev'ry heart and tongue.

DEM HERZEN JESU SING; ALOYS SCHLOER, 1805–1852
TR. BY ALBANY JAMES CHRISTIE, 1817–1891

275 Virgin-Born, We Bow Before Thee

88 77 D

MON DIEU PRETE-MOI L'OREILLE

LOUIS BOURGEOIS, C. 1510–1561
HARM. BY CLAUDE GOUDIMEL, 1514–1572

1. Virgin-born, we bow before thee; Blessed was the womb that bore thee; Mary, mother meek and mild, Blessed was she in her child. Blessed was the breast that fed thee; Blessed was the hand that led thee; Blessed was the parent's eye That watched thy slumb'ring infancy.

2. Blessed she by all creation, Who brought forth the world's Salvation, Blessed they for ever blest, Who love thee most and serve thee best. Virgin-born, we bow before thee; Blessed was the womb that bore thee; Mary, mother meek and mild, Blessed was she in her child.

REGINALD HEBER, 1783–1826

276 Virgin-Born, We Bow Before Thee
88 77

QUEM PASTORES GERMAN 14TH CENT. CAROL

1. Virgin-born, we bow before thee; Blessed was the womb that bore thee; Mary, mother meek and mild, Blessed was she in her child.
2. Blessed was the breast that fed thee; Blessed was the hand that led thee; Blessed was the parent's eye That watched thy slumb'ring infancy.
3. Blessed she by all creation, Who brought forth the world's Salvation, Blessed they for ever blest, Who love thee most and serve thee best.
4. Virgin-born, we bow before thee; Blessed was the womb that bore thee; Mary, mother meek and mild, Blessed was she in her child.

REGINALD HEBER, 1783–1826

277 Wake, Awake, for Night Is Flying
8 9 8 D 6 6 4 8 8

WACHET AUF

PHILIPP NICOLAI, 1556–1608
HARM. BY JOHANN SEBASTIAN BACH, 1685–1750

1. "Wake, awake, for night is flying,"
   The watchmen on the heights are crying;
   "Awake, Jerusalem, arise!"
   Midnight hears the welcome voices

2. Zion hears the watchmen singing;
   And all her heart with joy is springing;
   She wakes, she rises from her gloom;
   For her Lord comes down all glorious,

3. Now let all the heav'ns adore thee,
   Let men and angels sing before thee,
   With harp and cymbal's clearest tone.
   Of one pearl each shining portal,

And at the thril - ling cry re - joic - es:
The strong in grace, in truth vic - to - rious,
Where, dwell - ing with the choir im - mor - tal,

"Oh, where are ye, ye vir - gins wise?
Her Star is ris'n, her Light is come.
We gath - er round thy ra - diant throne.

The Bride - groom comes, a - wake! Thy
"Now come, thou Bless - ed One, Lord
No vi - sion ev - er brought, No

lamps with glad - ness take! Hal - le - lu - jah!
Je - sus, God's own Son, Hail! Ho - san - na!
ear hath ev - er caught, Such great glo - ry;

A CATHOLIC BOOK OF HYMNS • 295

With bridal care thyselves prepare To meet the Bridegroom, who is near."
The joyful call we answer all And follow to the nuptial hall."
Therefore will we eternally Sing hymns of praise and joy to thee.

Wachet auf, ruft uns die Stimme; Philipp Nicolai, 1556–1608
tr. by Catherine Winkworth, 1829–1878, alt.

278 Watchman, Tell Us of the Night
77 77 D

ABERYSTWYTH
JOSEPH PARRY, 1841–1903

1. Watchman, tell us of the night, What its signs of promise are.
Trav-'ler, what a wondrous sight: See that glory-beaming star.
Watchman, does its beauteous ray News of joy or hope foretell?
Trav-'ler, yes, it brings the day, Promised day of Israel.

2. Watchman, tell us of the night; Higher yet that star ascends.
Trav-'ler, blessedness and light, Peace and truth its course portends.
Watchman, will its beams alone Gild the spot that gave them birth?
Trav-'ler, ages are its own; See, it bursts o'er all the earth.

3. Watchman, tell us of the night, For the morning seems to dawn.
Trav-'ler, shadows take their flight; Doubt and terror are withdrawn.
Watchman, you may go your way; Hasten to your quiet home.
Trav-'ler, we rejoice today, For Emmanuel has come!

JOHN BOWRING, 1792–1872, ALT.

279 What Child Is This
87 87 WITH REFRAIN

GREENSLEEVES

ENGLISH FOLK SONG, 16TH CENT.
HARM. BY JOHN STAINER, 1840–1901

1. What Child is this, who, laid to rest, On Mary's lap is sleeping?
Whom angels greet with anthems sweet, While shepherds watch are keeping?
This, this is Christ the King, Whom shepherds guard and angels sing!
Haste, haste to bring him laud, The Babe, the Son of Mary!

2. Why lies he in such mean estate Where ox and ass are feeding?
Good Christian, fear, for sinners here The silent Word is pleading.
Nails, spear, shall pierce him through, The cross be borne, for me, for you:
Hail, hail, the Word made flesh, The Babe, the Son of Mary!

3. So bring him incense, gold, and myrrh, Come, peasant, king, to own him;
The King of kings salvation bring, Let loving hearts enthrone him.
Raise, raise the song on high, The Virgin sings her lullaby:
Joy, joy, for Christ is born, The Babe, the Son of Mary!

WILLIAM C. DIX, 1837–1898

280 What Star Is This
88 88

PUER NOBIS NASCITUR

TRIER MANUSCRIPT, 15TH CENT.
ADAPT. BY MICHAEL PRAETORIUS, 1571–1621

1. What star is this, with beams so bright, More lovely than the noonday light? 'Tis sent to announce a newborn King, Glad tidings of our God to bring.

2. 'Tis now fulfilled what God decreed, "From Jacob shall a star proceed;" And lo! the eastern sages stand To read in heav'n the Lord's command.

3. O Jesus, while the star of grace Impels us on to seek thy face, Let not our slothful hearts refuse The guidance of thy light to use.

4. To God almighty, heav'nly Light; To Christ, revealed in earthly night, To God the Holy Spirit raise An endless song of thankful praise!

QUAE STELLA SOLE PULCHRIOR; CHARLES COFFIN, 1676–1749
TR. BY JOHN CHANDLER, 1806–1876, ALT.

281 Whate'er Our God Ordains Is Right
87 87 44 88

WAS GOTT TUT
Weimar Gesangbuch, 1681

1. What-e'er our God or-dains is right; Ho-ly his will a-bid-eth;
   I will be still what-e'er he doth, And fol-low where he guid-eth.
   He is my God; Though dark my road, He holds me that I
   shall not fall; Where-fore to him I leave it all.

2. What-e'er our God or-dains is right; He nev-er will de-ceive me;
   He leads me by the prop-er path; I know he will not leave me.
   I take, con-tent, What he hath sent; His hand can turn my
   griefs a-way, And pa-tient-ly I wait his day.

3. What-e'er our God or-dains is right; Though now this cup, in drink-ing,
   May bit-ter seem to my faint heart, I take it, all un-shrink-ing;
   Tears pass a-way With dawn of day; Sweet com-fort yet shall
   fill my heart, And pain and sor-row shall de-part.

4. What-e'er our God or-dains is right; Here shall my stand be tak-en;
   Though sor-row, need, or death be mine, Yet I am not for-sak-en;
   My Fa-ther's care Is round me there; He holds me that I
   shall not fall, And so to him I leave it all.

Was Gott tut das ist wohlgetan; Samuel Rodigast, 1649–1708
tr. by Catherine Winkworth, 1829–1878, alt.

282 When I Survey the Wondrous Cross
88 88

HAMBURG
LOWELL MASON, 1792–1872

1. When I survey the wondrous cross
On which the Prince of glory died,
My richest gain I count but loss,
And pour contempt on all my pride.

2. Forbid it, Lord, that I should boast
Save in the death of Christ, my God:
All the vain things that charm me most,
I sacrifice them to his blood.

3. See, from his head, his hands, his feet,
Sorrow and love flow mingled down!
Did e'er such love and sorrow meet,
Or thorns compose so rich a crown?

4. Were the whole realm of nature mine,
That were a present far too small:
Love so amazing, so divine,
Demands my soul, my life, my all.

CRUCIFIXION TO THE WORLD BY THE CROSS OF CHRIST; ISAAC WATTS, 1674–1748

283 When I Survey the Wondrous Cross
88 88

ROCKINGHAM

SECOND SUPPLEMENT TO PSALMODY IN MINIATURE, 1783
HARM. BY EDWARD MILLER, 1735–1807

1. When I survey the wondrous cross
On which the Prince of glory died,
My richest gain I count but loss,
And pour contempt on all my pride.

2. Forbid it, Lord, that I should boast,
Save in the death of Christ my God;
All the vain things that charm me most,
I sacrifice them to his blood.

3. See, from his head, his hands, his feet,
Sorrow and love flow mingled down;
Did e'er such love and sorrow meet,
Or thorns compose so rich a crown?

4. Were the whole realm of nature mine,
That were a present far too small;
Love so amazing, so divine,
Demands my soul, my life, my all.

CRUCIFIXION TO THE WORLD BY THE CROSS OF CHRIST; ISAAC WATTS, 1674–1748

284 When Morning Gilds the Skies
666 666

LAUDES DOMINI   JOSEPH BARNBY, 1836–1896

1. When morning gilds the skies, My heart awaking cries, May Jesus Christ be praised: Alike at work and prayer To Jesus I repair; May Jesus Christ be praised.

2. When-e'er the sweet church bell Peals over hills and dell, May Jesus Christ be praised: O hark to what it sings, As joyously it rings, May Jesus Christ be praised.

3. My tongue shall never tire Of chanting with the choir, May Jesus Christ be praised: This song of sacred joy, It never seems to cloy, May Jesus Christ be praised.

4. Does sadness fill my mind? A solace here I find, May Jesus Christ be praised: Or fades my earthly bliss? My comfort still is this, May Jesus Christ be praised.

5. The night becomes as day, When from the heart we say, May Jesus Christ be praised: The powers of darkness fear, When this sweet chant they hear, May Jesus Christ be praised.

6. Be this, while life is mine, My canticle divine, May Jesus Christ be praised: Be this the eternal song Through ages all along, May Jesus Christ be praised.

BEIM FRÜHEN MORGENLICHT; KATHOLISCHES GESANGBUCH, WÜRZBURG, 1828
TR. BY EDWARD CASWALL, 1814–1878, ALT.

285 When the Patriarch Was Returning
87 87 77

ALL SAINTS
Gesangbuch, Darmstadt, 1698

1. When the Patriarch was returning, Crowned with triumph from the fray,
Him the peaceful king of Salem Came to meet upon his way;
Meekly bearing bread and wine, Holy priesthood's awful sign.

2. On the truth thus dimly shadowed Later days a luster shed;
When the great High-Priest eternal, Under forms of wine and bread,
For the world's immortal Food Gave his flesh and gave his blood.

3. Wondrous Gift! The Word who fashioned All things by his might divine,
Bread unto his body changes, Into his own blood the wine,
What though sense no change perceives, Faith admires, adores, believes.

4. He who once to die a Victim
On the Cross did not refuse,
Day by day upon our altars
That same Sacrifice renews,
Through his holy priesthood's hands,
Faithful to his last commands.

5. While the people all uniting
In the Sacrifice sublime,
Offer Christ to his high Father,
Offer up themselves with him;
Then together with the priest
On the living Victim feast.

Hoste dum victo triumphans
tr. by Edward Caswall, 1814–1878, alt.

286 When the Patriarch Was Returning
87 87 77

J.C. Bowen

1. When the Patriarch was returning
Crowned with triumph from the fray,
Him the peaceful king of Salem
Came to meet upon his way;
Meekly bearing bread and wine,
Holy priesthood's awful sign.

2. On the truth thus dimly shadowed
Later days a luster shed;
When the great High-Priest eternal,
Under forms of wine and bread,
For the world's immortal Food
Gave his flesh and gave his blood.

3. Wondrous Gift! The Word who fashioned
All things by his might divine,
Bread into his body changes,
Into his own blood the wine,
What though sense no change perceives,
Faith admires, adores, believes.

4. He who once to die a Victim
On the Cross did not refuse,
Day by day upon our altars
That same Sacrifice renews,
Through his holy priesthood's hands,
Faithful to his last commands.

5. While the people all uniting
In the Sacrifice sublime,
Offer Christ to his high Father,
Offer up themselves with him;
Then together with the priest
On the living Victim feast.

Hoste dum victo triumphans
tr. by Edward Caswall, 1814–1878, alt.

287 Who Are These Like Stars Appearing
87 87 77

ALL SAINTS GESANGBUCH, DARMSTADT, 1698

1 Who are these like stars appearing, These, before God's throne who stand?
Each a golden crown is wearing; Who are all this glorious band?
Alleluia, hark, they sing, Praising loud their heav'nly King.

2 Who are these in dazzling brightness, Clothed in God's own righteousness,
These, whose robes of purest whiteness, Shall their luster still possess,
Still untouched by time's rude hand? Whence came all this glorious band?

3 These are they who have contended For their Savior's honor long,
Wrestling on till life was ended, Foll'wing not the sinful throng;
These, who well the fight sustained, Triumph by the Lamb have gained.

4 These are they whose hearts were riven,
Sore with woe and anguish tried,
Who in prayer full oft have striven
With the God they glorified;
Now, their painful conflict o'er,
God has bid them weep no more.

5 These, th'Almighty contemplating,
Did as priests before him stand,
Soul and body always waiting
Day and night at his command:
Now in God's most holy place
Blest they stand before his face.

WER SIND DIE VOR GOTTES THRONE; HEINRICH SCHENCK, 1656-1727
TR. BY FRANCES ELIZABETH COX, 1812-1897

288 Who Is This, So Weak and Helpless
87 87 D

EBENEZER (WILLIAMS)   THOMAS J. WILLIAMS, 1869–1944

1. Who is this, so weak and helpless, Child of lowly Hebrew maid, Rudely in a stable sheltered, Coldly in a manger laid? 'Tis the Lord of all creation, Who this wondrous

2. Who is this, a Man of Sorrows, Walking sadly life's hard way, Homeless, weary, sighing, weeping Over sin and Satan's sway? 'Tis our God, our glorious Savior, Who above the

3. Who is this? Behold him shedding Drops of blood upon the ground! Who is this, despised, rejected, Mocked, insulted, beaten, bound? 'Tis our God, who gifts and graces On his church is

4. Who is this that hangs there dying While the rude world scoffs and scorns, Numbered with the malefactors, Torn with nails, and crowned with thorns? 'Tis our God, who lives forever 'Mid the shining

A CATHOLIC BOOK OF HYMNS

path has trod; He is God from ev - er - last - ing,
star - ry sky Is for us a place pre - par - ing,
pour - ing down; Who shall smite in ho - ly ven - geance
ones on high, In the glo - rious gold - en cit - y,

And to ev - er - last - ing God.
Where no tear can dim the eye.
All his foes be - neath his throne.
Reign - ing ev - er - last - ing - ly.

WILLIAM WALSHAM HOW, 1823-1897, ALT.

289 Who Is This, So Weak and Helpless
87 87 D

EIFIONYDD

JOHN AMBROSE LLOYD, 1815-1874

1 Who is this, so weak and help - less, Child of low - ly
2 Who is this, a Man of Sor - rows, Walk - ing sad - ly
3 Who is this? Be - hold him shed - ding Drops of blood up -
4 Who is this that hangs there dy - ing While the rude world

He - brew maid, Rude - ly in a sta - ble shel - tered,
life's hard way, Home - less, wea - ry, sigh - ing, weep - ing
on the ground! Who is this, de - spised, re - ject - ed,
scoffs and scorns, Num - bered with the mal - e - fac - tors,

308 • A CATHOLIC BOOK OF HYMNS

Coldly in a manger laid?
Over sin and Satan's sway?
Mocked, insulted, beaten, bound?
Torn with nails, and crowned with thorns?

'Tis the Lord of all creation, Who this wondrous
'Tis our God, our glorious Savior, Who above the
'Tis our God, who gifts and graces On his church is
'Tis our God, who lives forever 'Mid the shining

path has trod; He is God from everlasting,
starry sky Is for us a place preparing,
pouring down; Who shall smite in holy vengeance
ones on high, In the glorious golden city,

And to everlasting God.
Where no tear can dim the eye.
All his foes beneath his throne.
Reigning everlastingly.

WILLIAM WALSHAM HOW, 1823-1897, ALT.

290 Word of God to Earth Descending
87 87

DRAKE'S BROUGHTON   EDWARD ELGAR, 1857–1934

1. Word of God to earth descending, With the Father present still,
Near his earthly journey's ending Hastes his mission to fulfill.

2. Well the traitor's kiss fore-knowing, Miracle of love divine,
See his hands himself bestowing In the hallowed Bread and Wine.

3. Holy body, blood all precious, Giv'n by him to be our food,
With them both he doth refresh us, Formed like him of flesh and blood.

4. Mighty Victim, earth's salvation,
Heav'n's own gate unfolding wide,
Help thy people in temptation,
Feed them from thy bleeding side.

5. Unto thee, the hidden manna,
Father, Spirit, unto thee,
Let us raise the loud hosanna,
And adoring bend the knee.

VERBUM SUPERNUM PRODIENS; THOMAS AQUINAS, 1227–1274
TR. BY ROBERT CAMPBELL, 1814–1868

291 Worship the Lord in the Beauty of Holiness
12 10 12 10

WAS LEBET WAS SCHWEBET   *Rheinhardt Manuscript*, Üttingen, 1754

1. Worship the Lord in the beauty of holiness; Bow down before him, his glory proclaim; Gold of obedience and incense of lowliness Bring, and adore him: the Lord is his name!

2. Low at his feet lay your burden of carefulness, High on his heart he will bear it for you, Comfort your sorrows, and answer your prayerfulness, Guiding your steps as may best be for you.

3. Fear not to enter his courts in the slenderness Of the poor wealth which is all that you own. Truth in its beauty and love in its tenderness, These are the off'rings to lay at his throne.

4. These though we bring them in trembling and fearfulness,
He will accept for the Name that is dear,
Mornings of joy give for evenings of tearfulness,
Trust for our trembling and hope for our fear.

5. Worship the Lord in the beauty of holiness;
Bow down before him, his glory proclaim;
Gold of obedience and incense of lowliness
Bring, and adore him: the Lord is his name!

John S. B. Monsell, 1811–1875, alt.

292   Ye Holy Angels Bright
66 66 88

DARWALL'S 148TH   JOHN DARWALL, 1731–1789

1. Ye holy angels bright, Who wait at God's right hand, Or through the realms of light Fly at your Lord's command, Assist our song, for else the theme Too high doth seem for mortal tongue.

2. Ye blessed souls at rest, Who ran this earthly race, And now, from sin released, Behold the Savior's face, God's praises sound, as in his sight With sweet delight ye do abound.

3. Ye saints, who toil below, Adore your heavenly King, And onward as ye go Some joyful anthem sing; Take what he gives and praise him still, Through good or ill, whoever lives.

4. My soul, bear thou thy part, Triumph in God above: And with a well-tuned heart Sing thou the songs of love; Let all thy days till life shall end, Whate'er he send, be filled with praise.

RICHARD BAXTER, 1615–1691, ALT.; HAMPDEN GURNEY, 1802–1862

293 Ye Watchers and Ye Holy Ones
88 88 WITH ALLELUIAS

LASST UNS ERFREUEN
GEISTLICHE KIRCHENGESÄNGE, COLOGNE, 1623
HARM. BY RALPH VAUGHAN WILLIAMS, 1872–1958

1. Ye watchers and ye holy ones, Bright seraphs, cherubim, and thrones, Raise the glad strain, Alleluia! Cry out, dominions, princedoms, powers, Virtues, archangels, angels' choirs: Alleluia! Alleluia! Alleluia! Alleluia! Alleluia!

2. O higher than the cherubim, More glorious than the seraphim, Lead their praises, Alleluia! Thou bearer of th'eternal Word, Most gracious, magnify the Lord: Alleluia! Alleluia! Alleluia! Alleluia! Alleluia!

3. Respond, ye souls in endless rest, Ye patriarchs and prophets blest, Alleluia! Alleluia! Ye holy twelve, ye martyrs strong, All saints triumphant, raise the song: Alleluia! Alleluia! Alleluia! Alleluia! Alleluia!

4. O friends, in gladness let us sing, Supernal anthems echoing, Alleluia! Alleluia! To God the Father, God the Son, And God the Spirit, Three in One: Alleluia! Alleluia! Alleluia! Alleluia! Alleluia!

J. ATHELSTAN RILEY, 1858–1947

294   Ye Who Own the Faith of Jesus
87 87 D

DAILY, DAILY   19TH CENT. FORM OF MARIA ZU LIEBEN

1. Ye who own the faith of Jesus, Sing the wonders that were done
When the love of God the Father O'er our sin the vic-t'ry won,
When he made the Virgin Mary Mother of his only Son.

2. Blessed were the chosen people Out of whom the Lord did come,
Blessed was the land of promise Fashioned for his earthly home;
But more blessed far the Mother She who bare him in her womb.

3. Wherefore let all faithful people Tell the honor of her name,
Let the Church, in her foreshadowed, Part in her thanksgiving claim;
What Christ's Mother sang in gladness Let Christ's people sing the same.

Hail Mary, Hail Mary, Hail Mary full of grace.

VICTOR STUCKEY STRATTON COLES, 1845–1929

295 Ye Who Own the Faith of Jesus
87 87 87 6

DEN DES VATERS SINN GEBOREN
JOHANN A. FREYLINGHAUSEN, 1670–1739
HARM. FROM *ZION HARFE*, 1855

1. Ye who own the faith of Jesus, Sing the wonders that were done When the love of God the Father O'er our sin the vict'ry won, When he made the Virgin Mary Mother of his only Son.
2. Blessed were the chosen people Out of whom the Lord did come, Blessed was the land of promise Fashioned for his earthly home; But more blessed far the Mother She who bare him in her womb. Hail, Mary, full of grace.
3. Wherefore let all faithful people Tell the honor of her name, Let the Church, in her foreshadowed, Part in her thanksgiving claim; What Christ's Mother sang in gladness Let Christ's people sing the same.

VICTOR STUCKEY STRATTON COLES, 1845–1929

INDICES

INDICES

I.	FIRST LINES WITH TUNES	320
II.	TUNES WITH FIRST LINES	326
III.	LITURGICAL	331
	PROPER OF SEASONS	331
	PROPER OF THE SAINTS	333
	COMMONS	333
	RITES	334
	MASSES FOR VARIOUS NEEDS AND OCCASIONS	335
IV.	TOPICAL	336
V.	METRICAL	342
VI.	SCRIPTURAL PASSAGES RELATED TO HYMNS	ONLINE

Online indices address for fast searching:

www.catholicbookofhymns.com/index/

I. INDEX OF FIRST LINES WITH TUNES

1	Abide With Me	EVENTIDE
2	Accept, Almighty Father	
3	All Glory, Laud, and Honor	ST. THEODULPH
4	All Hail the Power of Jesus' Name	CORONATION
5	All People That on Earth Do Dwell	OLD HUNDREDTH
6	All You Who Seek a Comfort Sure	KINGSFOLD
7	Alleluia! Alleluia! Hearts to Heaven	HYMN TO JOY
8	Alleluia! Alleluia! Let the Holy Anthem Rise	ALLELUIA! ALLELUIA!
9	Alleluia! Sing to Jesus	HYFRYDOL
10	Almighty God, Your Word Is Cast	DUNDEE
11	Angels From the Realms of Glory	REGENT SQUARE
12	Angels We Have Heard on High	GLORIA
13	As With Gladness Men of Old	DIX
14	At the Cross Her Station Keeping	STABAT MATER
15	At the Lamb's High Feast We Sing	SALZBURG
16	Ave Maria! Thou Virgin and Mother	
17	Away in a Manger	CRADLE SONG
18	Be Joyful, Mary	REGINA CAELI
19	Be Thou My Vision	SLANE
20	Beautiful Savior, Mightiest in Mercy	ST. RICHARD GWYN
21	Before the Day's Last Moments Fly	TE LUCIS ANTE TERMINUM
22	Bethlehem, of Noblest Cities	MERTON
23	Bethlehem, of Noblest Cities	STUTTGART
24	Bless Me, Befriend Me	
25	Blessed Jesus, at Thy Word	LIEBSTER JESU
26	Blest Guardian of All Virgin Souls	
27	Bread of the World	EUCHARISTIC HYMN
28	Bread of the World	RENDEZ Á DIEU
29	Bright the Vision That Delighted	LAUS DEO (Redhead)
30	Brightest and Best	LIEBSTER IMMANUEL
31	Brightest and Best	MORNING STAR
32	Bring Flowers of the Rarest	QUEEN OF THE ANGELS
33	By the Blood That Flowed From Thee	
34	By the First Bright Easter Day	MENDELSSOHN
35	Christ Is Made the Sure Foundation	WESTMINSTER ABBEY
36	Christ, the Fair Glory of the Holy Angels	CAELITES PLAUDANT
37	Christ, the Glory of the Sky	CULBACH
38	Christ, the Lord, Is Risen Today	EASTER HYMN
39	Christ, the Lord, Is Risen Today	LLANFAIR
40	Christ, the Lord, Is Risen Today	VICTIMAE PASCHALI
41	Christ, the True Light of Us	O AMOR QUAM EXSTATICUS
42	Come Down, O Love Divine	DOWN AMPNEY
43	Come, Holy Ghost, Creator Blest	LAMBILLOTTE
44	Come, Holy Ghost, Creator Blest	KOMM, GOTT SCHÖPFER
45	Come, Holy Ghost, Creator, Come	SOUTHWOLD
46	Come, Holy Ghost, Who Ever One	LUDBOROUGH
47	Come, Holy Ghost, Who Ever One	O JESU, MI DULCISSIME
48	Come, My Way, My Truth, My Life	THE CALL
49	Come, My Way, My Truth, My Life	TUNBRIDGE
50	Come, Thou Almighty King	ITALIAN HYMN
51	Come, Thou Holy Spirit, Come	VENI SANCTE SPIRITUS
52	Come, Thou Long-Expected Jesus	STUTTGART

53	Come, Ye Faithful, Raise the Strain	GAUDEAMUS PARITER
54	Come, Ye Thankful People, Come	ST. GEORGE'S WINDSOR
55	Comfort, Comfort Ye My People	GENEVAN 42
56	Creator of the Stars of Night	CONDITOR ALME SIDERUM
57	Cross of Jesus	CROSS OF JESUS
58	Crown Him With Many Crowns	DIADEMATA
59	Daily, Daily, Sing to Mary	DAILY, DAILY
60	Daughter of a Mighty Father	
61	Dear Angel! Ever at My Side	
62	Dear Guardian of Mary	
63	Deck Thyself, My Soul, With Gladness	SCHMÜCKE DICH
64	Down in Adoration Falling	ST. THOMAS (Wade)
65	Draw Near and Take the Body of the Lord	COENA DOMINI
66	Eternal Father, Strong to Save	MELITA
67	Fairest Lord Jesus	SCHÖNSTER HERR JESU
68	Fairest Lord Jesus	ST. ELIZABETH
69	Faith of Our Fathers	ST. CATHERINE
70	Faith of Our Fathers	SAWSTON
71	Faith of Our Fathers	
72	Father, See Thy Children	GHENT
73	Firmly I Believe and Truly	DRAKE'S BROUGHTON
74	Firmly I Believe and Truly	MERTON
75	For All the Saints	SINE NOMINE
76	For the Beauty of the Earth	DIX
77	Forty Days and Forty Nights	HEINLEIN
78	From All Thy Saints in Warfare	KING'S LYNN
79	From All Thy Saints in Warfare	ST. THEODULPH
80	From the Depths We Cry to Thee	HEINLEIN
81	Full in the Panting Heart of Rome	WISEMAN
82	Glorious Things of Thee Are Spoken	BEACH SPRING
83	Glory Be to Jesus	WEM IN LEIDENSTAGEN
84	God of Mercy and Compassion	AU SANG QU'UN DIEU
85	God of Our Fathers	NATIONAL HYMN
86	God Rest You Merry, Gentlemen	GOD REST YOU MERRY
87	Good Christian Men, Rejoice	IN DULCI JUBILO
88	Great Saint in Heaven	
89	Great Saint Joseph	
90	Guardian Angel! From Heaven So Bright	
91	Hail, Glorious Saint Patrick	
92	Hail, Holy Queen Enthroned Above	SALVE REGINA COELITUM
93	Hail, O Star That Pointest	AVE MARIS STELLA
94	Hail, Queen of Heaven	STELLA (English)
95	Hail the Day That Sees Him Rise	LLANFAIR
96	Hail, Thou Living Bread	
97	Hail to the Lord's Anointed	ELLACOMBE
98	Hail to the Lord's Anointed	ES FLOG EIN KLEINS WALDVÖGELEIN
99	Hail, Virgin, Dearest Mary	QUEEN OF MAY
100	Hark! A Herald Voice Is Sounding	MERTON
101	Hark, My Soul	SURGE
102	Hark! The Herald Angels Sing	MENDELSSOHN
103	Hark! The Sound of Holy Voices	MOULTRIE
104	Hear Thy Children, Gentle Jesus	
105	Hear Thy Children, Gentle Jesus	
106	Heart of Jesus, We Are Grateful	

107	Help, Lord, the Souls That Thou Hast Made	REQUIEM
108	Holy God, We Praise Thy Name	GROSSER GOTT
109	Holy, Holy, Holy	NICAEA
110	Holy, Holy Name of Jesus	
111	Holy Light on Earth's Horizon	BLAENWERN
112	Holy Spirit, Lord of Light	VENI SANCTE SPIRITUS
113	How Firm a Foundation	FOUNDATION
114	I Heard the Voice of Jesus Say	KINGSFOLD
115	I Know That My Redeemer Lives	DUKE STREET
116	I Sing the Mighty Power of God	ELLACOMBE
117	Immaculate Mary	LOURDES HYMN
118	Immortal, Invisible, God Only Wise	ST. DENIO
119	In His Temple Now Behold Him	ST. THOMAS (Wade)
120	In the Bleak Midwinter	CRANHAM
121	In This Sacrament, Sweet Jesus	
122	In This Sacrament, Sweet Jesus	
123	Infant Holy, Infant Lowly	W ŻŁOBIE LEŻY
124	It Came Upon the Midnight Clear	CAROL
125	It Is a Thing Most Wonderful	HERONGATE
126	Jerusalem, My Happy Home	LAND OF REST
127	Jesu! The Dying Day Hath Left Us Lonely	NOCTE SURGENTES
128	Jesus Christ Is Risen Today	EASTER HYMN
129	Jesus Christ Is Risen Today	EASTER HYMN (Monk)
130	Jesus, Jesus, Come to Me	
131	Jesus, Keep Me Close to Thee	
132	Jesus, My Lord, My God, My All	SWEET SACRAMENT
133	Jesus, My Lord, My God, My All	SAWSTON
134	Jesus, the Very Thought of Thee	ST. AGNES
135	Jesus, Thou Art Coming	
136	Jesus, Thou Art Coming	
137	Joy to the World	ANTIOCH
138	Joyful, Joyful, We Adore Thee	HYMN TO JOY
139	King of Kings Is He Anointed	
140	Lead, Kindly Light	SANDON
141	Let Thy Blood in Mercy Poured	JESUS MEINE ZUVERSICHT
142	Lift Up Your Heads	TRURO
143	Light of All Days	TALLIS' CANON
144	Lo, He Comes With Clouds Descending	HELMSLEY
145	Lo, He Comes With Clouds Descending	ST. THOMAS (Wade)
146	Lo, How a Rose E'er Blooming	ES IST EIN' ROS' ENTSPRUNGEN
147	Lo! Round the Throne	ERSCHIENEN IST DER HERRLICH TAG
148	Long Live the Pope!	PAPAL HYMN
149	Look, Ye Saints! The Sight Is Glorious	BRYN CALFARIA
150	Lord, Accept the Gifts We Offer	BRYNTIRION
151	Lord, Enthroned in Heavenly Splendor	ST. HELEN
152	Lord, for Tomorrow and Its Needs	PROVIDENCE
153	Lord Jesus, Think on Me	SOUTHWELL
154	Lord Jesus, When I Think of Thee	WORD OF FIRE
155	Lord, Who at Cana's Wedding Feast	
156	Lord, Who at Thy First Eucharist	UNDE ET MEMORES
157	Lord, Who Throughout These Forty Days	ST. FLAVIAN
158	Love Divine, All Loves Excelling	BLAENWERN
159	Love Divine, All Loves Excelling	HYFRYDOL

160	Maiden Mother, Meek and Mild	ORIENTIS PARTIBUS
161	Michael, Prince of Highest Heaven	
162	Mother Dear, O Pray for Me	CATHOLIC HARP
163	Mother Dearest, Mother Fairest	
164	Mother of Christ	MOTHER OF CHRIST
165	My God, Accept My Heart This Day	
166	My Song Is Love Unknown	LOVE UNKNOWN
167	My Soul Doth Long for Thee	
168	Now, My Tongue, the Mystery Telling	DOWLING
169	Now, My Tongue, the Mystery Telling	GRAFTON
170	Now Thank We All Our God	NUN DANKET
171	Now That the Day-Star Glimmers Bright	FARRANT
172	O Blessed Saint Joseph	MARIA ZU LIEBEN
173	O Breathe on Me, O Breath of God	ST. COLUMBA (Irish)
174	O Christ, Our Hope	LOBT GOTT, IHR CHRISTEN
175	O Christ, the Heavens' Eternal King	CHURCH TRIUMPHANT
176	O Come, All Ye Faithful	ADESTE FIDELES
177	O Come and Mourn With Me Awhile	ST. CROSS
178	O Come and Mourn With Me Awhile	
179	O Come and Mourn With Me Awhile	
180	O Come, Divine Messiah	VENEZ, DIVIN MESSIE
181	O Come, Little Children	IHR KINDERLEIN, KOMMET
182	O Come, O Come, Emmanuel	VENI EMMANUEL
183	O Day of Rest and Gladness	ES FLOG EIN KLEINS WALDVÖGELEIN
184	O Food to Pilgrims Given	INNSBRUCK
185	O for a Thousand Tongues to Sing	AZMON
186	O God, Our Help in Ages Past	ST. ANNE
187	O Godhead Hid, Devoutly I Adore Thee	AQUINAS
188	O Jesus Christ, Remember	AURELIA
189	O Jesus Christ, Remember	
190	O Jesus, King Most Wonderful	ST. ANNE
191	O Kind Creator, Bow Thine Ear	TALLIS' CANON
192	O Little Town of Bethlehem	FOREST GREEN
193	O Little Town of Bethlehem	ST. LOUIS
194	O Lord, I Am Not Worthy	NON DIGNUS
195	O Praise Ye the Lord	LAUDATE DOMINUM
196	O Purest of Creatures	MARIA ZU LIEBEN
197	O Queen of the Holy Rosary	ACH GOTT VOM HIMMELREICHE
198	O Queen of the Holy Rosary	ELLACOMBE
199	O Sacrament Most Holy	O SACRAMENT MOST HOLY
200	O Sacred Head, Surrounded	PASSION CHORALE
201	O Sacred Heart	LAURENCE
202	O Sacred Heart, O Love Divine	
203	O Sacred Heart, What Shall I Render Thee	
204	O Salutaris Hostia	DUGUET
205	O Salutaris Hostia	WERNER
206	O Sanctissima	SICILIAN MARINERS
207	O Saving Victim	DUGUET
208	O Saving Victim	HERR JESU CHRIST
209	O Saving Victim	WERNER
210	O Splendor of God's Glory Bright	PUER NOBIS NASCITUR
211	O Star, for Whose Pure Light	FARLEY CASTLE
212	O Strength and Stay	STRENGTH AND STAY
213	O Trinity of Blessed Light	BROMLEY
214	O Trinity of Blessed Light	DANBY
215	O What Their Joy and Their Glory Must Be	O QUANTA QUALIA

216	O Wondrous Sight! O Vision Fair	WAREHAM
217	O Word of God Incarnate	MUNICH
218	O Worship the King	HANOVER
219	On Jordan's Bank	WINCHESTER NEW
220	On This Day, O Beautiful Mother	BEAUTIFUL MOTHER
221	On This Day, the First of Days	LÜBECK
222	Once in Royal David's City	IRBY
223	Only-Begotten, Word of God Eternal	ISTE CONFESSOR
224	Panis Angelicus	SACRIS SOLEMNIIS
225	Praise God! Who in His Grace	
226	Praise, My Soul, the King of Heaven	LAUDA ANIMA
227	Praise to the Holiest in the Height	BILLING
228	Praise to the Lord	LOBE DEN HERREN
229	Raise Your Voices, Vales and Mountains	
230	Rejoice, Rejoice, Believers	LLANGLOFFAN
231	Rejoice, the Lord Is King	DARWALL'S 148TH
232	Ride On, Ride On in Majesty	WINCHESTER NEW
233	Round the Lord in Glory Seated	RUSTINGTON
234	Savior of the Nations, Come	NUN KOMM DER HEIDEN HEILAND
235	See, Amid the Winter's Snow	CHRISTMAS MORN
236	See, Amid the Winter's Snow	
237	See the Conqueror Mounts in Triumph	REX GLORIAE
238	Silent Night	STILLE NACHT
239	Sing, My Soul, His Wondrous Love	ST. BEES
240	Sing Praise to God Who Reigns Above	MIT FREUDEN ZART
241	Sing Praise to the Lord	LAUDATE DOMINUM
242	Sing We Triumphant Hymns of Praise	LASST UNS ERFREUEN
243	Sing With All the Saints in Glory	RUSTINGTON
244	Songs of Thankfulness and Praise	SALZBURG
245	Soul of My Savior	ANIMA CHRISTI
246	Soul of My Savior	
247	Sweet Heart of Jesus	
248	Sweet Sacrament Divine	DIVINE MYSTERIES
249	Sweet Savior, Bless Us Ere We Go	SUNSET
250	Take Up Your Cross	BRESLAU
251	Take Up Your Cross	ERHALT UNS, HERR
252	Tantum Ergo	ST. THOMAS (Wade)
253	Tantum Ergo	UNSER HERRSCHER
254	The Advent of Our King	ST. THOMAS (Williams)
255	The Angel Gabriel	GABRIEL'S MESSAGE
256	The Church's One Foundation	AURELIA
257	The Day of Resurrection	CHARTRES
258	The Day of Resurrection	ELLACOMBE
259	The Day of Resurrection	LANCASHIRE
260	The Fiery Sun Now Rolls Away	ANGELUS
261	The First Noël	THE FIRST NOWELL
262	The Glory of These Forty Days	ERHALT UNS, HERR
263	The God of Abraham Praise	LEONI
264	The King of Love	ST. COLUMBA (Irish)
265	The Strife Is O'er	VICTORY
266	The Sun Is Shining Brightly	
267	The Sun Is Sinking Fast	ST. COLUMBA (Irons)
268	There Is a Green Hill Far Away	HORSLEY
269	There's a Wideness in God's Mercy	GOTT WILL'S MACHEN

270	There's a Wideness in God's Mercy	IN BABILONE
271	Through the Red Sea	STRAF MICH NICHT
272	'Tis Good, Lord, to Be Here	SWABIA
273	'Tis the Month of Our Mother	
274	To Jesus' Heart All Burning	COR JESU
275	Virgin-Born, We Bow Before Thee	MON DIEU PRETE-MOI L'OREILLE
276	Virgin-Born, We Bow Before Thee	QUEM PASTORES
277	Wake, Awake, for Night Is Flying	WACHET AUF
278	Watchman, Tell Us of the Night	ABERYSTWYTH
279	What Child Is This	GREENSLEEVES
280	What Star Is This	PUER NOBIS NASCITUR
281	Whate'er Our God Ordains Is Right	WAS GOTT TUT
282	When I Survey the Wondrous Cross	HAMBURG
283	When I Survey the Wondrous Cross	ROCKINGHAM
284	When Morning Gilds the Skies	LAUDES DOMINI
285	When the Patriarch Was Returning	ALL SAINTS
286	When the Patriarch Was Returning	
287	Who Are These Like Stars Appearing	ALL SAINTS
288	Who Is This, So Weak and Helpless	EBENEZER (Williams)
289	Who Is This, So Weak and Helpless	EIFIONYDD
290	Word of God to Earth Descending	DRAKE'S BROUGHTON
291	Worship the Lord in the Beauty of Holiness	WAS LEBET WAS SCHWEBET
292	Ye Holy Angels Bright	DARWALL'S 148TH
293	Ye Watchers and Ye Holy Ones	LASST UNS ERFREUEN
294	Ye Who Own the Faith of Jesus	DAILY, DAILY
295	Ye Who Own the Faith of Jesus	DEN DES VATERS SINN GEBOREN

II. INDEX OF TUNES AND FIRST LINES

278	ABERYSTWYTH	Watchman, Tell Us of the Night
197	ACH GOTT VOM HIMMELREICHE	O Queen of the Holy Rosary
176	ADESTE FIDELES	O Come, All Ye Faithful
285	ALL SAINTS	When the Patriarch Was Returning
287	ALL SAINTS	Who Are These Like Stars Appearing
8	ALLELUIA! ALLELUIA!	Alleluia! Alleluia! Let the Holy Anthem Rise
260	ANGELUS	The Fiery Sun Now Rolls Away
245	ANIMA CHRISTI	Soul of My Savior
137	ANTIOCH	Joy to the World
187	AQUINAS	O Godhead Hid, Devoutly I Adore Thee
84	AU SANG QU'UN DIEU	God of Mercy and Compassion
188	AURELIA	O Jesus Christ, Remember
256	AURELIA	The Church's One Foundation
93	AVE MARIS STELLA	Hail, O Star That Pointest
185	AZMON	O for a Thousand Tongues to Sing
82	BEACH SPRING	Glorious Things of Thee Are Spoken
220	BEAUTIFUL MOTHER	On This Day, O Beautiful Mother
227	BILLING	Praise to the Holiest in the Height
111	BLAENWERN	Holy Light on Earth's Horizon
158	BLAENWERN	Love Divine, All Loves Excelling
250	BRESLAU	Take Up Your Cross
213	BROMLEY	O Trinity of Blessed Light
149	BRYN CALFARIA	Look, Ye Saints! The Sight Is Glorious
150	BRYNTIRION	Lord, Accept the Gifts We Offer
36	CAELITES PLAUDANT	Christ, the Fair Glory of the Holy Angels
124	CAROL	It Came Upon the Midnight Clear
162	CATHOLIC HARP	Mother Dear, O Pray for Me
257	CHARTRES	The Day of Resurrection
235	CHRISTMAS MORN	See, Amid the Winter's Snow
175	CHURCH TRIUMPHANT	O Christ, the Heavens' Eternal King
65	COENA DOMINI	Draw Near and Take the Body of the Lord
56	CONDITOR ALME SIDERUM	Creator of the Stars of Night
274	COR JESU	To Jesus' Heart All Burning
4	CORONATION	All Hail the Power of Jesus' Name
17	CRADLE SONG	Away in a Manger
120	CRANHAM	In the Bleak Midwinter
57	CROSS OF JESUS	Cross of Jesus
37	CULBACH	Christ, the Glory of the Sky
59	DAILY, DAILY	Daily, Daily, Sing to Mary
294	DAILY, DAILY	Ye Who Own the Faith of Jesus
214	DANBY	O Trinity of Blessed Light
231	DARWALL'S 148TH	Rejoice, the Lord Is King
292	DARWALL'S 148TH	Ye Holy Angels Bright
295	DEN DES VATERS SINN GEBOREN	Ye Who Own the Faith of Jesus
58	DIADEMATA	Crown Him With Many Crowns
248	DIVINE MYSTERIES	Sweet Sacrament Divine
13	DIX	As With Gladness Men of Old
76	DIX	For the Beauty of the Earth
168	DOWLING	Now, My Tongue, the Mystery Telling
42	DOWN AMPNEY	Come Down, O Love Divine
73	DRAKE'S BROUGHTON	Firmly I Believe and Truly

326 • A CATHOLIC BOOK OF HYMNS

290	DRAKE'S BROUGHTON	Word of God to Earth Descending
204	DUGUET	O Salutaris Hostia
207	DUGUET	O Saving Victim
115	DUKE STREET	I Know That My Redeemer Lives
10	DUNDEE	Almighty God, Your Word Is Cast
38	EASTER HYMN	Christ, the Lord, Is Risen Today
128	EASTER HYMN	Jesus Christ Is Risen Today
129	EASTER HYMN (Monk)	Jesus Christ Is Risen Today
288	EBENEZER (Williams)	Who Is This, So Weak and Helpless
289	EIFIONYDD	Who Is This, So Weak and Helpless
97	ELLACOMBE	Hail to the Lord's Anointed
116	ELLACOMBE	I Sing the Mighty Power of God
198	ELLACOMBE	O Queen of the Holy Rosary
258	ELLACOMBE	The Day of Resurrection
251	ERHALT UNS, HERR	Take Up Your Cross
262	ERHALT UNS, HERR	The Glory of These Forty Days
147	ERSCHIENEN IST DER HERRLICH TAG	Lo! Round the Throne
98	ES FLOG EIN KLEINS WALDVÖGELEIN	Hail to the Lord's Anointed
183	ES FLOG EIN KLEINS WALDVÖGELEIN	O Day of Rest and Gladness
146	ES IST EIN' ROS' ENTSPRUNGEN	Lo, How a Rose E'er Blooming
27	EUCHARISTIC HYMN	Bread of the World
1	EVENTIDE	Abide With Me
211	FARLEY CASTLE	O Star, for Whose Pure Light
171	FARRANT	Now That the Day-Star Glimmers Bright
192	FOREST GREEN	O Little Town of Bethlehem
113	FOUNDATION	How Firm a Foundation
255	GABRIEL'S MESSAGE	The Angel Gabriel
53	GAUDEAMUS PARITER	Come, Ye Faithful, Raise the Strain
55	GENEVAN 42	Comfort, Comfort Ye My People
72	GHENT	Father, See Thy Children
12	GLORIA	Angels We Have Heard on High
86	GOD REST YOU MERRY	God Rest You Merry, Gentlemen
269	GOTT WILL'S MACHEN	There's a Wideness in God's Mercy
169	GRAFTON	Now, My Tongue, the Mystery Telling
279	GREENSLEEVES	What Child Is This
108	GROSSER GOTT	Holy God, We Praise Thy Name
282	HAMBURG	When I Survey the Wondrous Cross
218	HANOVER	O Worship the King
77	HEINLEIN	Forty Days and Forty Nights
80	HEINLEIN	From the Depths We Cry to Thee
144	HELMSLEY	Lo, He Comes With Clouds Descending
125	HERONGATE	It Is a Thing Most Wonderful
208	HERR JESU CHRIST	O Saving Victim
268	HORSLEY	There Is a Green Hill Far Away
9	HYFRYDOL	Alleluia! Sing to Jesus
159	HYFRYDOL	Love Divine, All Loves Excelling
7	HYMN TO JOY	Alleluia! Alleluia! Hearts to Heaven
138	HYMN TO JOY	Joyful, Joyful, We Adore Thee
181	IHR KINDERLEIN, KOMMET	O Come, Little Children
270	IN BABILONE	There's a Wideness in God's Mercy
87	IN DULCI JUBILO	Good Christian Men, Rejoice
184	INNSBRUCK	O Food to Pilgrims Given
222	IRBY	Once in Royal David's City

223	ISTE CONFESSOR	Only-Begotten, Word of God Eternal
50	ITALIAN HYMN	Come, Thou Almighty King
141	JESUS MEINE ZUVERSICHT	Let Thy Blood in Mercy Poured
78	KING'S LYNN	From All Thy Saints in Warfare
6	KINGSFOLD	All You Who Seek a Comfort Sure
114	KINGSFOLD	I Heard the Voice of Jesus Say
44	KOMM, GOTT SCHÖPFER	Come, Holy Ghost, Creator Blest
43	LAMBILLOTTE	Come, Holy Ghost, Creator Blest
259	LANCASHIRE	The Day of Resurrection
126	LAND OF REST	Jerusalem, My Happy Home
242	LASST UNS ERFREUEN	Sing We Triumphant Hymns of Praise
293	LASST UNS ERFREUEN	Ye Watchers and Ye Holy Ones
226	LAUDA ANIMA	Praise, My Soul, the King of Heaven
195	LAUDATE DOMINUM	O Praise Ye the Lord
241	LAUDATE DOMINUM	Sing Praise to the Lord
284	LAUDES DOMINI	When Morning Gilds the Skies
201	LAURENCE	O Sacred Heart
29	LAUS DEO (Redhead)	Bright the Vision That Delighted
263	LEONI	The God of Abraham Praise
30	LIEBSTER IMMANUEL	Brightest and Best
25	LIEBSTER JESU	Blessed Jesus, at Thy Word
39	LLANFAIR	Christ, the Lord, Is Risen Today
95	LLANFAIR	Hail the Day That Sees Him Rise
230	LLANGLOFFAN	Rejoice, Rejoice, Believers
228	LOBE DEN HERREN	Praise to the Lord
174	LOBT GOTT, IHR CHRISTEN	O Christ, Our Hope
117	LOURDES HYMN	Immaculate Mary
166	LOVE UNKNOWN	My Song Is Love Unknown
221	LÜBECK	On This Day, the First of Days
46	LUDBOROUGH	Come, Holy Ghost, Who Ever One
172	MARIA ZU LIEBEN	O Blessed Saint Joseph
196	MARIA ZU LIEBEN	O Purest of Creatures
66	MELITA	Eternal Father, Strong to Save
34	MENDELSSOHN	By the First Bright Easter Day
102	MENDELSSOHN	Hark! The Herald Angels Sing
22	MERTON	Bethlehem, of Noblest Cities
74	MERTON	Firmly I Believe and Truly
100	MERTON	Hark! A Herald Voice Is Sounding
240	MIT FREUDEN ZART	Sing Praise to God Who Reigns Above
275	MON DIEU PRETE-MOI L'OREILLE	Virgin-Born, We Bow Before Thee
31	MORNING STAR	Brightest and Best
164	MOTHER OF CHRIST	Mother of Christ
103	MOULTRIE	Hark! The Sound of Holy Voices
217	MUNICH	O Word of God Incarnate
85	NATIONAL HYMN	God of Our Fathers
109	NICAEA	Holy, Holy, Holy
127	NOCTE SURGENTES	Jesu! The Dying Day Hath Left Us Lonely
194	NON DIGNUS	O Lord, I Am Not Worthy
170	NUN DANKET	Now Thank We All Our God
234	NUN KOMM DER HEIDEN HEILAND	Savior of the Nations, Come
41	O AMOR QUAM EXSTATICUS	Christ, the True Light of Us
47	O JESU, MI DULCISSIME	Come, Holy Ghost, Who Ever One

215	O QUANTA QUALIA	O What Their Joy and Their Glory Must Be
199	O SACRAMENT MOST HOLY	O Sacrament Most Holy
5	OLD HUNDREDTH	All People That on Earth Do Dwell
160	ORIENTIS PARTIBUS	Maiden Mother, Meek and Mild
148	PAPAL HYMN	Long Live the Pope!
200	PASSION CHORALE	O Sacred Head, Surrounded
152	PROVIDENCE	Lord, for Tomorrow and Its Needs
210	PUER NOBIS NASCITUR	O Splendor of God's Glory Bright
280	PUER NOBIS NASCITUR	What Star Is This
99	QUEEN OF MAY	Hail, Virgin, Dearest Mary
32	QUEEN OF THE ANGELS	Bring Flowers of the Rarest
276	QUEM PASTORES	Virgin-Born, We Bow Before Thee
11	REGENT SQUARE	Angels From the Realms of Glory
18	REGINA CAELI	Be Joyful, Mary
28	RENDEZ Á DIEU	Bread of the World
107	REQUIEM	Help, Lord, the Souls That Thou Hast Made
237	REX GLORIAE	See the Conqueror Mounts in Triumph
283	ROCKINGHAM	When I Survey the Wondrous Cross
233	RUSTINGTON	Round the Lord in Glory Seated
243	RUSTINGTON	Sing With All the Saints in Glory
224	SACRIS SOLEMNIIS	Panis Angelicus
92	SALVE REGINA COELITUM	Hail, Holy Queen Enthroned Above
15	SALZBURG	At the Lamb's High Feast We Sing
244	SALZBURG	Songs of Thankfulness and Praise
140	SANDON	Lead, Kindly Light
70	SAWSTON	Faith of Our Fathers
133	SAWSTON	Jesus, My Lord, My God, My All
63	SCHMÜCKE DICH	Deck Thyself, My Soul, With Gladness
67	SCHÖNSTER HERR JESU	Fairest Lord Jesus
206	SICILIAN MARINERS	O Sanctissima
75	SINE NOMINE	For All the Saints
19	SLANE	Be Thou My Vision
153	SOUTHWELL	Lord Jesus, Think on Me
45	SOUTHWOLD	Come, Holy Ghost, Creator, Come
134	ST. AGNES	Jesus, the Very Thought of Thee
186	ST. ANNE	O God, Our Help in Ages Past
190	ST. ANNE	O Jesus, King Most Wonderful
239	ST. BEES	Sing, My Soul, His Wondrous Love
69	ST. CATHERINE	Faith of Our Fathers
173	ST. COLUMBA (Irish)	O Breathe on Me, O Breath of God
264	ST. COLUMBA (Irish)	The King of Love
267	ST. COLUMBA (Irons)	The Sun Is Sinking Fast
177	ST. CROSS	O Come and Mourn With Me Awhile
118	ST. DENIO	Immortal, Invisible, God Only Wise
68	ST. ELIZABETH	Fairest Lord Jesus
157	ST. FLAVIAN	Lord, Who Throughout These Forty Days
54	ST. GEORGE'S WINDSOR	Come, Ye Thankful People, Come
151	ST. HELEN	Lord, Enthroned in Heavenly Splendor
193	ST. LOUIS	O Little Town of Bethlehem
20	ST. RICHARD GWYN	Beautiful Savior, Mightiest in Mercy
3	ST. THEODULPH	All Glory, Laud, and Honor
79	ST. THEODULPH	From All Thy Saints in Warfare
64	ST. THOMAS (Wade)	Down in Adoration Falling
119	ST. THOMAS (Wade)	In His Temple Now Behold Him

145	ST. THOMAS (Wade)	Lo, He Comes With Clouds Descending
252	ST. THOMAS (Wade)	Tantum Ergo
254	ST. THOMAS (Williams)	The Advent of Our King
14	STABAT MATER	At the Cross Her Station Keeping
94	STELLA (English)	Hail, Queen of Heaven
238	STILLE NACHT	Silent Night
271	STRAF MICH NICHT	Through the Red Sea
212	STRENGTH AND STAY	O Strength and Stay
23	STUTTGART	Bethlehem, of Noblest Cities
52	STUTTGART	Come, Thou Long-Expected Jesus
249	SUNSET	Sweet Savior, Bless Us Ere We Go
101	SURGE	Hark, My Soul
272	SWABIA	'Tis Good, Lord, to Be Here
132	SWEET SACRAMENT	Jesus, My Lord, My God, My All
143	TALLIS' CANON	Light of All Days
191	TALLIS' CANON	O Kind Creator, Bow Thine Ear
21	TE LUCIS ANTE TERMINUM	Before the Day's Last Moments Fly
48	THE CALL	Come, My Way, My Truth, My Life
261	THE FIRST NOWELL	The First Noël
142	TRURO	Lift Up Your Heads
49	TUNBRIDGE	Come, My Way, My Truth, My Life
156	UNDE ET MEMORES	Lord, Who at Thy First Eucharist
253	UNSER HERRSCHER	Tantum Ergo
180	VENEZ, DIVIN MESSIE	O Come, Divine Messiah
182	VENI EMMANUEL	O Come, O Come, Emmanuel
51	VENI SANCTE SPIRITUS	Come, Thou Holy Spirit, Come
112	VENI SANCTE SPIRITUS	Holy Spirit, Lord of Light
40	VICTIMAE PASCHALI	Christ, the Lord, Is Risen Today
265	VICTORY	The Strife Is O'er
123	W ŻŁOBIE LEŻY	Infant Holy, Infant Lowly
277	WACHET AUF	Wake, Awake, for Night Is Flying
216	WAREHAM	O Wondrous Sight! O Vision Fair
281	WAS GOTT TUT	Whate'er Our God Ordains Is Right
291	WAS LEBET WAS SCHWEBET	Worship the Lord in the Beauty of Holiness
83	WEM IN LEIDENSTAGEN	Glory Be to Jesus
205	WERNER	O Salutaris Hostia
209	WERNER	O Saving Victim
35	WESTMINSTER ABBEY	Christ Is Made the Sure Foundation
219	WINCHESTER NEW	On Jordan's Bank
232	WINCHESTER NEW	Ride On, Ride On in Majesty
81	WISEMAN	Full in the Panting Heart of Rome
154	WORD OF FIRE	Lord Jesus, When I Think of Thee

III. LITURGICAL INDEX
PROPER OF SEASONS

Advent Season

52	Come, Thou Long-Expected Jesus
55	Comfort, Comfort Ye My People
56	Creator of the Stars of Night
97-98	Hail to the Lord's Anointed
100	Hark! A Herald Voice Is Sounding
142	Lift Up Your Heads
180	O Come, Divine Messiah
182	O Come, O Come, Emmanuel
219	On Jordan's Bank
234	Savior of the Nations, Come
254	The Advent of Our King
277	Wake, Awake, for Night Is Flying
278	Watchman, Tell Us of the Night

Christmas Season

11	Angels, From the Realms of Glory
12	Angels We Have Heard on High
17	Away in a Manger
102	Hark! The Herald Angels Sing
120	In the Bleak Midwinter
124	It Came Upon the Midnight Clear
137	Joy to the World
176	O Come, All Ye Faithful
181	O Come, Little Children
192-193	O Little Town of Bethlehem
222	Once in Royal David's City
235-236	See, Amid the Winter's Snow
238	Silent Night
261	The First Noël
279	What Child Is This

Holy Family

222	Once in Royal David's City
See also	CHRISTMAS SEASON

Mary, Mother of God

16	Ave Maria! Thou Virgin and Mother
60	Daughter of a Mighty Father
93	Hail, O Star That Pointest
222	Once in Royal David's City
See also	CHRISTMAS SEASON

Epiphany

13	As With Gladness Men of Old
30-31	Brightest and Best
See also	CHRISTMAS SEASON

Baptism of the Lord

244	Songs of Thankfulness and Praise

Lenten Season

14	At the Cross Her Station Keeping
33	By the Blood That Flowed From Thee
57	Cross of Jesus
77	Forty Days and Forty Nights
80	From the Depths We Cry to Thee
157	Lord, Who Throughout These Forty Days
177-179	O Come and Mourn With Me Awhile
191	O Kind Creator, Bow Thine Ear
200	O Sacred Head, Surrounded
250-251	Take Up Your Cross
262	The Glory of These Forty Days
269-270	There's a Wideness in God's Mercy
282-283	When I Survey the Wondrous Cross

Holy Week

See	GOOD FRIDAY
	HOLY THURSDAY
	LENTEN SEASON
	PASSION SUNDAY

Passion Sunday (Palm Sunday)

15	At the Lamb's High Feast We Sing
33	By the Blood That Flowed From Thee
58	Crown Him With Many Crowns
142	Lift Up Your Heads
200	O Sacred Head, Surrounded
232	Ride On, Ride On in Majesty
See also	GOOD FRIDAY

Holy Thursday (Chrism Mass)

35	Christ Is Made the Sure Foundation
256	The Church's One Foundation

Holy Thursday
(Evening Mass of the Lord's Supper)

See	HOLY COMMUNION
	HOLY WEEK

Good Friday

6	All You Who Seek a Comfort Sure
200	O Sacred Head, Surrounded
268	There Is a Green Hill Far Away
282-283	When I Survey the Wondrous Cross

Easter Season

7	Alleluia! Alleluia! Hearts to Heaven
8	Alleluia! Alleluia! Let the Holy Anthem Rise
15	At the Lamb's High Feast We Sing
34	By the First Bright Easter Day

38-40	Christ, the Lord, Is Risen Today		*Christ the King*
53	Come, Ye Faithful, Raise the Strain	3	All Glory, Laud, and Honor
58	Crown Him With Many Crowns	4	All Hail the Power of Jesus' Name
115	I Know That My Redeemer Lives	9	Alleluia! Sing to Jesus
128-129	Jesus Christ Is Risen Today	58	Crown Him With Many Crowns
151	Lord, Enthroned in Heavenly Splendor	97-98	Hail to the Lord's Anointed
242	Sing We Triumphant Hymns of Praise	101	Hark, My Soul
257-259	The Day of Resurrection	139	King of Kings Is He Anointed
271	Through the Red Sea	142	Lift Up Your Heads
285-286	When the Patriarch Was Returning	174	O Christ, Our Hope
293	Ye Watchers and Ye Holy Ones	175	O Christ, the Heavens' Eternal King
		190	O Jesus, King Most Wonderful
	Ascension	218	O Worship the King
9	Alleluia! Sing to Jesus	231	Rejoice, the Lord Is King
58	Crown Him With Many Crowns	237	See the Conqueror Mounts in Triumph
95	Hail the Day That Sees Him Rise		
174	O Christ, Our Hope		*Corpus Christi*
231	Rejoice, the Lord Is King	9	Alleluia! Sing to Jesus!
242	Sing We Triumphant Hymns of Praise	65	Draw Near and Take the Body of the Lord
		83	Glory Be to Jesus
	Pentecost	207-209	O Saving Victim
42	Come Down, O Love Divine	*See also*	HOLY COMMUNION
43-44	Come, Holy Ghost, Creator Blest		
45	Come, Holy Ghost, Creator, Come		
46-47	Come, Holy Ghost, Who Ever One		
51	Come, Thou Holy Spirit, Come		
173	O Breathe on Me, O Breath of God		
210	O Splendor of God's Glory Bright		
See also	CONFIRMATION		

Ordinary Time

See TOPICAL INDEX

Solemnities of the Lord in Ordinary Time

Trinity Sunday

25	Blessed Jesus, at Thy Word
50	Come, Thou Almighty King
73-74	Firmly I Believe and Truly
103	Hark! The Sound of Holy Voices
109	Holy, Holy, Holy
183	O Day of Rest and Gladness
211	O Star, for Those Whose Pure Light
213-214	O Trinity of Blessed Light
221	On This Day, the First of Days

Sacred Heart

6	All You Who Seek a Comfort Sure
83	Glory Be to Jesus
114	I Heard the Voice of Jesus Say
158-159	Love Divine, All Loves Excelling
201	O Sacred Heart
202	O Sacred Heart, O Love Divine
203	O Sacred Heart, What Shall I Render Thee
245-246	Soul of My Savior

PROPER OF THE SAINTS

Immaculate Conception (8 December)
117 Immaculate Mary

Presentation of the Lord (2 February)
119 In His Temple Now Behold Him

Annunciation (25 March)
92 Hail, Holy Queen Enthroned Above
94 Hail, Queen of Heaven
196 O Purest of Creatures
255 The Angel Gabriel

Birth of John the Baptist (24 June)
55 Comfort, Comfort Ye My People
219 On Jordan's Bank

Assumption (15 August)
117 Immaculate Mary

Triumph of the Cross (14 September)
57 Cross of Jesus
174 O Christ, Our Hope
282-283 When I Survey the Wondrous Cross

All Saints (1 November)
69-71 Faith of Our Fathers
75 For All the Saints
103 Hark! The Sound of Holy Voices
147 Lo! Round the Throne
233 Round the Lord in Glory Seated
243 Sing with All the Saints in Glory
287 Who Are These Like Stars Appearing

All Souls (2 November)
69-71 Faith of Our Fathers
75 For All the Saints
115 I Know That My Redeemer Lives
287 Who Are These Like Stars Appearing

COMMONS

Common of the Dedication of a Church

35 Christ Is Made the Sure Foundation
225 Praise God! Who in His Grace
256 The Church's One Foundation

Common of the Blessed Virgin Mary

16 Ave Maria! Thou Virgin and Mother
92 Hail, Holy Queen Enthroned Above
94 Hail, Queen of Heaven
111 Holy Light on Earth's Horizon
117 Immaculate Mary
196 O Purest of Creatures

Common of Apostles

69-71 Faith of Our Fathers
103 Hark! The Sound of Holy Voices
215 O What Their Joy and Their Glory Must Be
233 Round the Lord in Glory Seated
287 Who Are These Like Stars Appearing

Common of Martyrs

69-71 Faith of Our Fathers
75 For All the Saints
103 Hark! The Sound of Holy Voices
215 O What Their Joy and Their Glory Must Be
233 Round the Lord in Glory Seated
287 Who Are These Like Stars Appearing

Common of Pastors

264 The King of Love

Common of Doctors of the Church

75 For All the Saints

Common of Virgins

See also ALL SAINTS (NOVEMBER 1)
COMMON OF MARTYRS

Common of Holy Men and Women

See also ALL SAINTS (NOVEMBER 1)

RITES

Baptism for Children

- 35   Christ Is Made the Sure Foundation
- 256   The Church's One Foundation

See also   EASTER SEASON
               ALL SAINTS

Christian Initiation of Adults

- 35   Christ Is Made the Sure Foundation
- 256   The Church's One Foundation

See also   EASTER SEASON
               CONFIRMATION
               HOLY COMMUNION
               ALL SAINTS

Confirmation

- 112   Holy Spirit, Lord of Light
- 256   The Church's One Foundation

See also   PENTECOST
               ALL SAINTS

Funerals

- 115   I Know That My Redeemer Lives
- 126   Jerusalem, My Happy Home
- 264   The King of Love

See also   ALL SOULS
               EASTER SEASON

Liturgy of the Hours

Office of Readings

- 10   Almighty God, Your Word Is Cast
- 25   Blessed Jesus, at Thy Word
- 143   Light of All Days

Morning Prayer

- 171   Now That the Day-Star Glimmers Bright
- 284   When Morning Gilds the Skies

Evening Prayer

- 1   Abide With Me
- 16   Ave Maria! Thou Virgin and Mother

Night Prayer

- 21   Before the Day's Last Moments Fly
- 127   Jesu! The Dying Day Hath Left Us Lonely
- 140   Lead, Kindly Light
- 260   The Fiery Sun Now Rolls Away
- 267   The Sun Is Sinking Fast
- 272   'Tis Good, Lord, to Be Here

See also   PROPER OF SEASONS
               PROPER OF SAINTS
               COMMONS
               TOPICAL INDEX: PRAISE

Worship of the Eucharist outside Mass

- 108   Holy God, We Praise Thy Name

MASSES FOR VARIOUS NEEDS AND OCCASIONS
See also TOPICAL INDEX: PRAISE

VOTIVE MASSES

Holy Trinity

    See   TRINITY SUNDAY

Holy Cross

    174   O Christ, Our Hope
    282-283   When I Survey the Wondrous Cross
    See   CHRIST THE KING
             HOLY WEEK

Holy Eucharist

    See   ORDER OF MASS: COMMUNION

Precious Blood

    4   All Hail the Power of Jesus' Name
    33   By the Blood That Flowed From Thee
    83   Glory Be to Jesus
    141   Let Thy Blood in Mercy Poured
    245-246   Soul of My Savior
    See also   HOLY COMMUNION

Holy Spirit

    See   CONFIRMATION
             PENTECOST

Blessed Virgin Mary

    See   COMMON OF THE BLESSED VIRGIN MARY

Angels

    24   Bless Me, Befriend Me
    36   Christ, the Fair Glory of the Holy Angels
    61   Dear Angel! Ever at My Side
    90   Guardian Angel! From Heaven So Bright
    103   Hark! The Sound of Holy Voices
    108   Holy God, We Praise Thy Name
    161   Michael, Prince of Highest Heaven
    195   O Praise Ye the Lord
    226   Praise, My Soul, the King of Heaven
    243   Sing With All the Saints in Glory
    287   Who Are These Like Stars Appearing
    292   Ye Holy Angels Bright
    293   Ye Watchers and Ye Holy Ones

Apostles

    See   COMMON OF APOSTLES

All Saints

    See   ALL SAINTS (1 NOVEMBER)

MASSES FOR THE DEAD

Funerals

    See   ALL SOULS (2 NOVEMBER)
             EASTER SEASON
             FUNERALS

Marriage

    158-159   Love Divine, All Loves Excelling

Order of Mass

    9   Alleluia! Sing to Jesus
    15   At the Lamb's High Feast We Sing
    65   Draw Near and Take the Body of the Lord
    83   Glory Be to Jesus
    108   Holy God, We Praise Thy Name
    245-246   Soul of My Savior
    See also   TOPICAL INDEX: PRAISE

Ordination

    35   Christ Is Made the Sure Foundation
    114   I Heard the Voice of Jesus Say
    256   The Church's One Foundation

Pastoral Care of the Sick

    114   I Heard the Voice of Jesus Say

Penance

    114   I Heard the Voice of Jesus Say
    153   Lord Jesus, Think on Me
    269-270   There's a Wideness in God's Mercy
    See also   TOPICAL INDEX: PRAISE

Religious Profession

    35   Christ Is Made the Sure Foundation
    114   I Heard the Voice of Jesus

IV. TOPICAL INDEX

Adoration

- 3   All Glory, Laud, and Honor
- 4   All Hail the Power of Jesus' Name
- 7   Alleluia! Alleluia! Hearts to Heaven
- 8   Alleluia! Alleluia! Let the Holy Anthem Rise
- 9   Alleluia! Sing to Jesus
- 19   Be Thou My Vision
- 50   Come, Thou Almighty King
- 58   Crown Him With Many Crowns
- 75   For All the Saints
- 76   For the Beauty of the Earth
- 83   Glory Be to Jesus
- 85   God of Our Fathers
- 97-98   Hail to the Lord's Anointed
- 109   Holy, Holy, Holy
- 118   Immortal, Invisible, God Only Wise
- 165   My God, Accept My Heart This Day
- 167   My Soul Doth Long for Thee
- 170   Now Thank We All Our God
- 174   O Christ, Our Hope
- 186   O God, Our Help in Ages Past
- 195   O Praise Ye the Lord
- 207-209   O Saving Victim
- 211   O Star, for Those Whose Pure Light
- 221   On This Day, the First of Days
- 231   Rejoice, the Lord Is King
- 263   The God of Abraham Praise
- 284   When Morning Gilds the Skies
- 289   Who is This, So Weak and Helpless
- 291   Worship the Lord in the Beauty of Holiness

See also PRAISE

Angels

- 255   The Angel Gabriel
- *See*   LITURGICAL INDEX: ANGELS

Beauty

- 76   For the Beauty of the Earth
- 291   Worship the Lord in the Beauty of Holiness

Benediction

- 108   Holy God, We Praise Thy Name
- 204-205   O Salutaris Hostia
- 207-209   O Saving Victim
- 252-253   Tantum Ergo

Blessed Sacrament

- 135-136   Jesus, Thou Art Coming
- 184   O Food to Pilgrims Given
- 187   O Godhead Hid, Devoutly I Adore Thee
- 248   Sweet Sacrament Divine

See also HOLY COMMUNION

Children

- 72   Father, See Thy Children
- 104-105   Hear Thy Children, Gentle Jesus
- 130   Jesus, Jesus, Come to Me
- 132-133   Jesus, My Lord, My God, My All
- 125   It Is a Thing Most Wonderful
- 165   My God, Accept My Heart This Day

Church

- 35   Christ Is Made the Sure Foundation
- 69-71   Faith of Our Fathers
- 75   For All the Saints
- 76   For the Beauty of the Earth
- 256   The Church's One Foundation
- 277   Wake, Awake, for Night Is Flying

City of Our God

- 22-23   Bethlehem, of Noblest Cities
- 82   Glorious Things of Thee Are Spoken

Comfort and Consolation

- 1   Abide With Me
- 6   All You Who Seek a Comfort Sure
- 25   Blessed Jesus, at Thy Word
- 55   Comfort, Comfort Ye My People
- 106   Heart of Jesus, We Are Grateful
- 113   How Firm a Foundation
- 114   I Heard the Voice of Jesus Say
- 115   I Know That My Redeemer Lives
- 126   Jerusalem, My Happy Home
- 264   The King of Love
- 269-270   There's a Wideness in God's Mercy
- 291   Worship the Lord in the Beauty of Holiness

Commitment

- 69-71   Faith of Our Fathers
- 221   On This Day, the First of Days
- 287   Who Are These Like Stars Appearing

Courage

- 69-71   Faith of Our Fathers
- 113   How Firm a Foundation
- 250-251   Take Up Your Cross
- 264   The King of Love

Creation

- 54   Come, Ye Thankful People, Come
- 69-71   Faith of Our Fathers
- 76   For the Beauty of the Earth
- 118   Immortal, Invisible, God Only Wise
- *See also*   ADORATION AND PRAISE
-     THANKSGIVING

Cross

- *See*   LITURGICAL INDEX: HOLY CROSS

Death

- *See*   LITURGICAL INDEX: FUNERALS
- *See also*   COMFORT AND CONSOLATION
-     ETERNAL LIFE

Dedication of a Church

- *See*   LITURGICAL INDEX: COMMON OF THE DEDICATION OF A CHURCH

Eternal Life

- 9   Alleluia! Sing to Jesus
- 13   As With Gladness Men of Old
- 154   Lord Jesus, When I Think of Thee
- 165   My God, Accept My Heart This Day
- 212   O Strength and Stay
- 264   The King of Love

Evening

- *See*   EVENING PRAYER
- *See also*   ADORATION AND PRAISE
-     THANKSGIVING

Faith

- 10   Almighty God, Your Word Is Cast
- 65   Draw Near and Take the Body of the Lord
- 69-71   Faith of Our Fathers
- 73-74   Firmly I Believe and Truly
- 75   For All the Saints
- 113   How Firm a Foundation
- 118   Immortal, Invisible, God Only Wise
- 294-295   Ye Who Own the Faith of Jesus
- *See*   HOPE AND TRUST

Family Life

- 76   For the Beauty of the Earth

First Communion

- 2   Accept, Almighty Father
- 132-133   Jesus, My Lord, My God, My All
- 194   O Lord, I Am Not Worthy
- 199   O Sacrament Most Holy
- 245-246   Soul of My Savior
- *See also*   HOLY COMMUNION

Forgiveness

- *See*   LITURGICAL INDEX: PENANCE
- *See also*   MERCY

Freedom

- 15   At the Lamb's High Feast We Sing
- 52   Come, Thou Long-Expected Jesus
- 53   Come, Ye Faithful, Raise the Strain
- 54   Come, Ye Thankful People, Come
- 58   Crown Him With Many Crowns
- 97-98   Hail to the Lord's Anointed
- 174   O Christ, Our Hope
- 180   O Come, Divine Messiah
- 182   O Come, O Come, Emmanuel
- 263   The God of Abraham Praise
- 265   The Strife Is O'er

God the Father (Creator)

- 5   All People That on Earth Do Dwell
- 66   Eternal Father, Strong to Save
- 118   Immortal, Invisible, God Only Wise
- 221   On This Day, the First of Days
- 226   Praise, My Soul, the King of Heaven
- 240   Sing Praise to God Who Reigns Above

Grace

- 4   All Hail the Power of Jesus' Name
- 10   Almighty God, Your Word Is Cast
- 43-44   Come, Holy Ghost, Creator Blest
- 45   Come, Holy Ghost, Creator, Come
- 46-47   Come, Holy Ghost, Who Ever One
- 50   Come, Thou Almighty King
- 56   Creator of the Stars of Night
- 65   Draw Near and Take the Body of the Lord
- 73-74   Firmly I Believe and Truly
- 76   For the Beauty of the Earth
- 83   Glory Be to Jesus
- 113   How Firm a Foundation
- 118   Immortal, Invisible, God Only Wise

165	My God, Accept My Heart This Day
170	Now Thank We All Our God
180	O Come, Divine Messiah
195	O Praise Ye the Lord
263	The God of Abraham Praise
269-270	There's a Wideness in God's Mercy

Guardian Angel

24	Bless Me, Befriend Me
36	Christ, the Fair Glory of the Holy Angels
61	Dear Angel! Ever at My Side
90	Guardian Angel! From Heaven So Bright

Guidance

1	Abide With Me
85	God of Our Fathers
113	How Firm a Foundation
114	I Heard the Voice of Jesus Say
140	Lead, Kindly Light
170	Now Thank We All Our God
264	The King of Love

Harvest

54	Come, Ye Thankful People, Come
76	For the Beauty of the Earth
See also	THANKSGIVING

Healing

See LITURGICAL INDEX: PASTORAL CARE OF THE SICK

Heaven

See ETERNAL LIFE

Holy Communion - Eucharist

2	Accept, Almighty Father
132-133	Jesus, My Lord, My God, My All
194	O Lord, I Am Not Worthy
199	O Sacrament Most Holy
224	Panis Angelicus
245-246	Soul of My Savior
249	Sweet Savior, Bless Us Ere We Go

Holy Father

81	Full in the Panting Heart of Rome
148	Long Live the Pope

Holy Ghost ~ Holy Spirit

See LITURGICAL INDEX: CONFIRMATION PENTECOST

Holy Name

110	Holy, Holy Name of Jesus
See also	LITURGICAL INDEX: HOLY NAME

Home and Trust

35	Christ Is Made the Sure Foundation
97-98	Hail to the Lord's Anointed
113	How Firm a Foundation
114	I Heard the Voice of Jesus
115	I Know That My Redeemer Lives
126	Jerusalem, My Happy Home
186	O God, Our Help in Ages Past
264	The King of Love

Jesus Christ

20	Beautiful Savior, Mightiest in Mercy
25	Blessed Jesus, at Thy Word
35	Christ Is Made the Sure Foundation
36	Christ, the Fair Glory of the Holy Angels
37	Christ, the Glory of the Sky
41	Christ, the True Light of Us
67-68	Fairest Lord Jesus
75	For All the Saints
76	For the Beauty of the Earth
113	How Firm a Foundation
114	I Heard the Voice of Jesus Say
130	Jesus, Jesus, Come to Me
131	Jesus, Keep Me Close to Thee
158-159	Love Divine, All Loves Excelling
174	O Christ, Our Hope
185	O for a Thousand Tongues to Sing
217	O Word of God Incarnate
256	The Church's One Foundation
284	When Morning Gilds the Skies
See	LITURGICAL INDEX: ADVENT
	CHRISTMAS
	LENT
	HOLY WEEK
	EASTER
	CHRIST THE KING

Joy

5	All People That on Earth Do Dwell
48-49	Come, My Way, My Truth, My Life
53	Come, Ye Faithful, Raise the Strain
69-71	Faith of Our Fathers
76	For the Beauty of the Earth
115	I Know That My Redeemer Lives
126	Jerusalem, My Happy Home
158-159	Love Divine, All Loves Excelling
195	O Praise Ye the Lord
231	Rejoice, the Lord Is King
263	The God of Abraham Praise

Judgment

- 54 Come, Ye Thankful People, Come
- 56 Creator of the Stars of Night
- 100 Hark! A Herald Voice Is Sounding
- 231 Rejoice, the Lord Is King
- *See* SECOND COMING

Justice

- 97-98 Hail to the Lord's Anointed
- 118 Immortal, Invisible, God Only Wise
- 269-270 There's a Wideness in God's Mercy

Lamb of God

- 15 At the Lamb's High Feast We Sing
- 58 Crown Him With Many Crowns

Life

- 118 Immortal, Invisible, God Only Wise
- 171 Now that the Day-Star Glimmers Bright
- 183 O Day of Rest and Gladness
- *See* CREATION

Light

- 111 Holy Light on Earth's Horizon
- 112 Holy Spirit, Lord of Light
- 213-214 O Trinity of Blessed Light
- 217 O Word of God Incarnate
- 230 Rejoice, Rejoice, Believers

Love (God's Love for Us)

- 25 Blessed Jesus, at Thy Word
- 158-159 Love Divine, All Loves Excelling
- 227 Praise to the Holiest in the Height
- 264 The King of Love
- 268 There Is a Green Hill Far Away
- 269-270 There's a Wideness in God's Mercy
- 282-283 When I Survey the Wondrous Cross

Love (Our Love for God)

- 2 Accept, Almighty Father
- 174 O Christ, Our Hope
- 268 There Is a Green Hill Far Away

Marriage

- *See* LITURGICAL INDEX: MARRIAGE

Mary

- 111 Holy Light on Earth's Horizon
- 220 On This Day, O Beautiful Mother
- 229 Raise Your Voices, Vales and Mountains

Month of May

- 32 Bring Flowers of the Rarest
- 94 Hail, Queen of Heaven
- 111 Holy Light on Earth's Horizon
- 266 The Sun is Shining Brightly
- 273 'Tis the Month of Our Mother
- 275-276 Virgin-Born, We Bow Before Thee
- *See* LITURGICAL INDEX: COMMON OF THE BLESSED VIRGIN MARY

Mercy

- 226 Praise, My Soul, the King of Heaven
- 228 Praise to the Lord
- 269-270 There's a Wideness in God's Mercy
- *See also* LITURGICAL INDEX: PENANCE

Ministry and Mission

- 4 All Hail the Power of Jesus' Name
- 10 Almighty God, Your Word Is Cast
- 69-71 Faith of Our Fathers
- 97-98 Hail to the Lord's Anointed
- 250-251 Take Up Your Cross

Morning

- 109 Holy, Holy, Holy
- 221 On This Day, the First of Days
- *See* ADORATION
- *See also* PRAISE
- LITURGICAL INDEX: MORNING PRAYER

Petition

- 10 Almighty God, Your Word Is Cast
- 18 Be Joyful, Mary
- 25 Blessed Jesus, at Thy Word
- 35 Christ Is Made the Sure Foundation
- 43-44 Come, Holy Ghost, Creator Blest
- 45 Come, Holy Ghost, Creator, Come
- 46-47 Come, Holy Ghost, Who Ever One
- 50 Come, Thou Almighty King
- 52 Come, Thou Long-Expected Jesus
- 56 Creator of the Stars of Night
- 77 Forty Days and Forty Nights
- 85 God of Our Fathers
- 92 Hail, Holy Queen Enthroned Above
- 94 Hail, Queen of Heaven
- 126 Jerusalem, My Happy Home
- 140 Lead, Kindly Light
- 142 Lift Up Your Heads
- 157 Lord, Who Throughout These Forty Days
- 180 O Come, Divine Messiah
- 182 O Come, O Come, Emmanuel
- 200 O Sacred Head, Surrounded
- 207-209 O Saving Victim
- 245-246 Soul of My Savior
- 277 Wake, Awake, for Night Is Flying

A CATHOLIC BOOK OF HYMNS • 339

Poor Souls

    107   Help, Lord, the Souls That Thou Hast Made

Pilgrimage

    113   How Firm a Foundation
    114   I Heard the Voice of Jesus
    140   Lead, Kindly Light
    186   O God, Our Help in Ages Past
    264   The King of Love
    277   Wake, Awake, for Night Is Flying

Praise

    108   Holy God, We Praise Thy Name
    226   Praise, My Soul the King of Heaven
    227   Praise to the Holiest in the Height
    228   Praise to the Lord
    229   Raise Your Voices, Vales and Mountains
    239   Sing My Soul, His Wondrous Love
    240   Sing Praise to God Who Reigns Above
    241   Sing Praise to the Lord
    244   Songs of Thankfulness and Praise
    263   The God of Abraham Praise
    281   Whate'er Our God Ordains Is Right
    See   ADORATION

Priesthood

    See   LITURGICAL INDEX: ORDINATION
    See also   MINISTRY AND MISSION

Providence

    9   Alleluia! Sing to Jesus
    115   I Know That My Redeemer Lives
    170   Now Thank We All Our God
    186   O God, Our Help in Ages Past
    228   Praise to the Lord
    240   Sing Praise to God Who Reigns Above

Reconciliation and Concern

    See   LITURGICAL INDEX: PENANCE
    See also   LOVE (OUR LOVE FOR EACH OTHER)
                    MERCY

Repentance

    See   LITURGICAL INDEX: PENANCE

Rosary

197-198   O Queen of the Holy Rosary

Sacred Heart of Jesus

    6   All You Who Seek a Comfort Sure
    106   Heart of Jesus, We Are Grateful
    201   O Sacred Heart
    202   O Sacred Heart, O Love Divine
    203   O Sacred Heart, What Shall I Render Thee
    247   Sweet Heart of Jesus
    274   To Jesus' Heart All Burning
    See   LITURGICAL INDEX: SOLEMNITIES SACRED HEART

Saint Joseph

    62   Dear Guardian of Mary
    89   Great Saint Joseph
    172   O Blessed Saint Joseph

Saints

    88   Great Saint in Heaven
    See   LITURGICAL INDEX: PROPER OF SAINTS

Second Coming

    20   Beautiful Savior, Mightiest in Mercy
    54   Come, Ye Thankful People, Come
    58   Crown Him With Many Crowns
    100   Hark! A Herald Voice Is Sounding
    142   Lift Up Your Heads
144-145   Lo, He Comes With Clouds Descending
158-159   Love Divine, All Loves Excelling
188-189   O Jesus Christ, Remember
    216   O Wondrous Sight! O Vision Fair
    230   Rejoice, Rejoice, Believers
    See   JUDGEMENT

Service

    See   MINISTRY AND MISSION

Shepherd

    5   All People That on Earth Do Dwell
    200   O Sacred Head, Surrounded
    264   The King of Love

Social Action and Concern

    85   God of Our Fathers
    See   MINISTRY AND MISSION

Suffering

    See   LITURGICAL INDEX: LENT
                    HOLY WEEK
                    PASTORAL CARE OF THE SICK
    See also   COMFORT AND CONSOLATION

Temptation

- 1   Abide With Me
- 77   Forty Days and Forty Nights
- 111   Holy Light on Earth's Horizon
- 113   How Firm a Foundation
- 143   Light of All Days
- 157   Lord, Who Throughout These Forty Days
- 171   Now that the Day-Star Glimmers Bright

Thanksgiving

- 54   Come, Ye Thankful People, Come
- 73-74   Firmly I Believe and Truly
- 76   For the Beauty of the Earth
- 170   Now Thank We All Our God
- 231   Rejoice, the Lord Is King

Trinity

See   LITURGICAL INDEX: TRINITY SUNDAY

Truth

- 48-49   Come, My Way, My Truth, My Life

Unity

- 35   Christ Is Made the Sure Foundation
- 256   The Church's One Foundation

Vocation

See   MINISTRY AND MISSION

Witness

See   MINISTRY AND MISSION

Word

- 10   Almighty God, Your Word Is Cast
- 25   Blessed Jesus, at Thy Word
- 50   Come, Thou Almighty King
- 113   How Firm a Foundation
- 217   O Word of God Incarnate
- 223   Only-Begotten, Word of God Eternal

V. METRICAL INDEX

4 6 88 4
201   LAURENCE

557 557
206   SICILIAN MARINERS

56 56 56 5
20   ST. RICHARD GWYN

56 8 55 8
67   SCHÖNSTER HERR JESU
68   ST. ELIZABETH

64 66
267   ST. COLUMBA (Irons)

65 65
83   WEM IN LEIDENSTAGEN

65 65 D
135, 136   Jesus, Thou Art Coming

66 4 666 4
50   ITALIAN HYMN

66 66
93   AVE MARIS STELLA

66 66 88 or Hallelujah Meter (HM)
231, 292   DARWALL'S 148TH
166   LOVE UNKNOWN

66 66 88 66
248   DIVINE MYSTERIES

666 666
284   LAUDES DOMINI

66 77 78 55
87   IN DULCI JUBILO

66 84 D
263   LEONI

66 86 or Short Meter (SM)
153   SOUTHWELL
254   ST. THOMAS (Williams)
272   SWABIA

66 86 D or SMD
58   DIADEMATA
167   My Soul Doth Long for Thee

66 11 D
42   DOWN AMPNEY

67 67 66 66
170   NUN DANKET

74 74 674
271   STRAF MICH NICHT

76 76
194   NON DIGNUS
199   O SACRAMENT MOST HOLY

76 76 with refrain
274   COR JESU

76 76 D
188, 256   AURELIA
257   CHARTRES
97, 116, 198, 258   ELLACOMBE
98, 183   ES FLOG EIN KLEINS WALDVÖGELEIN
53   GAUDEAMUS PARITER
78   KING'S LYNN
259   LANCASHIRE
230   LLANGLOFFAN
217   MUNICH
200   PASSION CHORALE
99   QUEEN OF MAY
3, 79   ST. THEODULPH
2   Accept, Almighty Father
189   O Jesus Christ, Remember

76 76 D with refrain
266   The Sun Is Shining Brightly

76 76 676
146   ES IST EIN' ROS' ENTSPRUNGEN

76 86 86 86 with refrain
162   CATHOLIC HARP

77 77
37   CULBACH
77, 80   HEINLEIN
221   LÜBECK
234   NUN KOMM DER HEIDEN HEILAND
160   ORIENTIS PARTIBUS
239   ST. BEES
101   SURGE
48   THE CALL
49   TUNBRIDGE

342   •   A CATHOLIC BOOK OF HYMNS

77 77 with alleluias
- 38, 128   EASTER HYMN
- 129   EASTER HYMN (Monk)
- 39, 95   LLANFAIR

77 77 with refrain
- 220   BEAUTIFUL MOTHER
- 12   GLORIA

77 77 D
- 278   ABERYSTWYTH
- 235   CHRISTMAS MORN
- 34   MENDELSSOHN
- 15, 244   SALZBURG
- 54   ST. GEORGE'S WINDSOR
- 40   VICTIMAE PASCHALI
- 33   By the Blood That Flowed From Thee
- 236   See, Amid the Winter's Snow

77 77 D with refrain
- 102   MENDELSSOHN

77 77 77
- 13, 76   DIX

776 776
- 184   INNSBRUCK

777 777
- 51, 112   VENI SANCTE SPIRITUS

78 78 with refrain
- 273   'Tis the Month of Our Mother

78 78 77
- 108   GROSSER GOTT
- 141   JESUS MEINE ZUVERSICHT

78 78 88
- 25   LIEBSTER JESU

84 84
- 152   PROVIDENCE

84 84 with refrain
- 92   SALVE REGINA COELITUM

85 84 7
- 18   REGINA CAELI

86 86 or Common Meter (CM)
- 185   AZMON
- 227   BILLING
- 10   DUNDEE
- 171   FARRANT
- 268   HORSLEY
- 126   LAND OF REST
- 107   REQUIEM
- 45   SOUTHWOLD
- 134   ST. AGNES
- 186, 190   ST. ANNE
- 173   ST. COLUMBA (Irish)
- 157   ST. FLAVIAN
- 61   Dear Angel! Ever at My Side
- 165   My God, Accept My Heart This Day

86 86 with refrain
- 202   O Sacred Heart, O Love Divine

86 86 with repeat
- 137   ANTIOCH
- 174   LOBT GOTT, IHR CHRISTEN

86 86 D or CMD
- 124   CAROL
- 6, 114   KINGSFOLD
- 155   Lord, Who at Cana's Wedding Feast

86 86 D with repeat
- 148   PAPAL HYMN

86 86 76 86
- 192   FOREST GREEN
- 193   ST. LOUIS

86 86 8
- 225   Praise God! Who in His Grace

86 86 86
- 4   CORONATION

86 86 86 with refrain
- 86   GOD REST YOU MERRY

86 86 87 85 85
- 139   King of Kings Is He Anointed

87 87
- 57   CROSS OF JESUS
- 73, 290   DRAKE'S BROUGHTON
- 269   GOTT WILL'S MACHEN
- 29   LAUS DEO (Redhead)
- 22, 74, 100   MERTON
- 264   ST. COLUMBA (Irish)
- 23, 52   STUTTGART
- 96   Hail, Thou Living Bread
- 121, 122   In This Sacrament, Sweet Jesus

87 87 with refrain
- 279   GREENSLEEVES
- 161   Michael, Prince of Highest Heaven
- 163   Mother Dearest, Mother Fairest
- 60   Daughter of a Mighty Father

87 87 D
- 8   ALLELUIA! ALLELUIA!
- 84   AU SANG QU'UN DIEU
- 82   BEACH SPRING
- 111, 158   BLAENWERN
- 59, 294   DAILY, DAILY
- 295   DEN DES VATERS SINN GEBOREN
- 288   EBENEZER (Williams)
- 289   EIFIONYDD
- 9, 159   HYFRYDOL
- 7, 138   HYMN TO JOY
- 270   IN BABILONE
- 103   MOULTRIE
- 237   REX GLORIAE
- 233, 243   RUSTINGTON
- 89   Great Saint Joseph
- 104   Hear Thy Children, Gentle Jesus
- 131   Jesus, Keep Me Close to Thee

87 87 D with refrain
- 106   Heart of Jesus, We Are Grateful

87 87 44 88
- 281   WAS GOTT TUT

87 87 444 77
- 149   BRYN CALFARIA

87 87 77
- 285, 287   ALL SAINTS
- 222   IRBY
- 286   When the Patriarch Was Returning

87 87 77 88
- 55   GENEVAN 42

87 87 87
- 150   BRYNTIRION
- 168   DOWLING
- 169   GRAFTON
- 226   LAUDA ANIMA
- 11   REGENT SQUARE
- 151   ST. HELEN
- 64, 119, 145, 252   ST. THOMAS (Wade)
- 253   UNSER HERRSCHER
- 35   WESTMINSTER ABBEY
- 110   Holy, Holy Name of Jesus

87 87 887
- 240   MIT FREUDEN ZART

87 87 88 77
- 123   W ŻŁOBIE LEŻY

87 87 12 7
- 144   HELMSLEY

88 7
- 14   STABAT MATER

88 77
- 276   QUEM PASTORES

88 77 D
- 275   MON DIEU PRETE-MOI L'OREILLE

88 87 with refrain
- 229   Raise Your Voices, Vales and Mountains

88 88 or Long Meter (LM)
- 260   ANGELUS
- 250   BRESLAU
- 213   BROMLEY
- 175   CHURCH TRIUMPHANT
- 56   CONDITOR ALME SIDERUM
- 214   DANBY
- 204, 207   DUGUET
- 115   DUKE STREET
- 251, 262   ERHALT UNS, HERR
- 282   HAMBURG
- 125   HERONGATE
- 208   HERR JESU CHRIST
- 44   KOMM, GOTT SCHÖPFER
- 46   LUDBOROUGH
- 41   O AMOR QUAM EXSTATICUS
- 47   O JESU, MI DULCISSIME
- 5   OLD HUNDREDTH
- 210, 280   PUER NOBIS NASCITUR
- 283   ROCKINGHAM
- 63   SCHMÜCKE DICH
- 177   ST. CROSS
- 143, 191   TALLIS' CANON
- 21   TE LUCIS ANTE TERMINUM
- 142   TRURO
- 216   WAREHAM
- 205, 209   WERNER
- 219, 232   WINCHESTER NEW
- 154   WORD OF FIRE
- 26   Blest Guardian of All Virgin Souls
- 178, 179   O Come and Mourn With Me Awhile

88 88 with alleluias
- 147   ERSCHIENEN IST DER HERRLICH TAG
- 242, 293   LASST UNS ERFREUEN

88 88 with refrain
- 132   SWEET SACRAMENT
- 81   WISEMAN

88 88 with repeat
- 43   LAMBILLOTTE

88 88 87 with repeat
- 71   Faith of Our Fathers

88 88 88
- 66 MELITA
- 69 ST. CATHERINE
- 94 STELLA (English)
- 249 SUNSET
- 182 VENI EMMANUEL

88 88 88 with repeat
- 70, 133 SAWSTON

888 with alleluias
- 265 VICTORY

89 8 D 66 4 88
- 277 WACHET AUF

96 76 76 76
- 197 ACH GOTT VOM HIMMELREICHE

98 98
- 27 EUCHARISTIC HYMN

98 98 D
- 28 RENDEZ Á DIEU

10 4 10 4 10 10
- 140 SANDON

10 10
- 65 COENA DOMINI

10 10 10 with alleluias
- 75 SINE NOMINE

10 10 10 10
- 245 ANIMA CHRISTI
- 1 EVENTIDE
- 211 FARLEY CASTLE
- 85 NATIONAL HYMN
- 215 O QUANTA QUALIA
- 19 SLANE
- 24 Bless Me, Befriend Me
- 246 Soul of My Savior

10 10 10 10 with refrain
- 90 Guardian Angel! From Heaven So Bright
- 203 O Sacred Heart, What Shall I Render Thee

10 10 10 10 10 10
- 156 UNDE ET MEMORES

10 10 11 11
- 218 HANOVER
- 195, 241 LAUDATE DOMINUM

10 10 12 10
- 255 GABRIEL'S MESSAGE

11 10 11 10
- 30 LIEBSTER IMMANUEL
- 31 MORNING STAR
- 212 STRENGTH AND STAY
- 16 Ave Maria! Thou Virgin and Mother

11 10 11 10 with refrain
- 88 Great Saint in Heaven
- 247 Sweet Heart of Jesus

11 11 with refrain
- 117 LOURDES HYMN

11 11 11 5
- 36 CAELITES PLAUDANT
- 223 ISTE CONFESSOR
- 127 NOCTE SURGENTES

11 11 11 11
- 187 AQUINAS
- 17 CRADLE SONG
- 113 FOUNDATION
- 72 GHENT
- 181 IHR KINDERLEIN, KOMMET
- 172, 196 MARIA ZU LIEBEN
- 118 ST. DENIO
- 62 Dear Guardian of Mary

11 11 11 11 with refrain
- 91 Hail, Glorious Saint Patrick

11 12 12 10
- 109 NICAEA

12 10 12 10
- 291 WAS LEBET WAS SCHWEBET

12 11 with refrain
- 32 QUEEN OF THE ANGELS

12 12 12 8
- 224 SACRIS SOLEMNIIS

14 14 4 7 8
- 228 LOBE DEN HERREN

Irregular
- 176 ADESTE FIDELES
- 120 CRANHAM
- 164 MOTHER OF CHRIST
- 238 STILLE NACHT
- 261 THE FIRST NOWELL
- 180 VENEZ, DIVIN MESSIE
- 130 Jesus, Jesus, Come to Me

A Catholic Book of Hymns

For a Singing Catholic Congregation

Editions

Pew Book

Organist & Choir Director

Choir

✝

Guides to using the hymnal,
and editions for organists
of various levels:

www.catholicbookofhymns.com

Sacred Music Library
636 Old 19 • Augusta, KY 41002
www.sacredmusiclibrary.com

INDICES

I.	FIRST LINES WITH TUNES	320
II.	TUNES WITH FIRST LINES	326
III.	LITURGICAL	331
	PROPER OF SEASONS	331
	PROPER OF THE SAINTS	333
	COMMONS	333
	RITES	334
	MASSES FOR VARIOUS NEEDS AND OCCASIONS	335
IV.	TOPICAL	336
V.	METRICAL	342
VI.	SCRIPTURAL PASSAGES RELATED TO HYMNS	ONLINE

Online indices address for fast searching:

www.catholicbookofhymns.com/index/